D0311924

Dawn French is presently fifty-one years old and almost entirely spherical. She trained as a teacher at the Central School of Speech and Drama but luckily for the kids at Parliament Hill School, she left teaching in 1981 to join the *Comic Strip* team. Dawn made six series and various specials of sketch-based hilariosity with another girl called Jennifer Saunders. She has done lots of other telly including *Murder Most Horrid*, *The Vicar of Dibley*, *Wild West*, *Jam and Jerusalem* and *Lark Rise to Candleford*. She also does acting in plays sometimes.

DEAR FATTY

With a sharp eye for comic detail and a wicked ear for the absurdities of life, Dawn French shows how an RAF girl from the West Country rose to become one of the best-loved comedy actresses of our time. Here Dawn French invites us into her most personal relationships with, among others, her mum and dad, her husband, her daughter and her friend Jennifer. Dawn reveals the people and experiences that have influenced her and that helped shape her comedy creations. She describes the experience of losing her beloved dad and later finding a tip-topmost chap in Lenny Henry. From raging about class, celebrity and bullying to describing the highs and lows of motherhood and friendship, *Dear Fatty* reveals the surprising life behind the smile.

DAWN FRENCH

DEAR FATTY

Complete and Unabridged

CHARNWOOD
Leicester

First published in Great Britain in 2008 by
Century, Random House
London

First Charnwood Edition
published 2009
by arrangement with
The Random House Group Limited
London

British Library CIP Data

French, Dawn.
  Dear Fatty
  1. French, Dawn. 2. Television actors and actresses- -
Great Britain- -Biography. 3. Comedians- -Great
Britain- -Biography. 4. Women comedians- -Great
Britain- -Biography. 5. Large type books.
  I. Title
  791.4'5'028'092–dc22

  ISBN 978–1–84782–840–8

Published by
F. A. Thorpe (Publishing)
Anstey, Leicestershire

Set by Words & Graphics Ltd.
Anstey, Leicestershire
Printed and bound in Great Britain by
T. J. International Ltd., Padstow, Cornwall

This book is printed on acid-free paper

For
Michelle Lillicrap
1968 – 2008
Stephen Hardy
1972 – 2008
Marjorie Emily French née Berry
1908 – Forever

Hoc Feci

SMALLER

lyrics by
Alison Moyet

Taken from the album *The Turn*

I used to dance to the drum in your chest
My feet on your feet, my head at your breast
You gave me a tune and I carry it still
And I promise my darling, that I ever will.

Dear You,

Hello. I have decided to think of this book as a memoir rather than an autobiography. As I understand it, the latter means that I have to be precise about chronology and touch on all aspects of my quite-dull-in-parts life. I think that would be quite dull because in quite a lot of parts my life has indeed been quite dull. You wouldn't want to read about those bits, believe me. Those bits would mainly be about puddings I've enjoyed and when I've set the washing machine on the wrong cycle and my quest for comfortable shoes, and the time I put a gun in a kitten's mouth. You don't want to know about that ol' faffle. So, I've decided instead to concentrate on those memories that are especially important or vivid to me. The parts of my life I can still remember the taste and feel and smell of. Otherwise we'd be here all day and I'm hoping you can be finished by lunchtime so's you can have a nap and watch *Loose Women*. (Are they really loose? I've seen no evidence thus far and I've watched a lot . . . Unless, of course, the looseness is *under* the table . . . oh dear.)

Here's what I've learned writing this book. Memory doesn't begin with or end in 'what happened'. In fact, I don't think it ends at all; it goes on changing, playing a kind of hide-and-seek with our minds. Some of my memories are nearly 50 years old now and sometimes the startling clarity of them makes me doubt their reality. Do all of the people I write to in these pages remember what I remember? My dad, mum, brother, daughter, friends, lovers and so on? I am lucky that I've kept diaries for large parts of my life on which I can anchor many of these memories. Even so, most of my diary-keeping is pure organisation and, annoyingly, doesn't tend to remind me of my true emotions at any particular juncture. For that I must rely on my rapidly deteriorating grey matter, and a lot of investigative chatter with my nearest and dearest. I shouldn't really be so surprised by the alarmingly speedy erosion of my memory, after all, my waistline has disappeared entirely. Like wearing a nappy or the Lost City of Atlantis, my waist is now only a vague memory or may even just be an ancient myth for all I know.

So, it's in this spirit of reminiscence that I offer you this memoir of my life. My life so far, that is. To this end, I have decided to tell my story through letters, because this way, I can address my life to the people I've actually lived it with. It's not that I don't want to tell it directly to you, it's more that I know these people well, and hopefully, by the end, you might know me well too. I do hope you enjoy it. If you do, feel free to tell all your friends. If not, please replace the book neatly where you found it, and if you're in a residential area, be thoughtful, and leave quietly. Thank you.

1

Dear Dad,

So, you're still dead. It's been 31 years and every day I have to remind myself of that fact, and every day I am shocked.

You and I only had 19 years together, and so when I think of you, I am still 19 and you are . . . What age were you? . . . To me, you were just the right age for a dad. Old enough to be clever and young enough to be handsome. Probably about the age I am now. Blimey, that's weird. I will soon be older than you ever got to be. That's not right somehow. A parent is supposed to be older at all times. The natural form is, *I* get older and you get . . . just old. *Then,* and only then, should you be permitted to die. Even that should happen in front of the telly after a bowl of stew and a cuddle up with your missus. Not the way you died. Not like that.

I'm not 19 any more, Dad, and so many things have happened that you haven't known, so I have decided to write this book for you. I want to remember our time together and I want to tell you about lots of stuff since. So far, it's been better than expected . . .

Dear Dad,

I'm having trouble remembering my very first memory. Each time I try I think I'm stealing other people's first memories that I've either read or been told of. I *can't* remember looking out of my pram at an adoring mother, I *can't* remember being shocked at the first sight of my own pudgy baby fingers, I *can't* remember the oddly delightful feeling of a nappy full of hot new poo. (Actually, on second thoughts, I can, but that came years later!)

There is something I *can* remember vividly, and when I experience it now, the effect is visceral. It takes me thundering right back to a mysteriously timeless but definitely very early blurry memory. The smell of my mother. Of Mum. A heady aroma that embodies birth and life and strength and sex and safety and fags. Whatever perfume she adds (currently she's favouring JLo's new honk, I noticed, when I was last in her bathroom — she's MoLo!), this smell is always there as the baseline, and for me it's magnificent and it announces that I'm home. I swear to God her cooking is flavoured with the same scent, which is why none of us can replicate her recipes. You have to be *her* to do it. I guess the scent is the code, the method of imprinting between a mother and child, and it is so potent. Sometimes even now I snuggle up to Mum just to get another headful to nourish me till the next visit.

I don't have such a strong early memory of you, Dad, although I do have one of something that happened when I think I was about two or three. I remember creeping into your bedroom while you two slept and crawling under your bed. I'm not quite sure why I did this but I suspect it was the thrill of being hidden while being so close. A sort of delicious invisibility. (I did the same thing again years later at boarding school — more anon.) It seems a bit pointless to eavesdrop when those you'd like your eaves to drop on are fast asleep, but I suppose the joy was in the anticipation. Anyroadup, you might remember, a frightening thing happened. The bed was the kind that had low metal bars and bare springs beneath, and I only just managed to squeeze under. I must have had my hand inside one of the springs when one of you moved, resulting in a crushing pain as my little fingers were trapped. I shrieked and woke you. You leapt out of bed, full of confusion and dadly alert. You reached under the bed and, with a bit of gentle coaxing, pulled me out to safety and I ran into Mum's arms for comfort (and most likely to smell that healing smell). All of this was fairly unremarkable except for one thing. You were completely naked and, although I was in agony, I couldn't take my eyes off that weird dark dangly wrinkled thing. What *was* it? I'd never seen you without your pants on and for some scrambled reason the first conclusion I jumped to was that

3

you were being attacked by some kind of nocturnal bed-intruding vicious hairy saggy mole-snake creature. Naturally the correct course of action, considering you had just rescued me from certain finger-death, was to reciprocate, so I lunged at your assailant with mighty force, thwacking it as hard as I could, trying to dislodge its tenacious teeth from your groin. However hard I hit, it would *not* let go or fall off and so I was forced to pull it like the keenest frontman on a tug-o'-war team. Inexplicably, both of you seemed helpless with laughter, and you even seemed to be resisting my help as you pulled on your pants and let the biting thing stay INSIDE them. What an idiot! I never saw it again so I guessed you'd had it put down at the vet's or perhaps left it at the zoo.

Dear Gary,

Dad was at RAF Valley and we were living in Holyhead, Anglesey, so I must have been three years old and you must have been six when Hunni the dog turned up. I don't know where she came from, but I remember she was named after a little girl called Honey Hindley-Maggs who you were at school with and who you lost your heart to. Did she know you named a dog after her? Did she feel special as a result of that I wonder? I think the dog, a cairn terrier, was officially supposed to be *your* dog, but I just want to let you know that she definitely preferred me and I loved her back with a fervent passion verging on the illegal.

After a certain amount of initial resistance she gave in to my efforts to make her lie down next to me for hours on end. Mostly because I restrained her firmly every time she tried to move. I was determined we would be spooning partners. I wanted to feel her tiny body breathing calmly, sleepily, next to mine and I wanted her to be like a Disney or Lassie dog, who could understand me and all my three-year-old problems, so I endlessly blethered on into her ear, which twitched throughout these no-doubt heartfelt monologues.

When I'd had enough of talking, which was a

long time, and she had fulfilled enough of my desire for her to be counsellor/friend/hot-water bottle, she was also very handy as a baby or dressing-up doll. Quite a lot of my doll clothes fitted her and even suited her. She looked better in pastels — it contrasted well with her sandy fur — and I was stunned by how becoming she was in a mob cap, although I had to bite holes in it for her ears to poke through. I think that if she had shown a bit more commitment, we *could* have squeezed more stuff on, but too much wriggling prevented any true representation of an entire outfit, complete with sunglasses and luggage.

One thing Hunni was *always* up for, probably due to the delicious taste, was liberal use of Mum's lipstick, a stunning burnt sunset-type orangey red. Wetness of nose, hirsuteness of lips and constant licking made application tricky but, with effort and tenacity, not impossible. The overall effect was stunning and in no small part reminiscent of early Dusty Springfield. Excellent.

Obviously, to achieve the baby image was a much simpler operation — lay dog on its back, put on nappy and insert dummy in mouth. Simple but effective. Hours of contented cooing and cradling followed. That's me contented of course, maybe not always her. Still, I'm pretty sure she favoured this sort of girly activity over the silly exploits *you* got up to with her — like walking, throwing and catching, running after rabbits or wrestling. Honestly, what were you thinking? She was a *dog!*

6

Dear Mum,

I've been thinking about what life must have been like for you around the time I was born, when Dad was stationed in Anglesey. When I look at pictures of you pushing me in a pram, with a toddler Gary by your side, you look so glamorous and so happy. Then I look at other pictures from that time. We must have been in RAF quarters but there I am having a bath in a bucket in the backyard. Maybe this was just for a laugh — we must have had a bathroom, surely? I know that the camp was miles from the local village and the shops in Caergeiliog and that you had to walk for hours to get a pint of milk. I also know that Anglesey is hellishly windy and flat and remote. I've seen photos where the trees are growing diagonal to the ground because the mighty maverick gales have battered them into submission. They look tipsy, like staggering drunks, lurching sideways against their inebriation. It must have been exhausting to drag both of us such a long way in that raging raw weather, and I know that often when you arrived at the shop, so relieved to be out of the bluster and so glad to see other grown-ups, it was very hurtful when people chose to speak Welsh only, to refuse to help you in English. I know you often felt lonely and rejected but for me there is a truly visceral connection. I prick up my ears when I hear Welsh, I pay more attention when I am around Welsh people. I like how dangerous and dark and a bit caustic and secretive they seem, and somehow I have fused that persistent stormy weather with my memories of that country and those seductive Taliesin people. I feel a curiously enduring connection, although by rights I'm not entitled to it. I was born there, but I wasn't bred there and I'm not *from* there, yet Wales and the Welsh prompt an acute sense of tribal belonging in me. Perhaps what I'm feeling is a distant sense of your alienation, Mum. Because you were made to feel the trespasser, I want to belong, on your behalf. Maybe it's a bigger issue. Dad's being in the RAF meant that you (and we) followed him wherever his work took us, so we didn't get to belong anywhere. Sometimes we were in our home for less than a year. You might have only just got a job, we might have only just settled at school, and we had to move on again. Sort of legit gypsies really. Moving to a new camp, new town, new county, but strangely and rather comfortingly, always the same house — same layout, same G-Plan furniture. We seemed to have very little of our own. Just ornaments and books and odd items with which to try and personalise yet another RAF standard red-brick house.

It's no wonder both Gary and I did so much sleepwalking and sleeptalking when we were growing up. We probably harboured our fair share of new-school stress, constantly having to try to carefully negotiate our way into new

8

groups of friends. It was chum war. There were tactics. The RAF kids were easy to befriend — they had the same itinerant experience and were sympathetic. It was the gangs of local kids that were harder to crack. They were fed up with forces kids turning up, and then buggering off before true friendships could be forged. They were often wary of us and quickly judged if we were worth the effort or not. I vividly remember that crucial testing time in the first few days of arriving anywhere new, when it was imperative to make a good show of yourself, make sure all your wares were on display attractively — humour, hipness, kindness (but with a hint of steel), intelligence, comprehensive knowledge of hit parade, courtesy, eloquence and skipping and twoball prowess. If that failed (which it usually did due to pathetic lack of élan in any of above skills), employ bribery and giftage techniques swiftly, sometimes even deploying own toys as bait. This was a supremely risky strategy and you stood to suffer a high incidence of collateral damage, sometimes losing four or more well-loved Sindys or even a pair of champion skates or a warrior set of clackers. No matter — this is the cost of war, no one said it would be pretty, and these casualties were the price we had to pay. We will never forget them. On rare occasions, this modus operandi backfired and we were judged to be spineless tossers for buying our friends' affections. Then, *and only then*, would I employ my master plan, a strategy that never failed, but demanded countless hours of tireless acting. I would concoct a terminal illness

— 'toxic spasm' was a good one, as was 'marrow fester' or 'trench head', or simply 'swollen blood'. All of these maladies meant I was not long for this world, and would elicit sympathy and pledges of eternal friendship from otherwise hostile enemy agents. RAF kid 1 — local kid nil. Result. I'm sorry, Mum, if it meant you regularly had to answer strange questions from concerned parents about your sickly daughter's tragic condition, but somehow I eluded retribution and moved on to the next camp with renewed vigour and no small relief that I could shake off my fatal ailment and be healthy again in readiness for the next bout of 'find some friends!'. This nomad life, which incidentally also rewarded us richly with experiences all over the country and later in Cyprus, was no doubt part of the nagging core feeling I had: that we didn't belong anywhere.

For you, though, it must have been very difficult to make a home. If it's any consolation, Mum, believe me when I say that everywhere we went was our home because you made it so. You were and are the absolute centre of all of us, and you kept us anchored when we could so easily have felt lost and confused. There might have been endless new doors but behind each one was you and Dad, making a safe and happy place for me to be. Any confidence I have had since stems from that one unassailable fact. I am loved.

Thank you.

Dear Dad,

I think I was about four years or so when you were posted to RAF Leconfield and we all moved to Yorkshire. Only now do I realise that I've lived in Yorkshire at all — I was so unaware of our personal geography then. I *did* know it was a long way from Grandma and Grandad French in Plymouth because I clearly remember those endless hours in the car on numerous family visits. Gary and I would physically fight the entire time, mean pinches and punches and stabs and Chinese burns. You tried word games and songs to distract us, but we were compelled to battle. That was our kid purpose. If we were scolded, we resorted to verbal taunts and competitive face-pulling, but in the main it was the corporal torture that was most excruciating and most thrilling. If any of our squabbling became too dangerous, or if he was winning, I would be sure to whinge loudly to you and appeal for justice. Gary called me 'the Foghorn' for this crime of breaking rank and grassing him up, and accused me of being 'a girl'. A girl?! How very low.

Another reason I recall these journeys is the smoke. God, the smoke! I don't know how many fags you and Mum were smoking a day but it *must* have been 100 each. You obviously

11

regarded these journeys as a perfect opportunity to catch up on any non-smoking minutes you may have carelessly frittered away not smoking, and so put in extra smoking time to get up to smoking speed. One cigarette lit the next and we travelled along in this stinking, acrid foggy tin box for hours. Gary and me and the dog in the back seat, sucking up thousands of fags' worth of used smoke and gasping for air in a desperate attempt to stay alive. Heaven forfend we should open the window. Mum would screech, 'You're letting in the cold air! Shut that immediately!' Yes, it would have been awful to allow fresh air to dilute the thick pea soup of swirling smog that had built up inside the car. I swear sometimes I couldn't see as far as the back of your head. How did you see out at all? Is this why you often inexplicably used the windscreen wipers on a perfectly clear day? For years I thought I was a sufferer of carsickness until I travelled in a smoke-free car and realised that smoke was the reason for my queasiness. Perhaps Gary's cries of 'Foghorn!' were more apt than we knew.

Anyroadup, I remember one particular journey back up North because there was only one topic of conversation the whole way. The Queen Mother. You told us that you had been selected as a typical serviceman, a chief technician with an average family — one boy, one girl, one nursery-school-teacher wife, dog (comes with or without clothes). A perfect family, safe and presentable enough to display to a visiting royal on a very special day for our air force base. She was coming to visit and inspect in two weeks' time! All I could think was, 'Why is she called the Queen Mother and not the Queen's Mother? Was my mum therefore the Dawn Mother?'

Apparently there was a *lot* of preparation to be made before she could possibly cross the threshold of our humble G-Plan, red-brick quarter. What?! What did we have to do? Surely, you suggested, she was supposed to take us as she found us, that was the whole point, wasn't it? Absolutely *not* as far as the Dawn Mother was concerned. Do you remember she flew into a flurry of excitement and didn't sit down or sleep once in those two weeks? *Everything* was dusted, mopped, antisepticked, hoovered, pinned up on the line and beaten, including us kids. Our house would be *perfect*, we would be perfect, it would be perfect. That Queen Mother would NOT find fault with us. We would do you proud. Gary and I had haircuts, new outfits — mine was a tartan kilt and new red patent-leather Start-rites which I had been longing for, so yay and respect to the Queen Mother for those; Gary's was a grey suit so he could be a perfect mini-man. The Dawn Mother had a twinset and a perm and you of course wore your uniform, which I always loved because you looked so spruced and tip-top and important. Who would have thought drab bluey-grey would suit anyone? You shone in it, and it shone on you, with all buttons and belts and medals and significant regalia-type badge things duly buffed till they glinted. Nothing less would do. Mum tried to get the same shine on our faces, using a chamois leather and Vim. Well, all right, *not* that, but something like it — Brasso

13

maybe? Gary's newly cut but still renegade thick hair was semi-tamed with liberal dollops of Brylcreem and Mum's spit on the crown. There were new socks and new pants all round. This alarmed me — was the mother of the Queen going to be inspecting our pants? This visit was seemingly more thorough than I had anticipated. Shit. Or rather, not shit. On pants, or anywhere. *No shit!*

We practised bowing and curtsying for hours until our backs and knees buckled and bled. We tried to rehearse being humble and quiet so that if the mother of the Queen 'chose to converse with our parents, she could do so in peace, please!'. The little pamphlet on royal etiquette gave us some tips: we were to speak only if spoken to (royal rules, not family rules), so — should we say hello, or wait to be said hello unto? Could we try on her crown? Or feed sugar lumps to the unicorns that would pull her pink carriage? After the initial 'Your Majesty' we were then to address her as M'am, rhymes with Spam, *not* M'arm rhymes with farm, and never M'erm . . . This threw me into a panic because I felt sure I would mistakenly call her Spam from start to end.

The day came and, boy, were we prepared and perfect. Beds made with crisp hospital corners, books neatly on shelves with spines facing *outwards*, teddies and dolls scrubbed and lined up on the pillow. The house smelt of furniture wax and Mr Sheen. A newly baked cake was on the table and the best — in fact, the *new* — china was arranged beside it, as if it were commonplace that we had high tea in porcelain lady-cups. The Dawn Mum was virtually still licking us clean like a mumcat when *SHE* arrived (do I remember it correctly, Dad?) in a *helicopter!* All the neighbours were out in the road to watch. She first went for a quick visit to a suitably presentable officer and his family at the other, pedigree, end of the camp. We were always segregated like this from the commissioned officers — they had posh detached houses with huge gardens front and back whereas us oiks lived in rows around a central play park (freshly painted for the visit — several children bore the marks on the arses of their best clothes).

And so we waited and waited for her to come. Finally, just when I was starting to get lockjaw from the rictus of holding my Queen-Mother-welcoming cheesy grin in readiness, she walked up our garden path. I had a quick glance at the stunning outfit with the matching huge hat (hang on, where's the bloody crown?!! She's forgotten the crown. Someone's nicked the crown! The crown for Chrissakes! Call the police!!), before taking a very low stoop into my ballet-influenced curtsy, holding my tartan skirt out at the sides for maximum effect so that the QM could view the wondrous calibre of the cloth. Gary did his gentlemanly bow simultaneously, and both of us remained like this for an uncomfortably long time — possibly two days. During our punishing rehearsals, we hadn't worked out when the correct moment for closure on the bow/curtsy should be. It was best to just stay there till a cough from you brought us both upright, if a bit dizzy. Looking at the photos of the event, the overlong bowing was the last thing you needed since it immediately became apparent that Gary had not washed the back of his neck. Ever. It was truly grimy from a seven-year build-up of gladiator-game mud. He brought shame on the House of French at this critical moment but I don't entirely blame him, because what happened next would overshadow the whole day for me and haunt my dreams for years to come. As I stood up from my deep curtsy, and the blood rushed away from my head, I blinked in the light and looked directly into the face of the mother of the Queen. She was about my height (I was four years old and three foot), which surprised me. Was she, in fact, a munchkin? Excellent! I smiled my special show-every-tooth-in-your-head smile, carefully avoiding saying hello first and definitely *not* calling her Spam (*don't* say hello Spam, *don't* say hello Spam). She then reciprocated with a huge ear-to-ear beaming smile and — horror of horrors — she had a mouthful of BLACK TEETH! What? Eh? No carriage, no crown and now she turns out to be a fully certified evil witch! And she's coming into *my* house! I was dumbstruck and with my heart beating fear in my ears, I hid behind your knees and grabbed on to your legs. I remember you trying to shake me off and you even did that dadfirmpull thing to remove me, but I wasn't going anywhere. I was holding on to your leg with the grip of a randy terrier, trying to make legpuppies with you. She was in our house, chatting and drinking tea for all the world as if she *wasn't* evil incarnate . . . She looked at Gary's train set, she asked polite questions and complimented us on our lovely neat house. Had no one else noticed? Perhaps true evil, the soldiers of SATAN, can only be seen through kid-vision? So why was my brother being so suckuppy? Didn't *he* know? Perhaps it's only *girl*-kid-vision that works? I knew what to do. Hold on to your leg and refuse to either speak to her or look her in the eye. So that's what I did. I said one word when she asked me about my school. I said, 'Nice.' That was it. That's all I gave her and that was only to appear civil to the unknowing humans, the fools who knew not who she truly was. She left our house and went off to spread her evil seed elsewhere, after 20 minutes or so. The scariest 20 minutes of my life. Does she get back in the helicopter or simply hop on her broomstick to get home? Does the Queen know what's in her midst? I'm only four, there's nothing more I can do. No one believes me. I'm helpless, hopeless, inconsolable.

I was left with this deep hidden fear for years, and then I happened to meet the QM at a reception for the arts many moons later and found her to still be alarmingly short, but much less evil, with lovely teeth.

Thanks, Dad, for the use of your leg that day. It saved my life.

Dear Hannah,

Right from the moment you were born, on Boxing Day 1993, and when I first looked into your eyes, I knew we were linked in a profound way. It feels a bit like we are twins born 40 years apart. I know you. Because I *was* you. I have watched you grow into your teenagehood, negotiating the assault course of your childhood using exactly the same techniques as I did. I see your thinking, I see your actions, I see your doubt, and I see your method and I know them as my own. Is it the family connection? I guess that must be a huge part of it. Is it some great cosmic joke that I should appear again in my brother's life as his daughter, just when he thought he was safe, a spooky mini me, to continue the torture? Whatever the reason, I am so glad you're here, that you're my niece and I cherish our mysterious sameness.

I can't apologise enough for the lifetime of comparison to me you have already had to, and will in the future, endure. The endless comments about how you and I are so similar must be agonising. I am quite often the culprit myself, even when I am aware of how tiresome and frankly frightening it must be for you. I remember when I was 14 like you, I thought anyone over the ripe old age of 40 might as well throw in the towel and die to alleviate their unsightly and off-putting decrepitude. Surely, it would be a favour to themselves and to everyone else if they just, like, weren't there? So I understand how alarming this comparison must seem. For a start, how could anyone be alive and *so* very fat?! What is the point of that? Well, all I can say is that I am just as surprised as you. I honestly cannot fathom the dimensions of this curious body I've been given. I was aware, from *very* early on, that it wasn't quite like anyone else's. None of the laws of physics, nature, chemistry, biology, art *or* universal order seem to apply. I know I am a human life form, but not as we know it, Captain. Why, for instance, am I *so* short? I know the Frenchies are not tall in the genes department, hailing as we do from labouring stock, heavy, beefy men who built the first tar roads in Cornwall and from fishermen who, again, need to be robust and sturdy to haul in their living. Surely, though, their proportions were not quite as startlingly dwarfish as my own? What is my physical category, actually? Plump? Rotund? Squat? Corpulent? Buxom, possibly, in poor light? No, I defy these definitions. I've seen folk who fit those descriptions and they are not like me. I am more hobbitish, with a big dollop of Weeble. You know, the ones that wobble but don't fall down? Except I do, due to alarming lack of foot size which might otherwise offer some stability. You would think that in return for the shocking lack of leg/arm/torso length, God might have been prepared to barter and bless me with elegant long fingers suitable for pianos and

19

rings, or even exquisite toes for sandal and nail-polish use. No no no. Not to be — got the dumpy Wall's sausage fingers and the cocktail sausage toes. Thanks, God. What about an aesthetically pleasing, well-arched neck? No no no. Got the full, direct-from-chin-to-chest fortification, with impressive turkey-gobble flaps attached. How generous of the Almighty to gift me with not just the one chin, but several reserve chins — lest I lose one? Or perhaps so that I might fashion a sail from my own face if I am stranded at sea on a raft?

Above all, what in the name of all that is holy is the purpose of these massive ocean-going buoy chests? I know bosoms are womanly but these surely belong to *many* women. How did I get the rations for the whole queue from here to the edge of the earth? Every time I see a flat-fronted woman, I want to apologise for my seemingly appalling greed. This is the kind of hoarding that gets you sent to your room with a stinging arse. I would happily share, given half a chance. I'd love to see my chipolata toes again — it's been so long. I'd love to hold a friend's baby without seeing that strange slavering glint in their eye when they bounce off what must seem to be enough food to propel them into their teens. I'd love to run and still see ahead on every other stride. I'd love to lie down on my back without gathering underarm beach balls. I'd love to pick up a bra catalogue and find my size in *all* ranges rather than turn each page ever more forlornly till I come across the trusted industrial 'Doreen' in white polyester — the only bap-scaffolding that comes in my staggering 42H. I have tried to customise the 'Doreen' so many times — I've added lace, I've hacked away at it with pinking shears to create a sexular-looking shelf-like effect, I've covered it in intriguing fabrics in an attempt to make it more comely. On one occasion, fortified by drink, I wore it back to front, which was ill-advised and dangerous to all in my immediate vicinity. I've hunted high and low and under and over and beyond and back to find beautiful, supportive equipment for these unfeasibly large norks. Thank God then, and June Kenton, for Rigby & Peller, a place where physical freaks like me can find refuge, get measured properly and finally get heaved into something nearly pretty. I don't think you're heading this way in the front upper department, Hannah, but if you do, fear not — I will guide you beyond the darkness, through the portal of light that is Rigby & Peller's door, with the comforting Queen's royal warrant above it. There shall you find mammiferous fulfilment and happiness.

Any road, I know you will look at me from time to time and dread the onset of this odd body shape. Fortunately, I think your mum's genes might save you. Evidence thus far points towards early intervention of good strong height genes. You even seem to have an actual neck, which goes in under the jaw and then down, providing you with a place where necklaces apparently go. How lucky you are. But should this fleshy strangeness befall you, I want to allay your fears a tiny bit and tell you that it's not all bad. I have discovered that big breasts can precede you into a room and announce the arrival of someone to be reckoned with. This can be very useful if you are feeling nervous or shy, because the knockers do the attitude for you; meanwhile, you have enough breathing time to let your courage catch up with them. I've also experienced big bosoms as a sort of theme park for boys. They just can't seem to resist them. Every single boy I have known intimately has been utterly entranced by them and can't wait to earn access so they can play all day. Of course, not all of them have been well apprenticed in the art of bosom management. A big tip I offer you is to give boys with very small hands a wide berth. It seems cruel to exclude them but, believe me, they can't seem to get past the turnstiles into the park. They just can't. You will have to train boys to treat the pleasure domes with all due respect and to cherish them like the magnificent cherishable things they are. You will have to gently discourage any unconfident twiddling or tuning, you will have to insist on their close face-shaving to avoid chafing or grazing. You will have to fight off all attempts at actual breastfeeding, which some boys seem to regress to with zealous and baby-like oversucking. I once had a situation where a total nincompoop created a kind of vacuum on one of my pinnacles and had to be jabbed hard in the cheek in order to force a release. Painful for both of us and potentially fatal for him. You will also experience, should you be similarly endowed, a kind of sisterly regard verging on rampant

22

jealousy from other women. They, too, wish to join in the fun or at least behold the actual wonders or at the very least hear tell of saucy chesticle adventures so as they might vicariously enjoy the thrills.

I once went to the theatre with a chum and noticed a woman in her fifties having a pre-show drink in the bar, with the most splendid front I have ever seen (the woman, that is, not the bar). She was very grand and she held herself so proudly. I was in awe. I couldn't stop looking at her, at them, at it, at the whole fabulous majestic thing. Imagine my delight when, quite by coincidence, she sat down next to me. I was breathless with admiration. She was glancing at the programme. I tried to resist, truly I did, but I couldn't — I leaned over and said, 'Excuse me, I hope you don't mind but I am compelled to tell you that you have the most magnificent bosom I've ever seen.' She looked beatifically at me over her bifocals and said, 'Yes. I know,' and smiled. And the lights went down and we watched the play side by side. Me and the lady with the remarkable chest. We didn't speak again. And it was delicious.

Don't forget that although you have a deal of 'French' blood in you, to a certain extent the shape of your body can be YOUR CHOICE. I've heard that exercise and a lean, healthy diet can make a big difference . . . I've always known this but I can't help it — personally, I would rather read a book or watch *Big Brother* than go to a gym and jump about with a flushed face. Whenever I have passed a gym, and I've passed many, I look in through the steamed-up windows and see sights I would only ever imagine in the nine circles of hell. Puffing red people grimacing in pain, leaking buckets o' sweat. My only experience of this behaviour was enforced PE torture at school. During most PE classes, I had only one thought in my head: 'One day, when I am the one in charge of me, I will never have to do this again.' And so it was. However, I have to admit that those who put themselves through it often look bonny in the end, so the fact is — you do have a choice. I am a sedentary person, I've got the kind of well-spread bum that is perfect for sitting and watching, and that's what I do best. I'm sorry to boast but I really am good at it.

Some things *are* worth moving for, and for those beloved and special activities I have been known to move with alarming speed and tip-top energy. The 'worth moving fast for' list is as follows: 1. doing sex, 2. swimming, 3. tennis, 4. walking by sea with dog, 5. going into town to get a pasty, 6. doing sex, 7. dancing, 8. running away from evil people, 9. running towards delightful people, 10. doing sex.

Talking of dancing, sweet pea, you are *so* good at it. I've seen you perform on lots of occasions and when I watch you, I nearly burst with joy. Dancing is *so* great, isn't it? I see you move and use your lovely body in such a way that I know you are feeding from the pleasure of it. You are supple and expressive and dazzling. I hope your enviable connection to your body and the confidence it gives you will last the rest of your life. That's the key, you know, confidence. I know for a fact that if you can genuinely like your body, so can others. It doesn't really matter if it's short, tall, fat or thin, it just matters that you can find some things to like about it. Even if that means having a good laugh at the bits of it that wobble independently, occasionally, that's all right. It might take you a while to believe me on this one, lots of people don't because they seem to suffer from a self-hatred that precludes them from imagining that a big woman could ever love herself because *they* don't. But I *do*. I know what I've got is a bit strange and difficult to love but those are the very aspects I love the most! It's a bit like people. I've never been particularly attracted to the uniform of conventional beauty. I'm always a bit suspicious of people who feel compelled to conform. I personally like the adventure of difference. And what's beauty, anyway?

Ever since I can remember people have told me I have a 'pretty' face. When I was little, I used to feel so chuffed and grateful for this, it seemed kind and flattering and I know it was meant to make me feel good. The older I got the harder I found it to hear. I sometimes had the distinct feeling that it was a not very clever way of saying 'Oh my God, look at your huge unpleasant body, at least you've got a nice symmetrical face for us to look at'. Which isn't quite the same as the innocent, honest compliment I thought it was. Now, even older, I have found myself really thinking about this whole 'pretty' thing. What is it? Correct amount of features in a pleasing formation? Lack of deformity? What?! My biggest problem is how can I accept the compliment when I haven't accomplished *anything?* I haven't even tried! I was given this face by my parents just like you were given yours by yours. That's all. Nothing accomplished — just luck.

Mind you, with us, Hannah, you and me, it's not just about the looks we share. Something else, something much more fundamental, is going on. We can share our fears and our joys equally. I don't mean by this you should do as I do, follow my example or be like me in any way. Definitely *NOT*! I just mean that I think I sort of *get* you, so rest assured I've got your back, babe, and I'll fight for your right to be whoever you best think you are, making lots of necessary and glorious mistakes along the way. Oh, the places you'll go . . .

Dear the Monkees,

This is a really hard letter to write, probably the hardest ever in my whole life of 11 years. I wish it could be a happier one for you to get but, alas and alack, it can't because sometimes in life you have to do something bigger than yourself. And this is it.

I expect most of your fans are silly teenagers who are in love with one of you and writes to that one over and over again just to gush and be licky. Well, right now let me assure you that's not me. It's that very reason of choosing someone out for special praise that has made me write this. I refuse to do it, whatever anyone in my school says. It's obvious from anyone who knows me that I always have loved Pete the most of all of you. Only because he is the good-lookingest and funniest for me. Also I really really love his crazy clothes the most, especially his trousers, which are simply nutty! He is also the kindest and caringest one of you all, which is important in life in the future, which I find super. But that's the thing. Even though he is definitely my favourite one over my grave till I die, I would never say so and make the others of you feel left out. No. That is wrong. So I write this letter to tell you that I love you *all* the same and that even though Davy is from my country of England and so really *he* should be my best one, to make everything easier if we got married to see all our families who are also English, although one of my aunties was from Cornwall at the start but that doesn't matter. No. It is best for all if we keep it the same and say I like each Monkee like the same as the next. So you can easily see how different I am to those other fans who only think about themselves and not your happiness. Especially Mickey, who probably hasn't got many fans just because of his face. And that isn't fair, is it?

There was a thing on telly which said you are coming to England to sing soon. Please can you let me know where and when so my mum can organise time off work to take me to it? You don't have to meet her, just me. Maybe they don't even let parents go backstage anyway? You will love England, we are crazy here too, like you, although we don't all walk in a crazy straight line together like you!

Which is *so* crazy! But I *do* have a purple maxi-skirt you will go crazy at if you see it. Please let me show it to Pete, who would love it the most.

Anyway, loads of luv 'n' stuff till forever.
Moo French (age 11)

Dear B.F,

Being balanced, both psychologically and emotionally, is supposed to be an attribute, isn't it? I'm not entirely convinced that it *is*, and I am further unconvinced that it is an attribute that can be attributed to me! I have often, even sometimes by you, my beloved Best Friend, been told that I am a 'balanced' person. Is that a compliment or, as I suspect in occasional paranoid interludes, is it, rather, a heinous insult which, while appearing to indicate that I might be measured and fair, really denotes a big ol' underbelly of dullitude? Is the apparent ability to empathise with both sides of a situation an enviable quality or is it a sort of curse which renders one incapable of having a definite opinion or position? I don't know — aaargh there, see? I can't even decide what I think about not deciding. I see merit and, equally, see fault and this all leads to much frustration and not just for me, but for those closest to me, like Jennifer, for instance, who is often exasperated by my interminable see-sawing.

People have suggested to me that I am unfeasibly fair because I am a Libran. This smacks of uber-hogwash to me. Scales, balance — bit obvious. No, I think if I *do* have this tendency, and as yet I'm unconvinced (there I go again . . .), it's because of a simple family relationship. Or rather, two concurrent and utterly opposite family relationships. The ones I have had with both of my grandmothers. My dad's mum, Grandma French (Marjorie), and my mum's mum, Grandma O'Brien (Lil). Two mighty women who both did much to shape me. I surely walk in their shoes, although one is a teeny-tiny sparkly perfect pointy ballroom-dancing satin shoe which I can barely squish the chipolatas into. The other is a colourful, loud, high and clacky ankle-strappy saucy strumpet of a shoe, too roomy for me, therefore inherently perilous!

Let me tell you about my experience of these two polar opposite matriarchs. First, Marjorie French née Berry, much beloved mum of my dad, and without a doubt the most precious familial woman in my life next to my mum. Typical of the Berry family, she is diminutive and compact with a kind smiley face and the sparkliest, naughtiest, most expressive eyes in the firmament. As I write this, she is 99 years old and by the time you read this, she will be 100.

Actually, many women from my dad's side of the family have been true stayers. There was *his* grandmother for instance, Great-Grandma Berry, who died a few days before we celebrated her 100th birthday, which was a bit disappointing and frankly inconvenient, considering the whole, wider (in every sense of the word) family had gathered from far reaches for a splendid knees-up. Not that her departure prevented us from having a rare ol' time — far from it. The

31

chair in which she *would* have been seated was boldly placed in prime position on the stage of the parish hall in Eggbuckland, Plymouth, where the party was held. This resplendent, empty throne was then lit with reliable old industrial used-for-thousands-of-Brownie-productions house lights. There was no doubt where the spotlight was: on 'she who was no longer with us', my very formal, slightly scary, jolly but brusque, impressively hirsute great-grandmother. The entire evening went ahead as planned with speeches, salutations, songs and dances for the benefit of the eerily empty chair. Any alteration from celebratory party to wake was virtually imperceptible. Uncle Boy played his accordion with great passion and gusto as usual, Auntie Barb played the piano, and various kids did a turn.

Later on in the evening, we had the traditional family party highlight — 'The Informative Dance of the Two Elderly Sisters', as it came to be known in inner family circles. Great-Auntie Doris (real name Maude) and Great-Auntie Win (real name Win) had been tirelessly rehearsing their latest offering in honour of their mother's special birthday. They regularly performed together, always choosing a subject to inform us about through the medium of the dance. On this occasion they decided to give us a whistle-stop tour through the history of dance itself. As they entered the room, arm in arm, we fell silent in respect of their mastery of this rarefied — in fact unique, I think — art form. The clacking of tap shoe on parquet was unmistakable and I was already breathless with anticipation. Not only did they dance on these occasions, but they also made their costumes. It took time to work out exactly what era the costume signified because at first sight they presented as two giant *It's a Knockout* balls of wool. On closer inspection, I soon gathered that they intended themselves to be Elizabethan. It was hard to distinguish exact details of the costume since the entire outfit was executed in crochet. Crocheted bodices, crocheted voluminous bustled skirts, crocheted headpieces, crocheted chatelaines, crocheted ruffs, crocheted cuffs, probably crocheted codpieces beneath. The overall effect was bulky to say the least, but that didn't prevent the indomitable aunties from launching gamely into a display that would be etched on my memory for ever. Marjorie, the younger sister, my granny, was positioned by a small cassette player and charged with the task of musical director/ technician. The tape consisted of ten or so samples of music from different ages spliced together and it was tricky for her to coordinate what we were to see with what we were to hear. But she was determined to stick with it. SILENCE. The sisters stood stock-still in the centre of the floor. The atmosphere was electric. Marjorie clicked the play button and thereafter we witnessed a dance spectacle the likes of which even Boris Yeltsin would have hesitated to embark upon. Yes, the outfit *was* sort of Elizabethan, and yes, the music *was* sort of a galliard, and yes, the great-aunties were a-leapin' and a-hoppin' about with a sort of lumbering Elizabethan gait. We were just about to applaud their magnificent display when they stopped suddenly, and froze in posed positions, while Marjorie fast-forwarded furiously to the next era of music. Out blasted the opening notes of a charleston riff, and the great-aunties yanked off their poppered-on Elizabethan outfits and tossed them aside to reveal cunningly concealed crocheted flapper dresses! AWESOME! They jumped about swinging their crocheted strings of beads in a frenzy of *Bugsy Malone*-type routines until, stop — fast forward — play, and now we're at a hoedown, and yet another outfit, this time complete with crocheted Stetson, is revealed. On and on they went through polka and jive and cancan and waltz and old-time ballroom and rock 'n' roll, all with utter disregard for chronology but with great attention to technique and giant poppers. It was during this display that I cast a look around our table — a delighted Mum, Gary and Gary's then fiancée, Susan. Susan's face was a picture of stunned horror camouflaged under a fixed polite smile. I instantly realised that, of course, our family was used to this kind of eccentric entertainment, but that as an incomer, she must have been wondering what kind of freakish troupe of mentalists she was about to marry into. (Needless to say, they didn't stay engaged for long.) The fabulous routine ended on a high with by then minimal crocheted coverage in the form of somewhat unsettling disco outfits, and there was the most enormous explosion of euphoric, rowdy approval from the entire family. Enough whooping and stamping for the dead to hear

— well, for one particular dead anyway — and enough clamouring to frighten off any possibly unsuitable future family members. A good night all round . . .

But anyway, I was wanting to tell you about Marjorie, sorry — just got sidetracked by that other memory. Yes, Marjorie — you've met her several times. You know that she's remarkable. A 99-year-old woman who insists on living independently, who will get down on the floor to play with any visiting toddler, who will race out to the kitchen to make a cup of tea (powdered tea, that is — an acquired taste), and offer a saffron bun to all comers. She is the anchor for a massive group of people, she is our family's history and our rock. She is the keeper of all the secrets and she is the purveyor of all the comfort and advice any of us need. She has never, ever made a judgement about me or anyone else in my earshot that isn't positive or encouraging. She might often have a good laugh at some twit's shortcomings or do funny impressions of people who amuse her for one reason or another, but she has no malice in her. None.

Recently I took from her house a handwritten manuscript (in faultless copperplate, I hasten to add) she has been writing for some time about her life. It only goes up to the births of her four children, but I wanted to have it typed up so that she could show it to the rest of the family. Reading this account of her life has been mind-blowing for me. The details of her tough but well-loved childhood on Dartmoor are phenomenal. Her descriptions of the clothes, the food, the house, the people, the jobs and the family are unique and golden. She lived in a tiny two-up two-down near Princetown and the goings-on of the prison were a major factor in the day-to-day lives of all who lived nearby. Some of the family worked in and around the prison; Uncle Frank's job was to direct the unpredictable leats (small freshwater streams which occasionally disappeared underground) towards the prison so that inmates could have water. She tells us about her father, Samuel James Berry, who drove the first car in the area, as a chauffeur, and about the crush she and her friends had on the new young pastor and how very often they were compelled to visit church during his sojourn there! She remembers exactly which pew her family sat in.

She writes of when she went into service for a family in Plymouth and she is discreet but frank about falling out with the father of the family. Her love for her siblings is palpable and her admiration for her parents through feast and famine is so moving. Her knowledge of the moor is astonishing, she learned so much about its landscape and wildlife, her Arcadian life dictated by the seasons and the mysterious supernature that permeates the area. Whenever I've taken her there for a jaunt in the car, she insists that we pull over here and there, so that she can tell me relevant stories, or strange moorland legends that live on. She remembers meeting my grandfather Leslie, who was tall and handsome and rode a motorbike and whom she kept waiting and waiting for his first kiss. And waiting. He drove through regular snowdrifts on high parts of the south moor to see her on their rare days off. He lost his bike once in a huge mound of snow and had to return to dig it out. The snowy weather even threatened to ruin their wedding day. Only a few guests made it and those who did had to dig a path to the church through a snow barricade! The occasion was even reported in the local press.

My Grandma French is a minx, always quick with a gag and a wink and, to be honest, quite saucy. She always kept a bodice-ripping 'Mandingo'-type book next to the loo — they were pure eye-poppin', gasping delights for me. On one of our moorland outings, I was directed to the impossibly tiny house her whole family lived in while her father was in service as a chauffeur to a posh family near Two Bridges. The big house where the posh family lived is next to the tiny house and is now a hotel. I suggested we went in for a cream tea and she said she couldn't possibly go in, that she wasn't 'allowed', which of course was a throwback to her childhood. Eventually I persuaded her and we sat and had a slap-up tea and a good gossip in a room she had previously been forbidden to enter, a trespass that somehow made our scones even more delicious!

As we were driving away, up the long driveway, she pointed at a big, bushy tree on the right-hand side and said, 'See that tree? That's where me and your grandad first . . . ' and she winked. First what?! First let him kiss her after waiting so long? First let him go 'upstairsies outsidies'? First held hands? Surely not

37

first . . . ?! Surely my granny wasn't telling me about her first bonk?! Was she? I asked her, carefully, and she just tapped her nose. So I guess I'll never know, but she obviously remembers it *very* clearly. Lucky her!

My grandad Les was a real catch, albeit a bit of a rogue. I remember he had an amazing thick shock of hair and huge hands. He was very manly and always busy. He had been a milkman, but later, when I was very young, he was a newsagent with his own little shop on a housing estate called Ernesettle in Plymouth. He got up early every day to do the papers and to run a mobile newsagent from the back of his van at the Bush factory nearby, providing all the workers at the start of their day with supplies of fags and sweets and papers. He managed his team of paper boys like an army squadron. I clearly remember the bottom room of the shop where the papers were sorted into the bags and numbered with stubby pencils so's the boys knew where to deliver them. It was a loud, vulgar, cheerful atmosphere. The place and the boys smelt of ink. There was shouting and rude jokes and cussing and *BOYS*. Lots of *BOYS*! Half an hour of raucous sorting and then the bags were hoisted over adolescent shoulders and the squadron was off yelling their goodbyes to 'Father', as they called my grandad, and then silence, and all that remained was the lovely smell of recent *BOYS*!

There was always a shop dog, an Alsatian, for protection. Carlo was the first one that I remember. A huge handsome dog (but then, I was smaller, so he was probably just Alsatian-sized), who was *so* patient and tolerant day after day. Sitting on the front step of the shop while endless children came up and hugged him and poked his eyes and tickled his ears and kissed his nose and fed him sweets. He put up with all this fussing without a single grumble — I know because I was the perpetrator of many of those protracted hugs and kisses, (obviously he preferred my embraces to all the other kids' . . .). Then one day I witnessed a shocking change in the behaviour of this dog that made me respect him and his like for ever after. Grandad had locked the shop at the end of the day and he was doing some finishing up in the bottom room, the sorting room. I was with him, and someone, mistakenly believing no one was at the shop, tried to break in at the door where we were. The dog switched into a total killing and maiming machine and barked and snarled and slavered at the inside of the door. It was a terrifying sight, and I couldn't quite believe it was the same dog. This was a supreme working dog with utter control over the right response at the right time. There were no break-ins at the shop when that dog was presiding. There were also no incidents of biting or grumpiness around the kids either. He was a bit of a hero for me. Carlo the Great.

Grandma and Grandad lived at the top of the hill near the shop, in St Budeaux, in a cosy little bungalow they bought when the whole road was first being built. They put down the deposit after they saw the foundations and Grandma still lives

39

in that same house today. Forty-odd years ago, the land between their house and down the side of the hill towards Ernesettle was all woodland with a huge creek at the bottom and Grandad would walk Carlo in this woodland every day. He even had a sort of allotment in there where he kept geese (his passion) and lots of chickens. I loved going on these steep walks with him and the dog, our breath visible in front of us and our feet crunching through fallen twigs and leaves. He told me frightening, cautionary stories about children who had died playing in that muddy old creek where the quick tides were very dangerous. It worked. I always stayed away.

I have many lovely memories of my grandad, a very powerful one being his eccentric obsession with bargains. If he found out that something, anything, was going for a song, he'd find a reason to get there and snaffle up the bargain, whether it was something he needed or not. Hence, for years, he had two pairs of enormous department-store front doors leaned up against his shed. He had no use for them as far as I knew, he'd just got them for a good price. Likewise, he used to go to jumble sales and pick up stacks of ties. So many in fact that eventually they had to move the thousands of ties into a caravan parked in their drive. Pretty soon it was impossible to get into the caravan at all, so really the caravan simply provided a gigantic metal covering to keep the millions of ties dry and warm. I suppose if anyone had thought to hitch the caravan to a car, the ties *could* have actually gone on holiday to the seaside.

Another love of Les's was his aviary. He had various versions that I can remember, but the main one was in a shed in the garden. He chiefly bred budgies but he also had parakeets and lovebirds and canaries and all sorts of other feathered wonders. We grandchildren often witnessed the amazing moment the eggs cracked and the stubbly little pink alien fledglings flapped and waddled into Grandad's nest-box world. Each one was a proper little miracle to him and therefore to us also. I never tired of seeing his huge hands delicately holding those tiny, colourful birds. They were calm in his gigantic palms and he handled them like jewels. He was not always so sensitive with us mini-humans. He was quick to chide or discipline us if we put a foot wrong, but he was also fair and ultimately wanted to have a laugh, so all was forgiven. We all loved him.

So, anyway, sorry, I keep trying to tell you about Marjorie but my mind buzzes around all these other potent and irresistible recollections. Where was I? Oh yes, I was telling you about how inspirational she is to me. It is an intense pleasure for me to know how deeply she is loved by so many. If at the latter end of my life I can claim a fraction of the profound and sincere affection that is felt for her, I will be happy. That is just what she is. Happy. So long as her beloveds are well, she asks for nothing more. She has always been generous with what matters most: her time and her care. Due to the impracticality of the geographical distance, she and I have always written to each other about once a month. In this way, she includes me in the vital family loop, making sure I know exactly what's happening with my cousins and my aunties and uncles. She tells me all about the new babies and the hilarious toddlers and the spats and the celebrations, the births and the deaths and the fabric of the lives of our little tribe. She makes sure I am not a 'celebrity', that I am a granddaughter, as equally cherished as the others. No more. She earths me so that any sudden lightning that strikes, be it some glitzy prize or scary trauma, can be grounded through me without toppling me. She is proud of me, but she is proud of all of us equally. She is one of the few people who doesn't give me a metaphorical top billing — because in our family there *is* no billing. I am safe in the certain knowledge that with her I can just be me and that is enough, she will always love me, flaws and all. She is my ultimate proof that love is *always* the answer. She is loved because she loves. What more is there?

It is my heaven to be around her. I recall sneaking into her room, and snuggling up in bed with her along with various cousins, on cold mornings after Grandad had gone to work. Condensation on the windows, and stories, sometimes read and sometimes made up. I remember fitting into her shoes when I was about six or so because her feet are so very tiny — I think she takes a size 2. Some of the shoes had heels, which felt very grownup, but there were other, special shoes that were magical because they were her ballroom-dancing shoes. High, dazzling, flawless golden Faerie Queene shoes . . . which *fitted* perfectly! Imagine the joy! She was a wonderfully gifted dancer and in her rather unlikely (height-wise) but strangely hypnotic and graceful partnership with Grandad, the two of them not only taught but won lots of trophies. Somehow, when we granddaughters tried these shoes on, we borrowed a tiny bit of her innate glamour and elegance. It was a rite of passage to pass through this halcyon, and cruelly short, phase of time when Grandma's shoes fitted.

There was one other phenomenal world that Grandma let us into. The parallel universe of wondrous joys that was . . . the loft. A small metal ladder would be winched down and, if we were lucky, she would invite us up the ladder and through the small attic opening in the ceiling of the hall. This was a portal to her personal domain which was in an entirely other galaxy. It was not a loft, it was a twinkling constellation where all the tiny little stars could shine, and each star was a doll.

A doll, sometimes still resplendent in his or her own little box. Dolls from every country in the world, proudly displaying their national costume in miniature glory. They were sent or given by family, friends, ex-paper boys, mothers of paper boys, anyone really who had travelled *anywhere*. Some dolls wore hand-knitted or hand-sewn outfits to celebrate every kind of weather, occasion, fashion trend, sport, film, etc. Some dolls were big and blousy, some were tiny and delicate. Some had roll-around eyes. Some had perfect little bags, gloves and shoes, some

43

had painted fingernails, others had eyelashes. It could so easily have been sinister, I see that as an adult, but it really wasn't, it was a staggering, magical collection that enchanted every kid who saw it. Like going into Santa's grotto at Christmas, it sparkled and gleamed and delighted us. I went up those little steps into the loft recently to find a small empty space with no trace of the former magic. I thought I might have dreamt it. I asked her if I had remembered it correctly and, again, she just winked and hugged me . . .

So that's Marjorie, my lovely dinky fairy grandmother who smells like cake and only comes up to my shoulder, who has sent me a tenner in every birthday card for 50 years and never once forgotten. A dainty little lady with a towering powerhouse of strength inside her who has guided us Berrys and Frenchies through two warfuls of hell and all kinds of sun and storms for ten decades. She is my yin and I call her Good Granny.

Then, of course, there is Evil Granny. The yang. Grandma O'Brien. Lillian. Fag Ash Lil. Did you meet her? I can't remember. She wasn't evil really — just very, very bad. She died a few years ago at the respectable age of 93, I think. Another stayer. Actually, some of the most fun I had in my teenage years was with her, but I was nearly always aware that whatever we were doing was probably illegal and certainly unhealthy. All around Lillian were lies. Lots of lies. She would encourage me to lie so as not to get into trouble if we were up to something illicit, she told me lies about her childhood and her marriages, she told her own kids lies about many things and she lied to get her own way. On top of that, we all lied around her — elaborate lies about how we were going to be abroad at Christmas so that we didn't have to witness more drink-fuelled rantings and bad moods. Lies about how much pocket money I had in my purse so that she didn't scrounge it all. Mostly little, practical lies, but lies nevertheless.

Lil was a tricky woman with a colourful history, a sharp tongue and a short fuse. Her family were from Cornwall, her mother was Sarah Babbage from Menheniot, who became a Collicott when she married. Grandma's favourite aunt, who eventually lived with her, was Aunt Fan Rainey née Babbage, who lived just outside Saltash at Stoketon Cross until she was too blind to cope. Lil herself had a first marriage nobody seems to know much about, to a boxer, and she lived in Polperro where my mum's eldest sister, Wendy, was brought up until Lil married my mum's dad, John McArthy Alfonso O'Brien, and came to live in Plymouth, which is in Devon, which is *A LONG WAY* from Cornwall. In the same way Yorkshire is a long way from Lancashire. A long way. McArthy was in the Royal Navy, then left and ran various pubs with Lil, who couldn't have been better placed to indulge in her favourite hobby of tasting lots and lots of alcohol . . . It was when the two of them were running a pub called the Antelope in the Octagon on Union Street in Plymouth, that my mum gave birth to my brother in the upstairs

45

room. A real Plymouth 'bey'! (boy)

From what I can gather, Lil didn't seem to have a single maternal bone in her body. This did not prevent her from having more children: my mum Roma, Terry, Owen and Michael. She seems to have regarded her kids as either troublesome pests or domestics, except her first-born, Wendy, who was prized, protected and praised. When my mum talks about her childhood, she describes herself as 'the scrubber' of the family, meaning, I hope, the cleaner. Their upbringing was pretty tempestuous with Lil dishing out physical and verbal abuse in equal measure. They learned to dodge her and it seems none of them could wait to leave home. But those stories are for them to tell, I can only recount *my* experience of Lil. By the time the grandchildren came along Lil had mellowed a bit. She could hold forth when in her cups and she could often be a complete selfish pain in the arse, but I loved how uncontrolled and tough she was. She was sly, and never short of a con or two, always on the lookout for a way to make a few bob, at whatever cost. At some point she had worked on a stall in the Pannier Market, a beautiful, light, airy covered market in Plymouth. She knew all the stallholders back then, both reputable and otherwise. There used to be a big trade in second-hand jewellery and she knew how and where to get a good deal. On one occasion, I had need of her skills in this murky area.

I was about 15 and a friend of mine from school, Patsy Ritchie, had invited me to come home with her to Gibraltar for the holidays. Her dad was very high up in the medical arm of the navy, a surgeon captain, and was stationed there. Patsy had been telling all of us about the quantity and quality of dreamy boys in Gibraltar, when all the navy kids returned home for the holidays, and she wanted me to come and share in the rich pickings. I desperately wanted to go, but didn't have the funds and my parents didn't have enough cash to spare. So my dad struck a deal with me: if I did a paper round for him for a month, he would pay my wages and then double it to make up the required amount. I can't remember exactly how much it was, but I *do* remember that however hard I worked on the paper round, I fell short by £40 even with Dad's help. Time was running out to buy a ticket, and mindful of the certainty that all the best Gibraltar boys would be cherry-picked if I didn't hurry up, I felt hopeless. Mum noticed how sad I was and came up with a brilliant, generous solution. She went and furtled about in the attic for a while and returned with a flat velvet box. She explained that inside was a set of jewellery which she had never liked — they were pearls and she had always superstitiously believed that they bring bad luck. However, she felt guilty about owning such beautiful jewellery and disliking it so much, so she was glad to give it to me as a sort of task. My mission, should I choose to accept it, was to take the jewellery to the market and get the best possible price for it. She said I would certainly be able to get £40 but that I should barter, vigorously. OK. Off I went to the market, feeling a bit nervous about the whole dealing issue but determined to make the cash.

As I entered the vast hall, who should pop up from nowhere like an elderly Rumpelstiltskin, but Lil. She was curious as to why I was there, we went for coffee and I explained my predicament. She asked me how much I needed. 'Forty quid,' I told her, 'or more.' She took the box with the pearls from me and told me to leave it up to her, that this was, after all, her world, that she knew all the tricks and would undoubtedly do a better deal than I ever could with my middle-class wimpy sales technique. She was, of course, absolutely right, so I sat tight nursing another revolting Nescafé until she returned, smirking, ten minutes later. 'Who's your favourite gran?' she said as she sat down and triumphantly counted out the tenners on the table. One, two, three, four — great, that's my target. Then, oh God, here comes more — five, six. £60! I couldn't believe it. What a result! Big victory hugs all round, more coffees and some celebratory dough cakes too, which I happily paid for, oh and some bread and cakes for her to take home for later. Of course, my pleasure.

Feeling delighted and a bit smug, I went straight to Mum to show her my winnings. She asked how I'd done and when I told her about the £60 she didn't look as pleased as I'd hoped. She asked which stall I'd decided to sell to and I explained about meeting Lil and letting her do the dirty deed. She grabbed my hand muttering things like 'I'll kill her' and 'canny old cow' and other, ruder, grumblings under her breath.

Within minutes, we were at my gran's flat in Rendle Street and Mum marched me in, demanding that Lil give me the rest of the dosh. 'Rest of it?! Eh?!' Lil looked a bit sheepish and eventually relented and reached into her handbag. Then laid three more tenners on the table. I was aghast. Mum said, 'And the rest . . .' Eventually there was £100 on the table. I was speechless. She had done a deal for £160, but she had decided to pocket £100 of it as a sort of commission. As far as she was concerned, I had what I needed and a bit extra, and she had something out of it too. She didn't see it as my mum did — nicking money from your own grandchild! — not at all. My mum had known all along the pearls were worth a lot; she wanted me to have the experience of finding that out and doing a good deal for myself; she hadn't anticipated Evil Granny interfering. I always kept my eye on Lil after that day. She was quick. Very quick. And slippery.

Lil loved to have a good time. A drink, a song, some darts and a fight would be the perfect evening for her. Any chance to put on a rabbit-skin fur coat, *lots* of lairy bling, a big gash of red lipstick and some click-clacky shoes was all right with her. She was a Beryl Cook painting come to life. She took me to arcades and pubs and bookies. I got drunk, I caught nits, I occasionally walked home on my own when she was too pissed to remember I was with her. It was never dull.

When her marriage broke down, she moved in to the council flat in Rendle Street where my two great-uncles lived, her brothers, Bill and Jim. Both had been badly injured in the war serving with the Royal Devonshires. Uncle Bill was still in terrible shock from the unspeakable sights he had seen in Belsen. Uncle Jim had to have a full-body skin graft and lost several fingers, when he was the last off the roof of a bombed building in Greenland. He was the sergeant and, thus, final man to go down a precarious rope which burnt and snapped, plunging him, on fire, to the ground where his legs and ankles broke. When he was at the field hospital, they had set his legs wrong and covered his burns in sticking plaster which took months to soak off when he returned to England, where his legs had to be broken again and reset. In later life, he was the projectionist at the Plaza cinema in the Barbican while Uncle Bill built submarines in the dockyard and slowly contracted the asbestosis which eventually killed him, although no one would admit it. Neither of these lovely old guys had married and I always found it touching that they slept, Morecombe and Wise-like, in the same big bed just like they had as young lads, trusting only in their loyalty to each other. This meant, however, that there was a spare room and Lil wasted no time foisting herself upon them and somehow convincing them that they needed her to look after them. They were managing perfectly well on their own and surely they'd suffered enough? Not only did she decide they needed this service but she also demanded payment for it! An extortionate pecuniary arrangement was set up, and those poor brothers were stuck with their monstrous sister, charging *them* for living in *their* home. Another brilliant coup for Lil.

It was during Lil's time at this flat that another elderly relative, the previously mentioned Aunt Fan, came to live out her final days with them. She spent most of the time in bed in Lil's room. She was a gentle, sweet lady who we all loved, and even Lil softened to care for her in those last weeks. Aunt Fan died in the room that I was later to share with Lil when I spent weekends there from boarding school because Mum and Dad lived a long way away. One weekend with Marjorie (ahh, lovely) and the next with Lil (eeeek!), on the pull-out camp bed at the bottom of the actual bed where Aunt Fan had JUST DIED! This spooked me out badly and I could never get to sleep until Lil came to bed. I gradually got used to Lil's mysterious nighttime routine . . .

11pm   Curlers, hairnet, into bed. Teeth out into glass of water. Set alarm. 'Night, maid!' Light out. Snore.

3am   Alarm goes off. Light on. Sit up. Put teeth back in. (Why?!!) Open flask. Pour water into cup. Drink. Teeth out. Sleep. Snore.

4am
5am   I am convinced I hear/see ghost of Blind Aunt Fan.
6am

7am   Up. Teeth in. Curlers out. Start day.

51

It's only now I understand that this strange behaviour was probably the curse of the truly alcoholic. The need to top up with GIN (not water) halfway through the night in order to survive without the shakes.

Much later on, after Bill and Jim had died and there had been an alarming chip-fat fire incident in yet another flat she lived in, Mum organised for Lil to move to an amazing sheltered housing flat in Devonport where she was very happy. A warden at the end of the corridor, big buttons to press for attention (perfect for an accomplished attention-seeker), regular bingo and a view of the Hoe and the Sound beyond. It was in this flat that Lil mounted her final evil assault. She decided to spend her time making endless stuffed woollen toys for us, the next generation, to torture *our* children with. I have hundreds of them, all ugly and truly frightening — hobgoblins and pixies and nasty bug-eyed Santas. My daughter recoiled every year as she unwrapped yet another knitted gargoyle. Lil was famous in family circles for giving the worst *ever* presents. One Christmas she put all previous years in the shade by giving us each a special ornament: a plastic yule log with two robins perched on it, made from mushrooms. MUSHROOMS! Gotta hand it to you, Lil, you are the undisputed champ. No one did worse presents than you, nor ever will . . .

When my career kicked off a bit in the eighties and occasionally a picture of me, or me and Fatty, turned up in a magazine, Lil would cut it out, mount it on card or frame it, and display it in a corner of her flat I liked to refer to as the 'temple'. After I married Len, his visage occasionally turned up there too, among the reverential display. Other cousins' graduation photos and wedding pictures and new baby photos were relegated to a tiny sideboard while more and more room was devoted to the expansion of the temple department. Once, after coming to see me perform in Plymouth, she demanded I sign a 4 x 6 publicity photo to her as follows: 'To my darling grandma, I love you *so* much, thank you for everything, from your devoted granddaughter, Dawn French xx.' This too was then placed at the temple altar. I tried several times to dismantle the temple since it caused me untold embarrassment and was beginning to send trouble ripples through the family, who were rightly furious. But she wasn't having it, and it would be up again the next day. Woe betide any visitor who might come in and *not* know I was related to her.

But y'know, even after all the weird and bad stuff she did, I was really sad when she died. I felt like a mould had been broken, probably for the best, but nevertheless we wouldn't witness its like again. In her curious way, she loved me very much and I loved her, but it was the kind of love you only show when you've got your full armour on, just in case of unpredictable attack.

At her funeral, I sat behind her offspring, my mum and my uncles all in a row. She had done much, mostly carelessly, to divide and harm them in her life but here they were, temporarily united in her death. Much as I reckon none of

53

them had a proper parent in her, I think they all recognised that she was a true survivor and a larger-than-life ballsy dame. So, just wanted to say: 'To my darling grandma, I love you so much, thank you for everything, from your devoted granddaughter, Dawn French xx.' I think she'd like that.

So, you see, these two women have had a massive influence on me. Two entirely different extremes, two entirely different legacies. And I am grateful to both because without either of these opposing powerful forces, I don't think I would stop to balance things up as often as I do. It may frustrate me, but it's just the way I am.

Dear Jack,

When I was about six and your dad was about eight, only a couple of years younger than you are now — we went with our mum and dad to live on a hot island in the Mediterranean called Cyprus. Our dad, your grandad, who sadly you never met (you would have loved him, and boy would he have loved you), worked for the Royal Air Force and his bosses sent him to live over there for a few years. At the time we arrived, a frightening war was taking place on the island to do with the people who live there called Cypriots wanting their country to be separate from Great Britain. There was also some fighting between the two different types of people who lived there, the Turks and the Greeks, who had a long history of disliking each other, so all in all it was pretty scary.

The first house we lived in was in a place called Nicosia, which is in the north of the island. The house was big and painted white and pink with iron railings round the balconies. There was an older house next door where a Greek family lived and we all became friends. The mother of the family was called Androniki and she was very loud and bossy but very kind to us. She never stopped kissing me and your dad — you can imagine how much he liked that!

55

NOT! This lovely lady always used to call me Haravghi Moo instead of Dawn. She explained that the Haravghi bit is the Greek for dawn, as in the sunrise at the start of the day, and the little 'Moo' bit on the end of the name was in fact 'Mou' and is the way Greek people call you darling, or sweetheart. So, all the time I lived in Cyprus, our family called me 'Haravghi Mou', which slowly changed to just the plain old 'Moo' that you will have often heard your dad call me. At least, I *hope* that's why he's calling me that. If we find out that he's just being rude, I will need you to kick him hard on the shins for me. I'll show you how. I'm an expert at torturing your dad physically. Stick with me, kid, and I'll teach you how to do it mentally one day, and then he will be overpowered and the French kingdom will be yours, all yours, ha ha! (Do loud evil cackling here, Jack.)

While we were living in the big white-and-pink house, quite a lot of fighting was going on nearby and we would often hear gunshots and loud bangs, which were terrifying. We had to be safely locked up in our house by a certain time in the evening, as did everybody else. This is called a curfew and it lasted for some time. Our dad was busy at work and occasionally couldn't get home in the evenings so we were confined to our house and reliant on the radio to get instructions from the people who were in charge of the British on the island. One day, they would tell us to hang Union Jack flags on our front door to tell everyone we were British and the next day they would tell us to take them down as soon as

56

possible. We were even told to pack up everything several times because we were being evacuated to a safer place. All of this was very confusing and frightening. Our mum, your granny, had to be very strong and she helped lots of other families in the same situation because she was what's called a 'senior wife', meaning, I think, that she had more experience of being married to a serviceman than some of the other wives.

I remember one day that was particularly alarming. Granny kept telling Gary and me not to look out of the window and down into the street. There were gunshots very close by and it was really dangerous to be near the windows. Of course, as you know, I am a champion nosy parker and was even worse when I was little, so being a Curious Caroline, I couldn't resist a peek. I have never forgotten what I saw. A man was lying on the road right next to our house. I knew straight away he was dead. He had lots of blood on him and was lying in a strange crumpled way that would really hurt if you were alive. He was a Turk and had been shot by his enemy, a Greek. Granny was aware that gunmen, snipers, were aiming at the roof of our building and anyone who was on it. Honestly, Jack, you won't believe what she did. She marched up to the roof (remember we were under the curfew and she wasn't really allowed to go out), *still* wearing her apron, and she shouted at the gunmen to go away and leave us alone, that she had a family with young children inside to protect and that they should know better. She told them they were welcome to go and kill each other elsewhere, but not near her family and friends, thank you very much. While she was saying all this, she was taking down her washing, which was flapping in the warm breeze, and she told them off for that too, for fighting near her clean washing! These were *real* soldiers with *real* guns in the middle of a *real* battle, Jack! As you know, Granny can be pretty fearsome when she wants to be, so — can you believe it? — they apologised and moved elsewhere to continue their deadly fight. Wow! My mum was a superheroine.

The body of the Turk stayed there on the road for a few days though, and I tried not to look but I kept wondering when the poor dead man would be returned to his family, who must have been feeling so sad not knowing where he was. Every time I looked, I felt sort of embarrassed. Like being dead is a very private thing and that somehow it was rude to stare, but I also felt that perhaps I was the only one caring that he had been cruelly abandoned. I felt I had to keep looking for him to matter. It was horrible. Then, one day, he was not there. He was *there*, then he was *not there*. He had been *alive* and then he was suddenly *not alive*. He was younger than my own dad, but he was dead, and that was hard to understand.

During this difficult time, Cyprus was divided into two parts with a big border across the middle of the island from left to right, west to east. North of this line belonged to the Turks and south of this line belonged to the Greeks. We were moved to an air force base in the south, called Akrotiri near Limassol, and although the island was still at war, we were much safer and we were all together with other RAF families and life returned to relatively normal.

Well, Jack, let me tell you what 'normal' was like. When you live in a country like that, people tend to get up very early and do their work in the morning before it gets too hot in the middle of the day, then people have lunch and a little sleep, called a siesta, and then people go back to work in the late afternoon when it's cool again. So, us kids would go to school between 7am and 12 noon and then we would go to the beach *all afternoon, EVERY DAY!!* Fantastic! Sometimes a grown-up who wasn't working would come with us but often we would be dropped there, a group of about a dozen RAF kids ranging in age from six to sixteen, given a picnic for lunch and then be picked up again just before dark. Those long sizzling afternoons have remained in my memory as some of the happiest times I've ever had. Swimming and splashing with your dad and our mates, building huts and dens and sand sculptures. Finding lizards and seeing what happens when they lose their tails. Watching chameleons strain to change colour to match their environment as camouflage, and placing them on tartan rugs to see if they could rise to the challenge! Exploring among huge ancient rocks both on land and in the sea. Hearing stories of Greek gods like Aphrodite, the goddess of love. Daring each other to dive-bomb into the sea from higher and higher rocks. Eating olives

59

and smelling eucalyptus. Never wearing shoes other than flip-flops. Having loads of freckles and nutty-brown skin and bleached-by-the-sun blonde hair. Pretending to be mermaids and pirates. Inventing our own underwater towns and having jobs in submerged shops and factories. Befriending strange dogs on the beach and worrying about their welfare. Playing with local kids and not noticing for one second that we didn't speak the same language. Learning from them where the best caves and treasures were. Keeping secrets for each other, cutting our fingers on purpose and fusing our blood to become a forever conjoined family. Snorkelling in brightly coloured masks and darting through shards of underwater light chasing fish and octopuses. Noticing how big your skin is and how remarkable hair follicles on your hand are in the magnified world of goggles and water. Having an indented mark around your eyes where your mask had become part of your skin after you'd suckered the mask off. Having dazzling white fingernails and toenails where the sand had exfoliated them. Avoiding greasy suntan lotion and actively feeling vitamins entering you through your skin. The unsurpassable, exhilarating sense of freedom. We would often be hugged and kissed by friendly old ladies in black who smelt of coffee and smoke. They reminded me of Androniki, our friend in the north, and we were all sad to hear that she and her family had been forced to leave their house and all their possessions in the middle of the night and flee to the south. Hard to imagine,

60

isn't it? Leaving behind everything you have worked for for years, knowing that another family is going to move in the next day among all your stuff and live the life you have been forced to leave. This made our constant moving seem insignificant.

Most of the time we lived on the RAF base, your dad seemed to be dressed as a Roman centurion, wielding a huge toy sword, and roaring. Does this sound a bit like you, I wonder? Gary was very close to a little dog who lived with us called Whiskey, who I think we inherited from another family that were leaving. This was common practice among forces families. Pets were constantly passed around since they couldn't be shipped home. He was a great dog, springy and keen, and could see no other purpose in life other than to play. He often came in quite handy as a centurion's mascot or a hunting dog in Gary's games. He was also an accomplished lilo surfer.

Away from the beach, my playtime was taken up with four main activities. 1. Roller skating. Up and down the road for hours on end. Not the sleek in-line Rollerblades like you have. No, these had four wheels, one in each corner on a metal frame which you strapped to your shoes. They were ugly to look at and ungainly on my feet and made a huge rumbling noise on the pavement, but as far as I was concerned, I was a swan, gliding up and down the road in all my elegant splendour. I was sort of addicted to roller skating and would occasionally do it well after bedtime and on into the night, I loved it so much. I didn't really learn any nifty tricks or turns, I just loved the rhythmic swaying and feeling of speed. 2. Horse riding. Not a real one, you understand, no — a horse's face painted on the end of our fence with strings attached for reins which I sat on and jiggled about on for hours (!) pretending to be in endless imaginary gymkhanas and western movies. Oh, the joy. 3. Hairdos. Your granny had a friend who was training to be a hairdresser and she needed hair models so Granny volunteered me. This lady was mainly perfecting the art of bridal hairstyling, so twice a week, I would be the proud owner of an elaborate 'do' — usually 'up', and festooned with masses of curls and plastic daisies — that's what we liked in the sixties. Often the do would include ornate hairpieces which would be deftly pinned in to look like I had an enormous amount of piled-up hair. Sometimes the hairdo would be so fancy and flamboyant and flowery that my neck could not support it and I would simply fall over. Not good for roller skating. 4. Ballet. I was a divine dancer, so light, so graceful and renowned the world over as a champion junior prima ballerina who could leap higher than anyone else in the land. The trouble was, all of this was only true IN MY HEAD! I loved my ballet classes but was very quickly brought down to earth when your dad spied on one of my classes and said we looked and sounded like a herd of hippos. I couldn't cope with the disappointment of the reality after that, and soon gave up ballet for good. I blame him for my lack of success in that area. I'm pretty sure I could have been internationally acclaimed.

I do remember some sad times in Akrotiri, when Granny found out her dad had died and she cried for hours in front of a blow heater we had which glowed red. I remember her red face and her shiny hot red eyes and not really knowing how to make it all right for her. I also remember two other lots of crying. Everyone seemed to burst into tears when we heard of the death of someone called JFK in 1963. This person — who? — with no name, just initials, was important in America and he had been shot when he was visiting someone. That's all I knew, but a lot of crying happened, so I decided to join in because it seemed quite fascinatingly dramatic and tragic. However, I didn't stop skating. Roller skating and sobbing. Simultaneously. Quite a skill.

A similar thing happened two years later when a man called Churchill died and Granny and Grandad were extremely sombre. I had a bit more of a clue about him. I'd seen pictures — he looked like a grumpy bulldog and smoked fat cigars and was important in the war. I wept a few tears that day too, but mainly to see how sorrow looked in the mirror.

Actually, you know, hard as it is to believe it now, Granny and Grandad were really 'groovy' young parents back then. They really loved each other and were always smooching and dancing. They loved pop music like the Beatles, and Grandad especially loved Nat King Cole and Ella Fitzgerald and the Ink Spots and the Platters, and Johnny Cash and Matt Monro.

A really special thing happened to me one Christmas, Jack. Houses in hot countries don't have chimneys so I was obviously very worried about how Santa was going to get in with all our stuff. Granny told me not to worry, that he would find a way. Well, you can understand, I found it hard to sleep due to the worry and fear of disappointment. At about midnight, I heard the faint, very faint sound of bells, which grew louder and louder until there was a definite thud on our rooftop that shook the house. I ran to the window and opened the shutters and right there, outside MY window, was Santa himself with his sack. He asked if he could come through my bedroom since there was no chimney, so of course I let him in and he went through to the front room where the tree was. He rustled about a bit and then came back through with the empty sack and told me to go back to bed. I did. Straight away. But then I heard the bells again, so I shot over to the window and saw Santa in his sleigh, being pulled by all the reindeer rising higher and higher into the sky. I saw it with my own eyes! When I told them all about it the next morning, my dad said I must have been dreaming because Santa never lets you actually see him, but I'll tell you something, Jack. I did see him. I did.

Dear Madonna (the Madonna, Mrs Guy Ritchie, not a Madonna, the mother of Christ),

About 25 years ago, a posh fat girl and I started a female double act. We decided straight away that it should be female because both of us are of the woman persuasion and consequently the choice seemed obvious. On reflection, I think we done good with that instinct, because after all these don't-seem-a-day-too-long years, we have staunchly remained as women, and thusly our double act is correctly gendered. My sources inform me that you too are feminine typed, so I am muchly hopin' this note will agree with you and all your womanly ways.

From the very start of our comedy exploits the other woman and I have endeavoured to include you in and around our skits and japes. By dint of the writin' of your name on a bit of Auntie BBC headed notepaper inside a sketch where you also speak the funny bits too, we have invited you to come out to play with us. This has happened repeatedly often, so much so that after we is receivin' back your numerous rejections out of hand, we is havin' to rewrite the aforementioned hilarioso sketches to be *about* you rather than *with* you in it. It goes without sayin', so I will, that every time you dolloped out the bucketful of NO to us, we was left with no other alley to go

65

up and wee in, than to ridicule you. Sometimes with bile and venomosity but always with gentle pokin'. We fervently hoped you would be watchin' with open eyeballs and a full heart and that you would eventually be comin' around to the idea of joinin' in rather than sittin' on the side with no friends and smelly pants. After all, we are not a crazy, we is the leadin' double act of ladies in the comedy department for, oooh, over timpty-two years already. No one else has come even close up our behinds, although presently there *are* a few clever new puppy funny girls doin' bitin' on our comedy heels, but that don't bother us too intensely for we is stoppin' soon, so they can be the toppest for all we care.

Just before the other one and I bow away from the lemon and limelight though, I would like to be tellin' you that you has made one big giant haystacks of a mistake, momma. You would of got to be in some funny clothes and do laughing, laughing all the livelong day, instead of just lookin' cool for everyone to see, and seekin' out the latest trend of clowns to be associated with, instead of the French and the Saunders act who have always loved you truly and madly and deeply. There was one time when we very nearly done it, do you remember? You was goin' to be up London, as were we at a simultaneous time, and there was a laugh-till-you-poo scene already written including of your good self. It was lookin' like gettin' close to bein' done but then suddenly you were sendin' off a faxular note explainin' your busyness with two unimportant and irrelevant things. One was the singin' and

66

actin' of Evita the Peruvian, and the other was the gestatin' of the baby of Lourdes. Honestly, what kind of other measly excuse would you be comin' up with futurely? Well, as it happens, and it did, you came up with absurdist and ever increasingly unreliable reasons to not take part. All of them were silly and did you no credit in the good lies department of skills.

So, mainly my reasoning is this: thank you for being so Teflon resilient with your tough rebukes and endless restraining orders on us. It has taught us a big lesson to not miss after double maths with Miss Alford, which is simply that you is got a humour bypass that takes the red bus route round the back of fun without stopping at the park-and-ride of titters, so you could of got on a happy shopper to cock a hoop. You twot!

But anyway, keep doin' singin' because that bit's good. Of that we are jointly agreed.

Good luck for evermore, whatever it is you do.

Dear Sarah Walton,

I had to write to you because you were one of the very few 'civvy' friends I made as a kid. As you know, us air force 'crab' brats generally stuck together but when we came to live at RAF Turn Hill near your house in Market Drayton in Shropshire, we hit it off straight away, didn't we? You were so welcoming to me at quite a tricky time. It was only tricky really because I was 11 years old and my body was a hive of hormonal confusion and my brain was a soggy pink sponge of girly emotion ready to drip with inexplicable tears at any moment. Plus, there was suddenly hair. Everywhere. Alarming.

I always valued the security of the RAF base where I knew all the faces, but there was something magical about your house. I remember it as big and rambling and friendly with a toasty country kitchen. Am I right, did it have a mezzanine with banisters where you could see the entire first floor as you went up the stairs? You had lots of animals, which was a major lure for me. There was a new litter of curly-haired chocolate-coloured puppies that was a source of great delight. We lay on your lawn for hours playing with them and naming them and hugging them and dressing them and not minding being bitten by their tiny sharp teeth. I recall you having a veritable menagerie of animals — cats and kittens and guinea pigs and rabbits and hamsters and even a donkey. Am I accurate about all this, OR have I had a rosy false memory where I have supplanted you with Dr Dolittle?! Whatever, I know how lovely it was to be in your orbit and how loving your family were towards me.

I do clearly remember when we decided to do a little double-act turn for a talent contest at our school. Was Mr Kitching the headmaster of the school, and was it next to a graveyard which meant I had to hold my breath *ALL DAY* so that bad spirits couldn't get in me, which meant that sports activities outside were a potentially fatal pastime, since one usually needs to breathe during sports, I find, especially if you're a bit fat, when you need to breathe *a lot*. We performed Esther and Abi Ofarim's extraordinary hit 'Cinderella Rockefella'. A call-and-response classic . . . I wore a leather jacket and took on the male role and you were the pretty one in the dress. We mimed, I freely admit that, but we went down a storm and, best of all, people LAUGHED! I can't remember whether we anticipated that response. I rather think we imagined they would be astounded by our accurate impersonations. So, two big lessons were learned by me on that day: 1. ham it up and give the audience permission to find you hilarious, and 2. it doesn't matter if your impressions are pants so long as they're funny. Oh, and 3. try to get the other one to wear the leather jacket and be the Boy as often as poss to avoid cumbersome costume and stubble rash. Thanks for being the first of several successful partnerships I've had on and off stage!

When you and I weren't at school or petting animals, or just petting, we did a lot of dreaming didn't we? Mainly about being bridesmaids. I loved those conversations about how our dresses would be, how our tresses would be, how very like princesses we would be ... If only somebody, ANYBODY, would ask us! I thought it would be quite good to offer ourselves as a pair, a brace of bridesmaids. We were, after all, a splendid match, similar height, same taste, which conveniently avoids any thundering bridesmaid-dress-choosing tantrums. We were friends, which surely helps to sidestep ugly bridesmaid rivalrous wars that inevitably end in tears and a certain amount of hair damage or, worse, hairpiece damage. We were prepared to practise brides-maid tandem walking for *hours* so's we could be perfectly harmoniously in step like a couple of highly trained pantomime-Cinderella-goes-to-the-ball-carriage-pulling white miniature ponies. Elegant, light and breezy with a perky symmetry, if a bit chunky. Clippety-clop, clippety-clop. Bliss. If we could, what flowers would we choose? What headpieces, what shoes? Heel or flat? Would there be gloves? Would we be permitted the tiny tremulous first step of a relationship with the forbidden love — make-up? Just a smattering of mascara perhaps or the lightest brushing of a mum's shimmery coral lipstick? Oh, we could only dream.

Then, one blessed day, it happened. My mum

told me that my beloved Uncle Owen and his lovely fiancée, the irrepressible Joan, were coming to visit and that the bride-to-be wanted to have a chat with me. They were due to be married and I could only hope that this was *the* conversation I'd been waiting for my *whole* life! At last, I was on the brink of bridesmaidhood for sure and boy was I going to enjoy it to the full, I was going to relish every crystal-slippered, lacey-gloved, teary-eyed, dew-droppy, rose-petally, acres of tuille and netty, glossy, girly moment. Every perfect moment. I wasn't going to forget you though, you were definitely part of the deal, although of course you weren't actually part of the family and had never actually met Joan, but somehow, through sheer righteous force of the plan's perfectness, I would surely persuade her that you were to be included.

The day of their visit came and after a seemingly endless lunch at our house, where no one even mentioned the wedding, Joan asked if we could go for a walk together. Oh my holy God. This was it. We had never 'gone for a walk' before. We circumnavigated Buntingsdale Lake while I politely answered well-intentioned questions about school and life and school. I wanted to yell 'Just ask me! Don't delay another second! I'm going to say yes! Ask me soon! Ask me now! Ask me!!' Eventually, after a marathon amount of walking, we finally sat down and I nearly wet myself with anticipation, I even had my 'No really, me? I'm so shocked! Of course, I'd be honoured' face prepared just below the skin ready to pop up and be seemingly aghast at

71

the surprise of the moment. Yes, yes, she started to talk about the wedding and all their plans . . . 'Yes! I will of course be your bridesmaid — look no further for a devoted handmaiden, you lucky bride, you,' I was thinking, but she hadn't actually asked yet, so I suppressed my excitement and cocked my head and tried desperately to appear to be listening. 'Hurry, hurry, I might faint if you don't get to it. You know you need me. Just ask! Oh, and by the way, my friend Sarah and I are sort of joined at the hip, could she be one too?' I thought. Hang on, now she was telling me about her family and all the little girls in it who would make suitable bridesmaids. 'Yes, yes, there will be a bevy of us and we will resemble a bower of delicate flower fairies as we follow you up the aisle holding your gossamer train aloft with our wands,' I thought. Oops, careful, floated off into my own head a bit too long there, and now her expression has changed to a sort of pitying frown while I have mistakenly retained my listening rictus. Oops, quickly change it to match hers. Yes, now we are both frowning and looking sad. Why are we looking sad? Tune in, Dawn, what is she actually saying? Something about too many nieces, odd numbers, how I will apparently have lots of other opportunities and for me not to be too upset, and am I OK? What is she telling me? My tear ducts seem to get wind of the devastating rejection before I do, and start to do impulse crying. Why am I crying? Auntie Joan has her arm around me and is apologising. Why? — OH — MY — ACTUAL — GOD! She has told me

I'm not one. I haven't passed. I'm not in. Not can bridesmaid be. Me no bridesmaid. No. Not. No. Out. Go. Begone. Not. No floatiness. No wings. No Sarah. No. None. No . . . No!! My *single solitary* reason to live, second to puppy-nuzzling of course, and third to Peter Tork worship, snatched away in a flea's heartbeat. It was quicksilver. It was there. Then it wasn't. I was a bridesmaid. Then I wasn't. Of course Joan had never said that I *would* be, but that's not the point. I *wasn't* going to be.

I managed to reassure her that despite my silly tears, I really didn't mind. After all, she wasn't being malicious, just honest. Yeah, sure I didn't mind. The rabid injustice of it all sputtered inside me until it grew into a full howling tornado of hurt and anger which made me want to spear all bridesmaids everywhere immediately with my red-hot sharpened rods of spite. The only reason I didn't is because I am execrably polite and monstrously mindful of others. Otherwise I would have joyfully taken lives, I would have happily abandoned myself to a bridesmaid killing spree of behemoth propor-tions and willingly languished in jail for ever to have that sweet taste of revenge on my lips for only a nanosecond. I wanted bridesmaid blood.

As it was, we returned home and through gritted teeth I explained to my mum that there was indeed to be a full complement of fluffy bridesmaids but that I was not to be one of them. Never mind, eh? Mum saw through my pretence instantly and knew I would nurse the resentment into a snarling, snapping, biting dangerous thing unless she took decisive displacement action. A week later we drove to Manchester and we spent too much money on an outfit for me that was fit for one purpose only — to upstage those fecking chosen ones, the bridesmaids. I ended up at that wedding in an eye-catching, extraordinary and (like all revenge buys) ill-advised get-up. It took the form of a bright pink trouser suit. The trousers were flared, the top was a cape with gold braided buttons at the Nehru neck. The hat was jockey-inspired, also pink. The blouse was frilly-fronted, also pink. The shoes were black patent leather with a T-bar. The socks were school (mistake). Certainly I was noticeable. If only for all the wrong reasons. I looked like an Austin Powers reject. Thank heavens that, a short while later, my very cool, jazzy, clever Uncle Mike and his equally groovy fiancée Trish finally granted my wish and asked me to be bridesmaid at their wedding. It was a real sixties wedding and Trish's lovely sister Heather had to play your part, Sarah, because we had moved by then, and also mainly because she was Trish's sister. Anyway, I got to do it and it was utterly dreamy and included gloves *and* a fancy hairdo *and* a small heel. Praise be.

I had to laugh years later when Len and I were married and his nieces Donna and Babette were my bridesmaids. Jackie, a different niece who I knew less well obviously felt a degree of this bridesmaid envy I speak of, and decided to turn up in a canary-yellow bridesmaid outfit of her own devising. She went a step further than me

74

and for that I applaud her. Bring on the bridesmaids! Let *all* women and girls invited to weddings come in their own bridesmaid outfits if they so choose!

I never found out if you managed to be one. Hope you did. Otherwise you might still be as dangerously murderous as I was.

Any time you want to do synchronised slow walking, with fabulous hairdos and matching accessories, let me know!

Dear Dad,

I am trying to book a holiday. It has to be one
week long and in the UK somewhere. We haven't
got enough time to go abroad, and besides, I
don't really want to do that — I'm feeling a bit
carbon-footprint guilty, plus I hate flying. Flying,
for me, is utterly exhausting, for the simple
reason that it is my duty (on behalf of *all* the
passengers, I hasten to add) to keep the plane in
the air by sheer force of my mind . . . If I lose
concentration for even a minute, the massive
metal crate will surely plummet earthwards and
hundreds of tragic deaths would be on my
conscience. Well, if we could *find* my conscience,
which will definitely have been ripped backwards
through my arsebum on impact. Woe betide I
should have a little kip — chaos would certainly
ensue if I did. I'm not sure how all the many
planes I'm *not* on stay up. There must be some
cosmic system whereby a mind/plane controller
like me is placed on each and every flight. I don't
know what the process is, but it is obviously
working. On the whole. All of this means that
any trip abroad involving a flight equals major
stress so I have to balance that out with how
relaxing the holiday is going to be. Since we only
have a week, two flights don't add up to funsville
for me. No, I want to find a British-based

76

holiday. Quite difficult considering the different needs, likes and dislikes of all three of us. I like sea, art, food, naps, telly and dog. Len likes books, heat, pictures, tunes, wine, comics and walks. Billie likes bed, phone, PlayStation, Facebook, iPod, boys and dark rooms. Usually we try to do a bit of all of the above, but that often results in no one being satisfied.

We *have* had some splendid holidays, the like of which we could never have imagined as kids. We often stay in private rented houses so as to keep away from eager Brits with camera phones. I don't normally mind if people want a quick photo, but I have an entirely different mindset when I'm on holiday, and I feel strangely shocked that my work-life 'stuff' like photos and autographs has intruded on my private family time. It just feels inappropriate and I get quite embarrassed. I find it hard that people don't read the obvious signals, when you're meandering about hand in hand with your old man and your kid, nosying in art galleries or quietly reading a book in the back of a cafe. It is so clear that I am off duty, so to speak. Some people can be unbelievably rude — we've had folk who pull up a chair at the table where we are eating, assuming, I suppose, that we would enjoy the addition of their company on a blatantly romantic, intimate occasion! We have experienced overexcited or drunk people standing on chairs and announcing to a whole piazza of unaware and frankly uninterested tourists that we are over there in the corner, look. We've had photos taken from the balcony of our hotel *into* the bedroom, and on one excruciating occasion, Len and I were on honeymoon in Kenya and the dining room full of Brits joined in a loud chant of 'We know what you've been doing' as we entered. Exit swiftly stage left. Room service, thank you, goodnight.

The worst ever occasion of such thoughtlessness wasn't on holiday, it was at a sports event with Billie. She is a bit of a dab hand at the ol' shot-put, and she's not bad at discus either, and running. In fact, if only she would believe it, she's a fantastic athlete, but she is so utterly self-effacing and tough on herself, that she virtually disables her ability purposely, so as to deal with it more easily. What a wonderful, curious, complicated young woman she is! Anyway, on occasion, she *does* allow herself to acknowledge her skills and she takes part in various athletic competitions as a member of her local club, Bracknell Athletics. Imagine that, Dad, I am the mother of an athletic kid! Who'd've thought it, eh? I have been suddenly launched into a world of tracksuits, running shoes, personal bests, pep talks, endless packed lunches, safety pins for numbers to be attached to shirts, energy drinks, pulled muscles, Deep Heat, orders of events, statistics, long circuitous journeys to old stadiums at the arse end of brown towns, and loud, utterly biased hollering from the stands. I have never been good at sport. I've given tennis and hockey and netball my best shot on a few occasions but not so's anyone would notice. Therefore, being part of a sporty backup team is quite a novelty and quite thrilling. I can be nearly sporty, vicariously, through her. The fab thing about a local athletics club is that it unites everyone, whatever colour, background, school, religion or anything else. I have been astounded to see the dedication of the coaches, all volunteers, to these kids, and equally the parents who sacrifice so much of their spare time to join in and support. The folk at Bracknell Athletics Club were immediately welcoming to Billie and to us, with a palpable sense of 'nothing special' — thankfully — just a new kid joining and some new parents supporting. We were in the team, therefore we had to pull our weight and join in.

The single most remarkable person I met there was Marcia Toft, a mum whose love for and pride in her own kids is a treat to witness. Her loving but firm handling of her posse and her dedication to their interests in the club really struck me. She is a ferociously intelligent woman who takes no shit from anyone but has a heart of candyfloss. The kind of person you wish had been your chum at school, a cheeky and protective force of nature. She knew instantly that I was floundering like a carp out of water in the fresh, new-to-me sporting world. I was not conversant with the rules, the etiquette, the form. She explained stuff to me, about the sports, the club, the officials, etc. She helped me to understand what to bring along to survive those long cold days as a spectator, and she provided the gateway into a community we had hitherto not known, and about which we were patently ignorant. I was tentative initially about our inclusion in this group of strangers, because I didn't want to assume any kind of overfamiliarity, but that fear was unfounded.

The day came for our club to be represented in the Southern Counties Women's League at Kingston. There were about eight to ten clubs competing and the stadium was heaving. Our Bracknell lot decided to camp out on the grass, close to the discus net and the shot-put sector. It was a warm but blustery day and the events went well for us. Lots of our kids were coming in the top three, and the continual announcements of results from the speakers mounted on poles around the ground bode well for us. The picnics were tasty, the kids were in tip-top form and the whiff of victory was in our nostrils. Then, something terrible happened. Billie had thrown well in her shot-put event and we thought she might even bag first place but couldn't be sure till the official announcement was made. There was a hubbub of group excitement building, and then the familiar, loud, tinny voice from the speaker announced: 'In the under 15s shot-put . . . third was Katie blah blah . . . with blah metres . . . second was Tanisha blah blah with blah metres and first was Billie Henry with blah blah huge amount of winning metres!' We started to cheer and I grabbed Billie for a victor's hug. But Mr Tinny Official hadn't finished his announcement. He went on . . . 'Billie Henry, whose mother, the celebrity DAWN FRENCH, is here with us today, ladies and gentlemen, sitting over there on the grass. Nice to see you out today with all the normal mums and dads!'

I'm sure on reflection he meant no harm, but his careless and misguided attention started the rumblings of a volcano of foaming fury inside me. It started a long way down, from a Gollum depth I didn't even know I had, somewhere infernally deep, around the soles of my feet, and it rose up very fast, gathering velocity and ferocity at an alarming rate. Past my spleen where it gathered bile, past my guts where it gathered acid, past my bladder where it gathered gall, through my belly where it gathered humiliation, through my blood where it gathered hotter blood, through my heart where it gathered resentment, through my throat where it gathered pepper and through my mind where it gathered guilt. During this internal tornado, I found myself in a reflex action, charging purposefully towards the official's booth on the other side of the track. Billie was tugging at me, pleading, 'No, Mum, it's OK. I don't mind! Just leave it!' but I was hell-bent on a meet and right retribution. I wanted to slaughter — nothing less would satisfy. Stomp-stomp over the field, getting closer and closer. All the while I could taste the sourness of the soup of emotional sewage boiling further and further up my craw and curdling in my mouth. I was going to give it to him in an eloquent but savage verbal attack he wouldn't forget. How dare he highlight me over my daughter's hard-won achievements? How dare he make this day about anything other than the kids? How dare he sully this lovely, pure, clean, happy moment with the filth of 'celebrity'?! As I approached the booth, I caught my first sight of the enemy, three elderly silvered ex-athletes in their authoritarian whites beaming at me with expectation and joy. I opened the door and the main culprit, Official Tin Voice, a lofty and superior old fox, greeted me with: 'More tea, vicar?!' What fresh hell was this? I was so staggered by his blindness and insensitivity that my hitherto torrent of emotional lava somehow instantly diluted. Instead of an explosion of precise and accurate verbal spew, landing all over his face and dripping down on to his Dazzy whiter-than-whites, my body made an alternative choice — to blubber like a baby. Oh dear God, no. Not now. Come on! I need some steel! I endeavoured to use words, but I couldn't. I only had access to vowels and tears and snot. This, maddeningly, prompted a big hug from all three of the enemy. I did manage to blurt out a version of the 'How dare you?!' speech, but it manifested itself mainly as 'My daughter! Blub blub my daughter!' which they understandably misread as over-effusive pride. Billie was crumbling with embarrassment behind me, and led me away to the car. By now I was only liquid, so I poured myself into the driver's seat and tried to compose myself while she packed the car with the detritus of our day out. Various members of our club came over to sympathise and to share their annoyance and offer support. The journey home was glum and sniffly for me. I felt that this was another opportunity to have a full and frank chat about the drawbacks of being in the public eye. We have often talked about it, and Billie is in no doubt about my utter disrespect for the culture of celebrity. I didn't get the chance to know how you would have felt Dad, about this strange phenomenon of celebrity befalling your own daughter. I suspect you would have mistrusted it as much as I do. In my opinion, fame, money and politics are among the most corrupting influences we live with. It is always wise to keep an eye on any creeping personal corruptions we know full well are happening. Fame is toxic. There *are* benefits, but even those are dangerous if you get too used to them. Mostly, recognition is debilitating. It disables your ability to judge or behave normally because you are constantly reacting to people's preconceived perceptions of what or who you are, or what you need and want. Plus, you are constantly on guard to resist the bluster of gushing praise which is blown up your bum. It's very tempting to swig from it, but it is a poisoned chalice. I find the status and value system in our country confusing — how have we come to this place where footballers and singers and jesters are prized above teachers and doctors and carers? Don't get me wrong — I don't underestimate the importance of entertainment, not at all, *BUT* why are we paying so much attention to the wrong people? I have benefited hugely from this perverse social structuring, I don't deny that. I don't feel guilty, I feel baffled. While life's hierarchies are so topsy-turvy, it is even *more* crucial not to confuse lustre with importance.

Anyway there I was, apologising to Bill for the idiocy of adults who are impressed with the wrong thing. I was explaining how helpless I felt when her achievement was eclipsed by a stupid error of judgement. I told her it would be so great to be able to turn off the fame knob when it suited and that is practically always when I am around her. Billie told me to chill out, that she sees it coming a mile off every time, and finds it *hilarious* to watch, anthropologist-like, the behaviour of supposedly normal humans around the shiny quicksilver that is celebrity. Of course she sees it, she is in the observer's seat where the view is all too clear. She found the whole episode funny and embarrassing, not least my phenomenally entertaining overreaction! She patted my hand and said, 'There, there, dearie, you'll get over it. You'll worry when no one notices you.' God, I hope that's not true.

Anyway, I started this letter talking about holidays because, given only a week to find a good one, I wondered whether we should hire a canal boat. I remember all those lovely holidays we had on that tiny fibreglass motorboat you bought. It was only a two-berth really, wasn't it? But Gary and I would sleep at the back, under the cover at night, while you and Mum were in the cabin. It was so exciting. Chugging around the canals and rivers during the day, negotiating the locks and the islands, and mooring up at night wherever we fancied. Reading Spike Milligan and *The Hobbit* aloud by the light of the tilley lamp and holding on whenever the wake of a passing vessel rocked us too hard. I loved that you assumed the role of captain too

84

seriously, that we had to use nautical terminology for everything and be mindful of safety issues at sea. Not that we ever were actually 'at sea'. We were on canals in Shropshire and Lincolnshire and Yorkshire and the Midlands. Family jokes started there and have never let up. Going to 'the head' (loo) in a bucket affair in a tiny cupboard where everyone could hear your business was a rich seam for laughs. Noises were mimicked and the loud gushing of Dad wee which resounded around the whole boat was masked with the cry of 'Horse!' since you would wee at the rate of a urineful carthorse. To this day, we still shout it to cover up the noise. And I clearly remember the time when Gary was staring at me in my swimsuit oddly, and suddenly exclaimed: 'Dad! Dawn's got bosoms coming out!' Only *all* of the Trent canal witnessed that special moment!

We must have looked an odd sight on the canal. You in an ostentatious captain's hat, barking navy lark orders at your junior matelots. Mum holding Poppet, our Westie, over the side so she could do her business, and a sparrow in a cage on deck. Oscar the sparrow, a little no-hoper fledgling who fell out of his nest when he was only a few minutes old, was miraculously nursed to full adult birdhood and only wanted to hang around with humans because he was convinced he was one. He was a pet we inherited when Uncle Tot and Auntie June were posted abroad and he came everywhere with us. It didn't occur to us that it was strange to have a wild bird in a cage. The door of the cage was often left open for him, and he would occasionally hop about and stretch his wings, but his preference was to stay near us, his human buddies, who were just like him, human. OK?! Now back off and make with the seed.

I can't remember ever going abroad on holiday as a kid. We went to Scotland once, and drove around looking at castles and mountains, didn't we? Gary and I were teenagers then and holidays with you guys were totally uncool. We would have preferred to be at home fumbling about with our boyfriends or girlfriends. I think my own kid has reached that same point. She agreed to come on a sailing holiday last year where we bobbed about exploring various Greek islands with cousins and nieces and nephews, but she was mainly preoccupied with sending texts home to friends saying things like 'Am being forced to be interested in Greece. Send help' and 'Dull parents laughing all day — why?' and 'Saw fit guy who seemed interested but no, yawn, we had to 'eat in a taverna' instead. So random.' Yes. I know I shouldn't be reading them. On her phone. After she's gone to bed. Checking if she's doing any international drug deals. Or looking for clues as to whether she's considering having sex. I know it's wrong, but I'm a pathological nosy parker and I can't resist. If it's any consolation, it takes ages to decipher them since the above messages read something like 'dl pts. Laffg al dy — ?' and 'Sw ft gy — intd — bt no, we 'et @ tvn'. Rndm Lol.' At least I have to work at it to invade her privacy. So, if she didn't really enjoy the Greek boat experience, is it likely she is going to enjoy the British canal experience, where she will have to live up close and personal with her 'dull parents' for a whole week? I think not. Mmmm, better rethink holiday idea. Maybe stay at home? All do stuff we want to in separate rooms? Sounds sublime.

Dear Billie,

When I was about 13, I was invited to a party by my friend Karen. I was *so* excited about this party because I knew that there was going to be a boy there called Mark who I really liked. Although we had some mutual friends and we had been in the same room on various occasions, he had paid me no attention whatsoever and was blissfully unaware that I existed at all. I found this heartbreaking and I was determined to get him to notice me. I planned to summon up my courage and somehow do this at the party that Saturday night. In order to impress him, I decided to wear my new purple suede hot pants. Hot pants were what we called shorts back then and they were the singular most fashionable item you could own. I saved up my pocket money for AGES, I did odd jobs for extra cash, and eventually I had enough to go to a big shop called Trago Mills and buy them. They didn't really fit me, they were far too tight, but I wanted them SO much I didn't mind how uncomfortable they were. Everyone wanted hot pants, but as is so often the cruel injustice of fashion they suited very few people. I *wasn't* one of those chosen few. It was definitely an advantage to be tall, thin and have long, shapely legs. I had none of these attributes but I convinced myself I could carry the hot pants off nevertheless. My whole outfit was new. Starting from the bottom up (the bottom of my legs, that is, not my actual bottom): brown suede wedge heels with espadrille straps around my Miss Piggy ankles. American tan tights. The bright purple suede hot pants with shiny buttons on the pockets. Above the waist was a considerable overflow of puppy fat, which was forced upwards and outwards by the too-tight waistband of the hot pants. On top of this was a cream cheesecloth smock top with stringy lacing down the front, slightly see-through, with flared sleeves. Many Indian bangles about the wrists. Large dangly earrings. Round my neck a homemade pendant made of bent horseshoe nails on a black leather thong. Long straight hair parted in the centre with no fringe, a bit like Ali MacGraw, but only a very tiny bit. Green suede shoulder bag with tasselly fringing. Big round sunglasses worn permanently on head. I glanced in the mirror and decided I looked pretty damned fine. Actually I didn't feel this at all but I knew I would have to fake feeling good in order to leave the house. So it was with this pretend confidence that I went to look for my dad to arrange my lift home. I was hoping to negotiate a later pickup just in case Mark might notice me! I met my dad in the hallway and he asked me to come in to the front room for a quick chat. He closed the door behind us, and asked me to sit down. My heart sank. I thought I was in for a good talking-to. I was right about that, but it wasn't the usual precautionary drill, it was something else. Something I've always remembered, especially if I'm feeling a bit insecure — which we all do sometimes, don't we?

It was a long time ago but, to the best of my memory, it went something like this:

Dad: Sit down, puddin'. Actually, before you sit down, give us a twirl. Wow, you look really lovely, a right bobby-dazzler. Are those shorts? Or lederhosen?

Me: They're hot pants, Dad.

Dad: Where did you get those? Millets?

Me: No, Dad, Trago Mills.

Dad: Well, you look very . . . pretty. They are quite short . . .

Me: Yes, because they're shorts.

Dad: I see, well you look really super in them. Very dandy. Super.

Me: Can I come home late?

Dad: Hold your horses there, missus. Before we talk about arrangements, there's something I want to say. What's that black stuff in your eyes by the way?

Me: Kohl.

Dad: Coal?

Me: No, Kohl. It's Indian. I've worn it before.

Dad: Have you? I've seen black stuff on *top* of your eyes before, and maybe something underneath the bottom bit but that looks like it's right inside . . .

Me: That's where it's supposed to go.

Dad: You might get conjunctivitis with that.

Me: I won't.

Dad: You might.

Me: It's . . . antiseptic.

Dad: Is it?

Me: No — but it's fine, trust me. Millions of Indian ladies haven't died of it yet.

Dad: Does it hurt?

Me: No.

Dad: It would hurt me.

Me: You're not wearing it.

Dad: No. I never would.

Me: Good. Be quite hard to explain if you did.

Dad: Some men wear eye stuff, in other countries . . . For instance, when I was in Aden —

Me: Anyway . . .

Dad: Anyway. This party tonight . . .

Me: It's fine, Dad. There won't be any alcohol.

Dad: I should hope not. Alcohol? You can't drink alcohol!

Me: I know. That's why there won't be any.

Dad: You're not allowed to buy it or drink it, young lady.

Me: I know.

Dad: It's against the law.

Me: I know.

Dad: No alcohol whatsoever. Do you understand?

Me: Yes.

Dad: Right, I'm trusting you on that —

Me: There won't be any.

Dad: There'd better *not* be any.

Me: There won't.

Dad: How do you know?

Me: Because Karen said so.

Dad: She said there wouldn't be any?

91

Me: Yes, because her parents'll be there, they're going next door during the party.

Dad: Nearby?

Me: Next door!

Dad: Good. If they weren't next door, would there be alcohol then?

Me: Don't know. Maybe.

Dad: There wouldn't.

Me: Wouldn't there?

Dad: No. I'm telling you. There wouldn't. OK?

Me: OK . . . Can I come home late?

Dad: Here's the thing I want to say . . .

Me: Can we hurry?

Dad: Shush. How much do you think Mum and I love you?

Me: Um . . . a lot?

Dad: More than a lot, Dawn. Much more. When you were born, you had scarlet fever, and for a couple of days there, it was a bit touch and go . . .

Me: I nearly died?

Dad: Yes, and when we thought we might lose you we realised just how much we loved you already, even your brother was worried . . .

Me: Yeah, worried I might survive . . .

Dad: Don't be facetious, which by the way is one of the few words in the English language with all the vowels in the correct order. No, we were all very anxious. It was then we knew that having a baby girl, having you, completed our little family. That's all we ever wanted. The four of us together for ever. We had so much to look forward to, so much to learn. So much to do, so much fun to have. Mum and I fought hard to be together and to make this family. I know it's been a challenge sometimes, with all the different relatives who have lived with us, all the travelling and moving and new schools. I know when I've had to go away on my own for work it's been hard for you all. We haven't had much money, no surplus certainly, but we have saved and shared everything together, haven't we? In this family, no one is lonely because we're always there for each other, the four corners that keep our square whole, each connected to and looking out for each other, equally. You are a vital part of that. You and your brother are our life, our reason and our happiness. We adore you both and we feel blessed to have you, and to witness you grow into the remarkable young people you are becoming. You are both so impressive! Truly, you are our world, our joy. Never forget what a treasure you are, and if your faith in that ever wobbles, have a look in the mirror and have confidence in what you see. You are a rare thing, an uncommon beauty, a dazzling, exquisite, splendid young woman. Look! You must know it's true, you're a corker. How lucky any boy would be to have you on his arm. They should fight tournaments to win your affection, they should kill for your favour. Don't you dare be grateful for their attentions, you utterly deserve it and, more than that, you deserve the very best. Don't think for one second you should settle for other people's rejects. *You* are the princess, you are the prize, so be choosy and take your time. You decide how, when and where, *not* them. They will wait. Of course they will. Who wouldn't wait for someone so priceless? There is no one better. Know this: if anything ever happened to you, Moo, our lives would fall apart, we would be devastated and this family would never be happy again. So, you must take care of yourself, you must guard against danger. When you are out of this house it is up to you to protect yourself, your reputation and your dignity. We love you and we need you.

OK. That's all. You can go now. And yes, you can come home late, 1 am at the outside, understand?

Me: Yeah . . . Thanks, Dad.

Then we had a big hug and off I went to the party, feeling ten foot tall and fabulous in my hot pants. Mark did come to talk to me that night, but I wasn't that interested. He wasn't really good enough, to be honest . . .

My dad gave me armour that night and I have worn it ever since. I could never quite buy the bit about being the best, but I *do* believe I am worth something. My self-esteem, still surprisingly intact after quite a few attacks, is still my strong centre, my metal, and I owe that to him. He

94

spoke honestly of his faith in me and it was such a sunshiny warmth that I grew towards it like a tomato plant.

The comforting thing is, Bill, I may not have my dad around any more but I do carry his values and his belief in me. When I think of what he said to me — every word applies to you. I'm so sorry you didn't get to meet him because he would have loved you so much and you would have loved him back. The only gift I can give you from him is this letter and the hope that you will read it, imagining his sentiments are addressed to you, through me and Dad. Hopefully, with time, you will come to know a greater and truer self-worth and know how valuable you are to us and to the family.

That's all. You can go now. Be home by 1 am at the outside, understand?

Dear David Cassidy,

It's very important that you read this letter because it is going to change your life in a BIG way. If this is being read by a minion or secretary or bouncer, I literally beg you to pass this on to David — he will thank you for it one day in the future. Big time. That of which, I can assure you.

David, if I may call you that, it feels so right to me, so natural, but I fear I may overstep my place to be so intimate so early on, but I am forced to be candidly open about my sheer knowledge in and about you, now and always. Let me put it like this — you don't know me yet but one day in our future when we stand high on a desert rock with the sun on our faces instead of frowns, looking at a golden sunset after an oh-so-perfect loving day, you will wonder how you ever *didn't* know me and how you ever survived and grew without me, both spiritually *AND* on the outside. Because, David, we are meant to be together, and to deny our hearts' true path to joy would just be foolish, never mind devastating. I have never, ever in my whole life known something to be so truly real. You probably get loads of post from silly teenage girls who immaturely try to adore you just because they fancy you. That isn't me. Let me make this clear, I *don't* fancy you, I *know* you. My soul knows your soul even though there is a crater of nothingness between us. Sometimes when I see you on telly, I don't even look, so that I won't be taken in by your sheer and true handsomeness. Oh yes, I know it's there, I know how fanciable you are, that is oh-so-obvious right from the start to me and whoreds of others but that's not what I'm here for. I am not just some here-today-gone-tomorrow sort of person who blows hot and cold like a feather in the wind blown about by air. Oh no. Believe me, my love for you is, was and always will be true and oh-so-real. Hunt high and low over hill and dale forever and a day and you will never find a heart as big as mine for you is.

David, I am worried about you at the moment. Every time I see you on telly, you seem to be surrounded by whoreds of yes-men and yes-women. Not when you are doing interviews obviously, they are probably secreted nearby then. But David, is that what you really want? So many people around you simply doing every-thing you do/do not want? It is exactly these kind of people who will prevent you from meeting me. (When I came to see you at Wembley I waited outside, in the midst of a baying mob, for over two hours until someone finally had the manners to tell us you had left the area right at the end of the show before we could even get there.) You see? If things carry on like this, we will never meet and then how would you feel?

I have put my address on the top of this letter so that you can write back to me and we can arrange to meet up away from all those endless looking eyes and listening ears. I can personally guarantee that you will find peace here in my house. I will make sure my parents are both out — they do sometimes go to archery together, so that would be a good time to come, on Thursday evenings. (Except at half-term when my brother comes home from boarding school and we are going on our boat on the Trent canal. Again. YAWN. I would much rather see you.) However we arrange it, I can assure you of peace and quiet and my 100% full attention, with snack refreshments and whatever drink you choose. Obviously I will have to buy those ahead of time so you will need to send me a list of your favourites, with *most* favourite as No. 1 and so on. (Bear in mind that we cannot always get American drinks here, e.g. soda pops or Popsicles or ice-cream sundaes etc., but we can get English drinks like Coke, Vimto or Kia-Ora squash. Plus my parents have got some sherry and a bottle of Asti Spumante if you so need or want.) When it comes to your transport here, I expect you will arrange that and I can get directions for you from the big roundabout near school or I can even call a taxi to pick you up from the station if necessary. But David, all that nickety-pickety arrangements stuff is for later, let's not ruin it now with all that.

There is something else I just want to mention now because I've been thinking about it. Other than the mega luv we will have for each other which I take for granted already, we will have to learn about each other's cultures and this might take some time, so we must be patient and tolerable about it. As of this moment, there is so much I don't know about your fair land, the United States of America, but believe me, I am an oh-so-hungry learner and am oh-so-keen to digest it all! Before long, I will be jivin' on the Sunset Strip, eating crabfish on the byoo and getting down all over the place! And perhaps, in time, you will come to love our crazy fish 'n' chips in newspaper and our coins with the head of the Queen on one side as a mark of respect. What a fascinating time we have ahead as a future. So, unlike most other couples who simply come from the same place and already know all this stuff, we will have so much more exciting exploration to do. I can't wait!

So, anyway, this is enough for you to take in all in one go so I will wait for your reply before I arrange anything. Please can you make sure it's you who writes or calls me rather than a servant/secretary? That would be better. Until we finally meet and instantly know how in luv we are and always will be forever and a day to the moon and back, I leave you with one last thought to abide. 'Could it be forever?' Oh yes, my love, it could, is my answer. My heart in yours, have courage,

Lotsaluv,

Moo French age 14

(This is a family nickname which comes from when we lived in Cyprus and has nothing to do with me looking like a cow! — as you will see from enclosed photo, which you are free to keep. I have another copy.)

Dear Dad,

I loved Lincoln, I thought it was the poshest city we had ever lived near. There was something grand about it. There's that big ancient bow arch you can walk under, and an elegant river that runs right through the middle, reminding you what an important place you're in. Plus of course a cathedral you can't miss. I haven't visited Lincoln since we left when I was 14 years old so maybe it isn't as impressive as my memory insists, but I clearly remember shopping there and being in awe.

RAF Faldingworth was also impressive to me, but in a different way. The quarters and the NAAFI were quite compact and cheery but the actual base where you worked seemed sprawling and, as I recall, a large part of it was empty and virtually derelict. There were plenty of big old buildings that must once have been — what? Billets or meeting rooms or training areas or messes or something? It was like being in a spooky episode of *The Avengers* or *The Prisoner* where someone nearly always ends up in a deserted military base doing plenty of fast running and hiding and dodging. The perfect location for a teenager to get up to eight kinds of no good. And sorry to say, Dad, we did. We had secret parties where I was introduced to the mixed blessing that is sweet cider. We had romantic liaisons behind the doors of storage cupboards. (Most of these were innocent fumblings resulting in flushed frustration, nothing more.) We had terrifying seances where we tried to summon up the spirits of dead relatives. I once attempted to connect with Grandad McCarthy and was utterly petrified when the glass on our home-made Ouija board hurtled around accurately spelling out various clues about our family which no other soul there could have known. I was shaken to the core by this creepy, seriously weird experience, but I didn't feel I could share it with you and Mum because it was so supremely bad to have done such a thing. Had I opened up a sinister portal through which my dead grandfather had been reluctantly sucked into our earthly plane? Was he going to haunt me from now on? Was he attached to me like some kind of astral teasel stuck on my jumper? I was freaked out for a while but lots of reassurance in the form of heavy petting with David Eccles alleviated my spiritual burden somehow. Ain't it always the case?! I have never fully understood what happened but I have learned enough to keep a respectful distance from any inexplicable phenomena since (except for watching Most Haunted of course, of which I am a devotee). This explains why I have never tried to communicate with you through any of these odd channels which I find too eerie and strange to understand. I do hope you haven't been sitting on the other side of that spiritual portal for these past 30 years, staring at the backside of a closed door waiting for someone to buzz you in. That *would* be awful. If that's the case, Dad, just lock up, turn off the lights and go to bed cos no one's comin'! Maybe we'll see you in the morning . . . Who knows.

Do you remember taking me to look around Caistor Grammar, my first experience of senior school? I only spent a year there but I had a good time except for the hideous weekly cross-country torture. Why do schools insist on hurting children with ugly running kits and near-death experiences of exercise which is too demanding? Has anyone ever died of PE? I think I did, several times. At the least, I learned to reject any suchlike activity in adult life. Thanks, school. Otherwise Caistor was just fine. It *was*, however, the venue for my first criminal activity. There was a sweet shop just outside the school gates and, yes, I can hear you, I *know* how little the return is on sweets, especially when kids are nicking the profits. As the granddaughter of a newsagent I knew all this and I knew it was wrong because you had impressed that on me at a *very* early age, *but* what you didn't know is that it was mandatory. Like a Herculean task, it was expected of you as a measly first-former to steal sweets for the older girls. You were a cretin and a smell if you didn't and you would also be forced to suffer the humiliation of being actually killed, which I didn't relish. So, you see, Dad, I stole in order to live. That's entirely different to stealing because you're just a greedy immoral grubby little twat, isn't it? That's my defence for my initial sticky-fingeredness. I have no such justification for what happened next.

There was an officer's daughter called Heather (not her real name. Her real name is Hannah Black). She was big and bold and brave. She *loved* stealing. It was her passion and she was extremely talented at it. Like many illicit skills, her excellent pilfering credits won her a lot of attention and much admiration. She was cool, she was a bobby-dazzler, she was a hep cat. She was *it*. I was swept along with this frothy tide of admirers, and somewhere along the way I convinced myself that stealing was actually OK, that it was only our parents' archaic morals that had fooled us into eschewing such exciting, rewarding delights. What did they know? They were ancient and ill-informed and, like, *so* establishment. I wanted to be like Heather. I wanted to be a proper thief, yay. We would go into town at lunchtimes and I would watch and learn from the Grand Mistress. She had no fear, she was cunning and stealthy and extremely smooth. My first attempt was in Smith's. She advised me to start small, with something inexpensive so I could feign ignorance if caught — after all, what is the *point* of stealing a packet of pencils, sir, it's hardly rich pickings, look, here, I have enough money in my purse if I really wanted them. Good ruse. OK, here I go — a packet of six pencils. The execution of the 'grab' was awkward and the packet edges grazed my flesh as I shoved it up my sleeve. I went a bit sweaty and telltale red in the face, but I did it — I nicked the pencils and propelled myself out of the shop as if bitten on the bum by a beaver.

My tutor was delighted with her protégée and promised a bigger, brighter, lucrative future if I stuck with her.

I went home that night and looked at my swag. Six lovely red pencils, sharp and perfect. My booty. Mine, all mine, and I hadn't parted with a sou of my precious pocket money. How great was this? Yes, it was. It was great. Wasn't it? So why wasn't I feeling great? Was it simply that I was back in the home environment and thus back under the old, outdated regime of morality? Surely I *should* be feeling great? Like Fagin-type of great? I didn't feel great — I felt awful. Full-of-guilt-and-self-loathing awful. Fagin-at-the-end-of-the-film-type awful. In the end, I tossed 'n' turned in bed, feeling steadily worse as the night wore on. I was plagued with guilt. It was a massive dragon breathing hot fire down my neck until eventually I could bear it no longer and I came to speak to Mum and confessed all. It gushed out of me like spew, my litany of felonious misdeeds — well, the one dastardly pencil one and some sketchy info about the lesser but still vile prior sweet-shop crimes. She was very understanding but said that you, Dad, needed to be brought into the loop to make the big decisions about how we should proceed now that she was fully informed of how hopelessly miscreant I was. So, you sat on my bed and what followed was the most serious and sobering conversation I had ever had. Thanks for holding my hand, by the way, but it didn't comfort me much during your frank assessment of the dire situation. You explained that in light of the extent of my villainous underhand dealings, there were only two options open to us. A, to call the police and inform them how bent I was, or B, to try and replace the contraband without anyone knowing. I had never known you be so solemn. You then commended me for my honesty and said it might take time to come to terms with the shame and the potential dishonour brought upon the House of French. Then you promised to make a decision the next morning and we went to bed.

Well, we were outside the door of Smith's at opening time. Putting those pencils back was SO difficult! People around me were noticing my shifty behaviour and looking at me with accusatory and disgusted glares, but, somehow, I replaced them. I left that shop and my former crooked life behind that day. I was no longer a low curr; I had cleaned up and was back on the straight and narrow, all thanks to your wise counsel. You surely saved me from a life of pure base wickedness. So that's good then.

Heather was disgusted and said she'd let me know when she'd found a spine donor for me. She went on to some truly awesome thieving, including large hi-fi equipment and TV sets. Eventually her dad found it all in a cupboard and she got a hiding from hell. Wonder what she's up to now? Probably something in government, I s'pect.

It was at that camp you set up the big youth club, wasn't it? I know you had done stuff like that before but this was the time I really noticed it because I was the age to appreciate it personally. I think you must have noticed how vulnerable bored teenagers are. Maybe you could see that shagging and stealing weren't going to lead us anywhere good, that we needed distractions. All of my mates loved you for it — you reclaimed a building from dereliction and we all decorated it till it was a perfect teen meeting place with a coffee bar, tuck shop, ping-pong, games and a dance floor with disco lights. I loved those dances except for one thing — you were *always there* keeping a watchful eye on the proceedings, so it was double difficult for Gary or me to get a snog or a puff. The kids there knew you well, and thought you were dead groovy and told us how lucky we were to have parents like you. This was only a small part of what you did for young people everywhere we went, and only now do I see what a phenomenally selfless thing it was to do. It took up a lot of your energy and often tested your patience, but Dad, you did a wonderful thing — you gave your time up to improve the lives of so many young men and women. I hope you knew how proud we were when you received the BEM in the honours list for this work, because we really were.

Dear David Eccles,

Oh heck, even writing your name there has given me a little flutter of flushed embarrassment. It is only momentary though, because if I scrunch my brain up hard enough to remember . . . yes, there it is — I can still smell your sweet breath and taste your divine lips. Your lovely, lovely mouth. How bloody fabulous it was to kiss you.

You weren't the absolute first. Sorry, I may have lied and told you that. Before you, there was a boy called Michael Le Pellier. I was about four I think, and the lip activity was very brief and not as entertaining as I might have hoped. We merely stood opposite each other and let our lips touch. That's all. Just touching. Eyes open. No movement. Like statues that have fallen towards each other and come to rest at the lips. It usually lasted for about two minutes and was supremely uneventful, although I was flattered that he had chosen me for the experiment. We did it at various intervals during the day at infant school while class carried on around us, and we joined in with all the normal activities either side of the kissing interludes. Eventually we agreed that it wasn't the best use of our time. We both preferred the sandbox play to the kissing so we cooled it off and only

108

engaged in the face-docking as a courtesy at the start and end of each day.

That was pretty much it till you came along when my Dad was posted to RAF Faldingworth in Market Rasen. As I recall, you were Gary's best friend on that camp, just before he went away to start boarding school in Plymouth, and even after, when he came home on holiday. I can't quite remember how we started with the kissing, I don't think we actually dated as such, did we? I was in hyperdrive with the ol' puberty hormones at the time and was raring to get out of the traps, so I doubt you had a chance of escaping. I loved how tall and funny you were (are?!) and I was doubly impressed with your Swiss army knife expertise, and the whole camouflage flak jacket and bobble hat thing you had going on. You looked liked you might go all Rambo at any moment and disappear into the forest to live on grubs and bark, start your own campfires from brushwood kindling and stab any evil-doers who crossed you. I liked that. Any teenage fugitive who could survive against the elements and, frankly, against a whole world which was against him was my kinda teenager. Of course, I didn't actually see any Swiss army knife action except perhaps a bit of whittling and some bottle-opening, but I was still impressed, just by the potential.

Both my parents were out at work all day and my bro and I were latchkey kids. We literally used to reach inside the letter box and fumble around for a piece of string that had a key on it to open the door. How was that OK? Why weren't we endlessly burgled? Why didn't we just have a key each? Every single other kid on the camp whose mum worked did the same thing and we all knew. Were those times more innocent? Was the neighbourly community ethos stronger? Were people more nosy or watchful, or less criminal? Dunno, but it meant that after school there were a good couple of hours of parent-free home time in which to pretend it was actually our own house and we could behave any bloody way we wanted. We could be true renegades and put chocolate powder in our milk or even chuck our knives and forks carelessly in the sink instead of carefully putting them there, thereby making quite a clatter. We could leave the fridge door ajar and we could play Deep Purple records at volume 6 and everything. So we did. Other kids would come round and sit about untidily, putting their feet up on the sofas *with* their shoes on and taking dangerous single sips of Amontillado sherry from a six-year-old bottle Lil had left. It tasted like vinegar, because by then it actually was, but it didn't matter, it was alcohol of sorts, and in a virtually teetotal household, that was precious. It was during these crazy, wild escapades that you and I eventually made contact. I was praying that you would fall under my bewitching spell when I caught your eye and gave you my well-practised come-hither head toss, the like of which I had seen working for Marilyn Monroe in films. I actually tried it on you about a dozen times before the bewitching-ness of it started to work. Bear in mind, I was a novice and some of my sexy self-lip-moistening may well have appeared to be uncontrollable dribble. I'm not sure how you held back for so long, but eventually you stopped kissing every single *other* girl available and gave in to my utterly resistible siren techniques. I lured you onto the rocks called Dawn with my eyelash-fluttering and doe-eyed prowess. I *think* that's what did it. Of course it could have been my enormous baps, but I prefer to think differently.

Do you remember the joy of sitting on that couch and doing industrial-strength kissing? Sometimes for an hour and 20 minutes without a break? The sudden revelation for me was that you can move your face about while in the throes of a delicious snog . . . And *breathe* . . . and make little snuffly, grunty noises of pleasure. You can even sing along to Deep Purple or Creedence Clearwater Revival, but that is less successful mid-clinch. The thousand ways of using your lips with someone else's lips — the nips and the sucks and the different pressures were a sensual wonderland — but the mother of all epiphanies was the power of the tongue. I don't know why, but no one had *ever* told me this was probable or possible or pleasurable. I can't imagine being thrilled at the prospect, even if anyone *had* told me. The thought of someone else's tongue anywhere near mine would have sent me into spasms of retching at that age, but the first time it actually happened was with you. When you tentatively and tenderly crept that hot powerful muscle into my mouth, I nearly swooned with ecstasy. Nobody had ever been inside me before, it was the most intimate and

111

carnal congress I had known, and I loved it. I was giddy with delight, and instantly became obsessed with you, with the potency of kissing you. I wanted to do it forever. Sometimes we kissed until my lips were bruised, and I even remember actually nodding off during one particularly gentle session. We were limpets stuck to the rock faces of each other. Every time we were forced to part, I practically died of heartache. I didn't know that my heart could physically hurt, that it could feel so sore. You may, of course, have been blissfully unaware of all that. I, however, am for ever indebted to you for showing me the ropes kiss-wise. You were a generous, accomplished instructor and it has been a struggle to find a match of your elan ever since. Perhaps we never can recapture the unique thrill of first love with its heady, exciting blood rush. Perhaps we're not supposed to. Perhaps other, later relationships have to be built on stronger foundations, more durable than pure kissing genius alone. A good kisser is hard to beat though, and hard to find; and believe me, I've tried!

It seems to have fallen to me to continue the quest for ever. Or at least as long as I can get away with it. I have never passed up the opportunity to lock on to the face of a willing party, male or female, in the pursuit of that rare beast, the talented kisser. In this particular hunt, I am bold and unshakeoffable. Sometimes I see people on the street, total strangers, I'd like to kiss. I fancy I can judge a contender from simple observation. Noticing how they speak, or eat or

112

laugh. I feel like an inspector, duty-bound to forage out an elite crack team of lip meisters. Equally, I feel that it falls to me to expose those who purport to have skills, but who are, in actuality, hopeless in the frontal face-sucking department. There are more of these charlatans than you would imagine. A tip: beware of anyone who regularly pouts. Pouting is the enemy of kissing, as the pouter has risked the perils of overdeveloped pouting muscles, often too toned to deliver a simple home-made soft smooch. I refer you to exhibit A — Sylvester Stallone. I have not visited that particular mush, but there again, I wouldn't want to, for that very reason. Nor his mother. Imagine. Oh dear me, no.

In my desire to test-drive as many lips as possible before I am too ancient and repulse my accomplices (I'm aware that, sadly, I may well have passed this point of no return), I really have endeavoured to plant one on as many coopera-tive others as possible. To that end I have been unfeasibly lucky. For an early Comic Relief, I decided to wangle a kiss from Hugh Grant by involving him in an elaborate ruse where I pretended to be a swollen version of his then beloved, Liz Hurley, wearing a giant version of 'that dress' she wore so effectively, with the safety pins down the side. I wore it with considerably less panache but with quadruple the comedy, I felt. Jen and I wrote the sketch with the sole intention of landing his lips on mine, and may I say, 'HOWZAT!' We raised a million quid, and carried on kissing throughout the break for the news, only stopping for toilet breaks and occasional refreshments. It was reminiscent of all those delicious Michael Le Pellier moments in the infants. Except it was Hugh Bloody Hell Grant! Very quickly I realised that if the reason was funny enough, I could elicit these smackers at a prodigious rate. Thus I have proceeded to claim quite a few impressive trophies along the way, and none of the participants have seemed in the slightest bit offended. Lucky me.

Just thought I might make a little list of some of the more memorable liptastic moments I've had in case you're interested. Try not to be too jealous.

1. Michael Le Pellier — functional and edifying.
2. A dog called Hunni — hairy.
3. You — heavenly.
4. Assorted guinea pigs (long AND short-haired) — split lips and large teeth — alarming.
5. A girl called Lisa — soft and fragrant and confusing, involved lipstick.
6. Assorted friends of brother — unremarkable, worse than guinea pigs.
7. A horse called Shula — huge velvety lips with spiky hairs, but bliss.
8. A farmer's son called Mark — new stubble, passionate.
9. Nick Brentford — meaningful and lingering.
10. A clever boy called Charlie who played Falstaff when I played Mistress Quickly — onstage, covered in talcum powder he

114

had put in his hair to age him. I longed for him to kiss me offstage but he wasn't interested.

11. A French sailor on the Hoe — cold, with nose dribble involved, but was given the little red pompom from his cap in return for the kiss, so v. romantic.
12. Plymouth College boys on Saturday nights at the OPM club — all tasted of cider or lager.
13. Various girls in dorm — but doesn't really count as was only practice.
14. Neil, a marine — light, almost not there.
15. Graham Inman — oh, how I wished.
16. Biker boys in the car park opposite Burgh Island — not a word spoken, furious and slavering and brief.
17. Jerry, the art teacher's son — sensitive but distant.
18. A chef at the Salcombe Hotel — utterly revolting. Bad teeth.
19. David Smyth, a navy sub lieutenant — many, many soft Irish kisses with lots of laughs in between.
20. Students of the acting course at Central — too self-interested, were only imagining kissing themselves.
21. Colin — wouldn't, shame.
22. A saxophone player — too much suck and blow.
23. Steve — first experience of a moustache. Furry.
24. A rugby player — gay. Lived with mother. Cried.

25. Scottie — gay. Fag-hag kisses. Good technique.
26. A Welsh actor — poetic, heart-stopping.
27. Keith Allen — bossy, smug, scary and ultimately disappointing.
28. A musician on the Red Wedge tour — exciting.
29. Robin Ellis-Bextor — very tall, stepladder needed.
30. Lenworth G. Henry — the brightest, the best. *Loves* kissing anywhere, anytime. The King of Kiss.
31. Every boy at the Comic Strip — joy in the workplace.
32. Jennifer Saunders — in a play — passed messages in note form or gum. Lovely.
33. Frances Barber — in *Murder Most Horrid* — temptress with fabulous upper lips (as opposed to lower, more intimate lips — I didn't go anywhere near those, honest).
34. Hugh Grant — professional with odd chuckle, very game.
35. Jonathan Ross — for a joke. Never again.
36. Boyzone — enjoyable, varied.
37. A cat's arse — less enjoyable, but better than Jonathan Ross.
38. Brad Pitt — angel in male form. A woman's mouth, bliss.
39. Johnny Depp — sweet, respectful, as if I was favourite aunt. Not long enough or full enough or penetrative enough. Resistant.
40. Jamie Theakston — second-best kisser in the world.
41. Stephen Tompkinson — skilled, heartfelt.

42. Clive Mantle — strong, savouring, powerful, with occasional slurping.
43. George Clooney — bold, unashamed, clasped my face in both hands.
44. Richard Armitage aka Guy of Gisborne, or 'Man of Pleather' — shy, giggling, loving.
45. Richard Curtis — kisses like a butterfly has landed on your lips.
46. Len Henry again — sorry, but truly, he's really good.
47. Oh yes, and Alison Moyet — in a video. She knows how, that girl.

So, you see, it's been quite a journey, liply speaking, and believe me, my work is not yet done. As long as I'm allowed to keep doing it, I'm going to persevere with my research. I have you to thank though, David Eccles, for starting me up, and keeping me revved. I intend to tick over until I stall, and I hope my final breath is on someone else's lips, doing this kissing thing you are so darn good at. Mwah mwah.

Dear Gary,

Perhaps I should finally, belatedly, apologise to you for writing rude notes for you to find in every drawer in your bedroom when you came home for the holidays from boarding school. My feeble excuse is that I had Mum and Dad entirely to myself when you were away and I was on the receiving end of some fabulous tip-top quality spoiling which was their displacement activity for missing you, I think. Still, that's no excuse for writing notes like 'Nobody here likes you — true' or 'Go back to Nam'! I didn't really know what 'Nam' was. I just knew it was bad and so it'd suit me for you to go there. Yes, I *should* apologise for that but then I also remember quite a lot of torture coming my way too. Besides the barrage of pinches and punches and Chinese burns, I was regularly pinned to the floor by you, as you clambered on top of me, your knees on my shoulders, while you waited the thousand years it took for saliva to gather in your open mouth and dribble slowly on to my writhing face from a height of two foot. That was pretty disgusting, wouldn't you say? So, yeah, actually, 'Go back to Nam', whydoncha!

Eventually, after a year at Caistor Grammar, I began the big boarding school experience myself. I think Mum and Dad knew that it was time for

118

me to be at the same school for longer than a year if there was any hope of some O levels. Like you, I went to board in Plymouth so's we could be a stone's throw from the wider family and, like you, the RAF paid the bill, which meant both of us were in schools with people who were well out of our social and economic class. I think boys are crueller about all that stuff and I suspect you had a harder time than me, although both of us seemed to keep friends from schooldays for years afterwards, so we must have forged *some* loving and lasting links along the way.

Thanks, by the way, for bringing home a variety of different chums in the holidays from Plymouth College. I appreciated these offerings. Most of them were of great interest to me! You must have been longing for me to get to 'big' school so I could reciprocate with my friends. You seemed to date most of them at one time or another. The stripey blazers and hideous school hats didn't seem to put off you or your mates, so didn't we all have a rare ol' time getting to know each other's friends far too well? I remember one incident where a boy from your school took me to a party in his car on a Saturday night and, forgetting that you were present, started boasting to his friends back in school on Monday morning about the many wild exploits we had been up to in the back of his small, dull car. All lies, of course, and according to your friends who related this to me later, you 'sorted him out'. I think that was my one and only date with that particular lying damn fool. Ta for that. I remember when you did something similar in Cyprus when some boys were trying to pull my gym pants down for a look when I was about six. Ta for that too. You have always been protective towards me and I do appreciate that, especially in later years when we have sometimes needed to look out for each other as the road to adultville has become evermore twisty and turny. Underneath your good humoured, easy going exterior Gary, I know you are made of strong stuff and I have been glad of it on lots of occasions.

I imagined St Dunstan's was going to be like 'The Four Marys' and that it would be one long round of midnight feasts and jolly hockey sticks with plenty of clandestine liaisons down the dingle thrown in. It wasn't, of course. It was a small, traditional girls' public school set in the grounds of a beautiful Gothic abbey, where staff and pupils rubbed along trying to do the education stuff the best way they could. Do you remember Hazel Abley, my headmistress, who I think you must have witnessed at speech days trying to rally the troops? She could be a fearsome sight, clacking up and down the long cobbled Hogwarts cloisters in her good shoes with her black gown flying up behind, like a giant bat with the sheer force of her speed and purpose. She was small and tough and extremely efficient. She taught us English with a special, inspirational interest in Chaucer and in the evenings she retired to her flat up many stairs in a tower at the far end of the chapel, from whence it felt like she could see into every single window of the school and directly into every single one of

120

our souls. Miss Abley was everything a good school head was supposed to be — fair but austere, and very, very clever.

In the evenings after supper, some of us boarders used to volunteer to help out in the kitchen. It wasn't quite as altruistic as it may sound, since this favour elicited two important returns: 1. big hugs from Lavinia the cook, who was huge and generous and loving and was a kind of temporary mum substitute in occasional, usually crepuscular moments of homesickness (I'm sure you remember those) and 2. Lavinia sometimes doled out goodies like biscuits and hot sweetened milk to accompany our task. Result.

Quite often Hazel Abley would pop in to the kitchen at this quieter vesperal time, and chat with Lavinia too. She might even have slippers on and be rinsing out a plate in the big industrial sinks. It was then that I saw her in a totally different, softer light. She too had come in to the kitchen to snatch a slice of homey warmth, to have a laugh and a cuddle and a biscuit from Lavinia. Perhaps sitting alone in a tower busying herself with omnipotence wasn't quite as satisfying as we had imagined. I had to confront the bald fact, in these curiously intimate moments when I saw her in 'civvies', that she was, after all, human, and what's more, I *really* liked her. I had to keep that to myself of course, I couldn't possibly break rank and defect to the teacher side, I shouldn't really even be speaking with the enemy, never mind sharing a tea towel.

Funny how we were all drawn to the kitchen,

to some vestige of home life, of normality, at the back end of the day, to calm us all before sleeping. Are we all always looking for home? Don't get me wrong, I wasn't the achingly sad and lonely type of boarder — I met plenty of those and their sorrow consumed them. I didn't feel like that, partly, I think, because it was made so clear to us, wasn't it, how difficult and strange it was for Mum and Dad to send us there in the first place. We don't come from a posh long line of generations of public-school sprogs, of whom it is expected they will be shushed away like bothersome flies. Kids who have no say in the matter, kids whose fathers and forefathers had the same experience at most likely the same schools. No, our mum and dad did *not* get this kind of education and they were determined that you and I would benefit from everything they were convinced they'd missed out on. The RAF would provide most of the fees, so that made possible an opportunity they'd only ever dreamt of for us. However, they still had to find the funds for uniform, books, trips, trunks, name tags and all the other endless minutiae of a boarder's requirements. In order to find this cash they gave up fags and holidays and treats. They made sacrifices so that we might have the privilege of what they considered to be an excellent education. You and I know of course that both of our schools were very minor public schools, and not really in that elite league of academically excellent establishments which afford an unspoken and mutually coded understanding among only themselves. An exclusive collusion which I only recognised later in life when I was constantly reminded that I *wasn't* part of it, whatever *it* was. The gradually dawning realisation that there is an underground class network buzzing away in parallel to your life, of which you know only one thing — you ain't invited.

I think, for both of us, the boarding-school experience was a challenge and a test of what was already a tenuous grasp on our sense of identity. We were kids from a working-class West Country background whose father's job meant we travelled so we didn't grow up where we belonged. Add to that a father who refused the chance of a commission out of the ranks because — why? — presumably he feared the judgement of those above him who he clearly knew to be from a different, higher class than his. He preferred to stay down, to be at the top of his game, in his 'rightful' place. He had no desire to prove himself to people he was *supposed* to, but often didn't, respect. On top of that, Mum hailed from an even lower class than Dad, and boy didn't she feel it when she first got together with him. She experienced plenty of snidery and even actual resistance to their marriage. I think it's true that Grandma and Grandad French didn't speak to her for a year or so when she married Dad and only relented when you, their first grandchild, came along and they couldn't resist the chance to know you. So, we had parents who felt the weight of class and limitation on their shoulders and were determined to push up, push through that prejudice. For them, education was

123

the answer. Boarding gave us stability; we wouldn't have to keep moving from school to school every time Dad was posted elsewhere. It gave us an alliance and a connection to the family to board in Plymouth and to spend time in the heart of the kin as I did every weekend. It also gave us a stepping stone into a class they had not entered, the middle class, that objectionable but desirable mysterious new place they believed you had to visit in order to earn your wings so's you could take off to wherever you wanted with your brand-spanking-new self-worth, unfettered by the ties they so clearly felt. They wanted us to become confident, brave people who would not be daunted by class or intellect or authority. In fact, they wanted us to achieve all three! As I see it, their intentions were honourable and sensible, they had no shame about their own personal histories, none at all, but they could see that there might be more opportunities for us if we opted for this route.

Of course, we experienced the other side of it too: it wasn't easy being the first from our family ever to go through the public-school system. We were mixing with kids who were very different to us economically and socially. I stayed some weekends with girls who had *ponies* in *meadows* and *sinks* in the corner of their bedrooms. Whose houses had driveways and beige carpets where you had to take your shoes off, where the heating was on all the time in the whole house! Girls who were presented with a new car on their seventeenth birthday. Girls who went skiing. All unfamiliar, all exciting, all *so* middle class, all so new. While I was busy building myself up into a frenetic excitable hysteria about this amazing new 'me', the family were very quick to deflate any delusions of grandeur and to bring me crashing back to earth. Grandad French was especially keen that I wouldn't forget who I was or where I was from. He teased me mercilessly about my awful swanky uniform and my newly posh turns of phrase. They would not hold with the slightest sniff of pretension or insincerity, thank goodness, because I certainly gave it a go. I tried on for size the mantle of public schoolgirl at ease with privilege and superiority, but I quickly realised it didn't suit me, and anyway, I didn't carry it off with enough flourish. Frankly, it was too fecking small! I regarded the whole confusing experience as fascinating drama — look how these people live, look how they think, look what they say, look what they wear, look what they love.

There were some girls who were much more familiar, some whose dads were in the forces like Nicky Varley, some who were on scholarships so were thrust in at the potato end of the pasty, some whose dads were butchers like Nikki Rowe, and some whose dads were the housemaster of your own brother's school like Jane Veale, or salty Salcombe girls who were just wild and adventurous and naughty like Kirsty Lamont. I loved being with those girls and I never detected an iota of grandeur about any of them, but they were in the minority. The problem with a small public school is that it is crammed with wannabe-in-a-bigger-better-public-school kids and parents. For me, this school was the height of everything our parents wanted for us, so I found the lofty disapproval of snobs insufferable. I couldn't fathom why it should trouble them so much that we were tiny and average. *This* was our school, our team, our tribe, our world, and my parents had made seismic sacrifices for me to be there and I loved it and felt proud to be part of it and I wasn't having any pompous princess telling me or my folks otherwise. I wore my Downton House badge with unquestionable pride and used my hockey stick as a cudgel to defend the honour of my team against any snivelling enemy wing attack. Hockey, with all its runny snot and ponytailed puffy red-facedness and mottled white/red leggedness, was the sport of choice if you wanted to feel valiance coursing through your veins. We rarely won a match but we forged everlasting tribal bonds, and bore the scars of our many defeats with pride. I still have them. Inside and out.

I remember coming to watch you doing the same thing playing rugby. Donating your knees and ears and teeth for brief moments of glory, and a profound sense of belonging. Funny, isn't it, how now that we are so much older, after both having lived in many different places, countries even, we have returned here, to the West Country, where we feel the strongest call. I don't think it's just the sea and the light and the green and the cream. I think there are echoes for both of us of those cold sports fields and those cold dormitories, of Mum's tears and Dad's brave face on the first day of term when she couldn't face dropping us off, and even he had a shaky lip. Of what it cost us as a family. Of discovering our sibling glue and liking it, liking the security of having a brother inextricably linked to me. Of our filial relationship with that area. Of the cries and cheers from the Green Army at Home Park when Argyle are playing, of the Hoe, Ivor Dewdney, Dingles and Looe. Echoes of grand-parents digging the ground for your roots to be secure. Knowing you'll return, and we have, haven't we? Not for the ghosts, but for the certainty of it all. For the familiar and the reminder.

Dear Fatty,

You and I have often talked about our respective school lives, the friends, the teachers, the whole caboodle. In fact, over the years, we have plundered that rich seam for material for our show. It would seem that we went to different schools inhabited by the same people! Confounding many people's perceptions of us, you went to the local grammar school and I went to public school, but when we have discussed our individual experiences, the difference is minimal, I think. So minimal that in one rather uncanny coincidence we even shared the exact same friend, but at different times. Her name was Camilla Leng. I think her dad was something impressive in the army and she lived for a short while in Plymouth and was in my class at school. She was a fantastic, larger-than-life character, a force of true naughtiness. It was Camilla who dared to attach notes declaring 'I'm so sexy' and 'Kiss me now' to the backs of the muted lavender cardigans of the most elderly teachers. It was Camilla who made loud rasping farting noises with her mouth while appearing totally innocent and straight-faced, thereby confusing teachers unable to apportion blame. It was Camilla who persuaded me to go into a long dark dripping cave by the river near Rock in

Cornwall, where we were searching for dabs in the sand. She made scary noises — screeches and wails — using her natural ventriloquist skills, each time claiming she was not to blame. It took me hours to stop my heart beating too fast, making me giddy. I loved being around her, basking in the heat of her boldness and her humour. Then, years later, I think it was during an interview, you and I discovered that we had *both* known her, and that before she came to Plymouth, she had lived near you and been your chum also. I bet you loved the same things about her that I did. Perhaps on some deeper level, we saw the Camilla Leng in each other years later when we finally met . . . ?

Both you and I also took care to judge the safest and most enjoyable route through the canyon of danger and death that is an all girls' school. Keep your enemies close and beware bandits and fair-weather friends. Dodge the quicksand and use the oldest, tallest, widest trees for shelter and camouflage. Occasionally it is important to prove your colours as a leader and instigator in order to earn respect, but, equally, it's vital to entertain and amuse your fellow troopers. Hence the clowning and the mimicry. Let's all have a good laugh because it's nigh impossible to laugh and hate simultaneously. I knew I could easily fulfil the job vacancy — 'jester needed for part-time peacekeeping duties in perilous jungle of minor independent girls' school' — so permitting a little break from bitchery and witchery.

St Dunstan's Abbey school in Plymouth was

no longer a convent when I arrived in 1970, but it had all the trappings of one: cloisters and chapel and towers and neatly planted nun-ish gardens. One of our main play areas was an old graveyard with the uprooted tombstones stacked against the wall. It was grey and Gothic and ghostly. The floors creaked and the wind whistled through the covered cloisters to whip our calves. In stark contrast to the cheerless ash grey of the building, some ancient sadist unburdened with any sense of fashion or flair had decided that dark blue, light blue and yellow stripes would be a good idea for a school uniform. We wore ties and blazers in this awful gaudy pattern and looked like escapees from a glee club for dwarfs. The hats were the final insult. Dark blue bowlers with a ribbon in the school stripe around the brim in winter, and boaters with the same ribbon in the summer. We might as well have been branded with 'twatty little toff' on our foreheads. We certainly attracted plenty of unwanted attention when we were out and about. Perhaps that was the idea, a collusion between parents and school to ensure that as the most garish, noticeable creatures in town, we would be less likely to go missing or slope off for illicit purposes. To that end, it worked, I think. However, I don't suppose whoever invented that uniform could have predicted what a thoroughly effective magnet it would prove to be for general abuse. There were some strange folk in town who regarded us as a kind of human coconut shy; they hurled verbal insults at us and, on some more frightening occasions, actual missiles — anything off the pavement would be fit for purpose to chuck at a precocious Abbey girl.

Yep, the uniform identified us all right. It marked us out as young, green (or rather dark blue, light blue and yellow) and supremely vulnerable. Never more so than on one particularly distasteful occasion.

Boarders at St Dunstan's were not, repeat NOT, allowed out without permission or parents between Monday morning and Friday evening. OK?! This rule was made crystal clear. The consequences were dire and could include capital punishment. Mind you, I would happily have chosen eternal Stygian darkness over the worst punishment of all, which was meted out for 'being seen outside school in uniform — but hatless'. If caught committing this heinous crime, we were subjected to the arse-wrenching humiliation of having to wear the hat ALL DAY at school. I experienced this once and it was grim. I still have therapy in order to forgive, forget and move on. Woe betide anyone who went out without permission — and death betide anyone who went out without permission *out of uniform*. However, one evening, a friend and I agreed we would risk extermination in order to go into town for half an hour. But we weren't total nihilists, we would, *of course*, wear our uniform. That way, if we *were* caught, we could beg for mercy citing the honourable and correct wearing of the uniform, and asking for that to be taken into consideration.

Intent on using a well-honed system of covert

timings, knockings and bribings of an 'insider' accomplice in order to get back in, we slipped out the side door and giggled all the way into town with excitement. We had a singular, important purpose. We needed to go into the Co-op and spend all of our pocket money on the photo-booth machine. We had planned a series of hilarious face contortions we knew would stick together to make a funny cartoon-style story about . . . well . . . about two girls in school hats in a photo booth in the Co-op, pulling faces. Excellent! With this task in mind, we dived into the back of the multi-storey Co-op, which led us through the food hall bit on our way to the front, where the photo booth was. We were just about to put our money in the machine when a burly man in a suit called out, 'Hey, you two — stop that!' We froze as he approached. 'What do you think you're doing?!' he asked, sternly. I ventured, 'We were just going to use the — ' but before I finished he interrupted, and my heart sank as he said, 'As you well know, one of you has stolen a packet of tights. I am the store detective and I clearly saw you sneak the tights under your jumper. You have two choices: A, we can call the police, and since you're Abbey girls that means informing your head; or B, you can choose to be searched and we can settle this matter here in the shop. You haven't actually left the shop as yet, so if the tights are returned to us, it's not technically stealing and it needn't go any further. It's up to you, but you need to decide immediately.' I flashed a look at my friend. I was furious with her — how could she

132

ruin our trip into town for a pilfered pair of tights? We both knew we would be in all kinds of trouble if anyone alerted the school, so we took the search option. We chose that option inside one glance. The decision was that quick.

The man instructed us to follow him and we went to the door that led onto the big staircase, which was ordinarily quite busy but unusually empty on this particular day. We went up one floor and I saw why there wasn't a soul around — there were scaffolding and ladders and paint-pots blocking the way. The Co-op was undergoing a makeover but the worksite was completely still, the men had obviously finished for the day. Big dust sheets covered the floor and stairs and hung from the ladders. He indicated that we should push past the dust sheets, so we did. I expected to find a door to an inner office of some kind, the place where they did the searches. A place with other people perhaps? Instead he stopped us behind the big canvas dust sheet and told us he would conduct the search right here himself. Although it did occur to me fleetingly that this was a strange place to do it, I was quite relieved that we didn't have to endure further humiliation with any other witnesses. He asked me to lift my jumper up, which I willingly did. After all, I was utterly innocent and he would find no contraband on me. No siree. On finding nothing, he asked if I had hidden them inside my blouse. Absolutely not, I said, have a look. He did, and he put his hands right round my back to check. All of this was done in a most professional way, you understand. Fast and emotionless. Had I hidden the packet *inside* my bra? I was aghast at this allegation, did he not realise I was the innocent one?! He then deftly checked *inside* my bra very thoroughly. Indeed. No sign, of course. Had I hidden the packet up my skirt? Inside my tights? Inside my pants? No I hadn't thank you very much, and please to check. Which he did. Very thoroughly. You see? Nothing. You have maligned me for nothing, you have misjudged me, sir. SHE is the thief, *that's* where you'll find them. I didn't say this out loud of course, but I was screaming it loudly inside my head, which thus far was the only place he hadn't thoroughly searched. He said that he suspected me initially but he had obviously been wrong, so NOW he searched *her* in exactly the same way. Very thoroughly indeed. She looked worried, which I took to be an unmistakable sign of guilt. As he proceeded further and further I was gobsmacked to see how well she had hidden this elusive packet of tights. Where *was* it? As he was searching inside her pants, she had pulled up her skirt and I saw that she was wearing her Dr White's belt, which meant she was having her period, or was 'on the blob' as we called it at school, misguidedly convinced that made it coded and covert. (God, do you remember those awful clunky things? A pink belt round the middle with a fastening front and back from which we suspended a small thick nappy-type pad from front to back. It was so cumbersome and useless, like walking around with a small chunky hammock between your legs. A hammock for mice.) I felt awful for her that she should have to undergo this horrible, shocking search at such a time but, after all, she HAD nicked the tights so she had kind of brought it on herself, for heaven's sake! I was amazed when his search proved fruitless. Had she secreted them internally? It was a mystery. He told us that we had been *very* clever with the hiding and to run along and not do it again.

We raced away from there so fast. Halfway back up the hill towards school we finally stopped running and sat on a wall to catch our breath. 'Where did you hide them?!' I puffed. 'I didn't nick any tights, I thought you had . . . ' It was only then we realised what had happened. A sleazy git had just groped us in the stairwell of the Co-op. He had expertly taken advantage of our obvious fear and lured us into a vulnerable situation where we were willing to let him fiddle with us, to let him put his filthy mitts all over us under the pretence of an official frisk. We were wholly complicit! Well, no, actually, not wholly because of course we were not aware of the intent. It was so easy for him. How many times did he do it to others? Did he ever do anything worse? I hadn't properly remembered the incident until I came to write this letter to you, and was thinking about the uniform and the unwanted attention it attracted, so I don't think I could ever claim that it scarred me in any deep way. Sadly, it has melted into my memory as just another one of those difficult and unpleasant moments that young women experience all the time with dirty old men. How many times did we turn round on a tube or train and see some sad old git's cock dangling out of his smelly old trousers? Admittedly this horrid man had gone a lot further and as the mothers of girls we would now reflect upon it with horror, imagining what *could* have happened. Instead, luckily, I was shaken but unhurt and I learned a big lesson about how crafty and manipulative predatory men can be. What strikes me as one of the worst aspects of the whole sorry episode was the fact that my friend and I kept this story to ourselves. We felt stupid and embarrassed and, most of all, we were so afraid because we were breaking a school rule! The priorities of a 13-year-old are admittedly difficult to fathom, but the fact is that school was our whole world and the fear of the consequences of breaking school rules was far greater than our concerns for our safety.

Have you and I taught our beloved daughters enough to keep them safe? While we pray they never have to face anything too scary, surely we also know they can learn to navigate their way through life by occasionally butting up against something a bit frightening and realising they can indeed cope with it. I don't savour the idea that they will no doubt witness a few unsightly limp willies on the tube, but perhaps those awkward and startling moments will strengthen their resolve to judge a dud and reject any unwanted attention in the future. Perhaps they will more readily tell those rude and uncouth codgers to cock right off. I wish I had.

Dear Madonna (the Madonna, the Yankee singer, not any old Madonna from religious history like The Da Vinci Code),

I is writin' to you for enquirin' about the procurement of the tiny brown baby. I seed you on the teleovision box sittin' all important next to a candlestick with flouncy drapin' all behind you like in a Meat Loaf video, explainin' to the news that you is wantin' *everybody* to be doin' the bringin' home from dark incontinence, many of the tiny babies that is not got family due to disease and fightin' and no money. They certainly did get bad cards to play life with, didn't they? Some of them doesn't get to live at all because celebrities from England and Yankees is snappin' their fingers every three seconds which means one of them has to die each time. That don't seem much fair, do it?

You is obviously done a kind thing. There's no miss doubt-pants about that. 'Cept I is scared for you somehow. Will the baby grow up wonderin' what the cock is gone on? Will he be doin' confusion about why he is the only one what looks like him? Maybe it would help if some Africas could be allowed to show him oils for skin and hair care or is you in charge of that with many a top stylist/dancer advisin' it? Will he be

137

permitted the tastin' of big mutton stews with flour and fat in with maize and cornflour nan breads on the side? Or is you wantin' only for him to be fed the macrobiotics with raws and no pop to drink whatsoever thank you? Will he be listenin' of the harmonionial voices with clever clickin' and ululation-type singin' from deep place inside with the beatin' of drums and stampin' of feet in rhythm of heartbeats and warm winds in strings of guitars what is made at home? Or will he be havin' to dance to electro disco rock pop videos of yourself with tight ladymen jumpin' all around you, doin' the adorin' and touchin' of you in private places for voguin' purposes? Will he be doin' the talkin' in the home-heard Chichewa words or will he be speakin' in American soundin' like English like you is, or posh soundin' cockernee like the gangster-type husband who is huntin' and shootin' in tweed strides at the weekend on a big peasant and pheasant estate, but durin' the week is neckin' pints of Irish foam and wearin' usual jeans and pumps, mate, with flat cap on the side jaunty angle?

Is you mainly thinkin' it don't matter as long as he is gettin' to stay alive, and have school and bikes and maids and hold hands with his new friendly pink family? Yes, you might be right about that, but sista, just watch out for when the baby does growin' and finds it all out. He might do some confusion about what all's been done. He might not warm to the rainbow family idea of many roots to put in a cultural stewpot for the equal lovin' of all, coat of many colours, side by

138

side on my piano keyboard oh lord why can't we? Watch out then for some shoutin' and stompin' and explainin' to do. But then again, he might not. He might just love it and say thanks Mum, with a big sloppy smacker. Have a make-up on hand to touch you up again if so . . .

That's all, so you can go about your busyness now, probably gettin' the bingo wings made to go away with pumpin' so you can instead have the toned sculpturalness we, the hungry magazine readers, have come to expect. Or p'raps you is upside down with yoga, gettin' bendy so you can kiss your own arsebum with ease? Hope so.

Take care, lotsa care.

Dear Nigel,

May I just say what a delight it has been to be your number-one fag hag all these years. May I also say that you deserve major regalia-type bling for the remarkably long and loyal service you have put in as BBF (Best Boy Friend). You ought to have a medal. But perhaps you would prefer an ankle bracelet? Needless to say, it will involve Diamonique in ample measure.

How I loved the teen-slouching around your kitchen table in Plympton with you and your twin bro Gareth, eating your mum's Welsh cakes, and raging about the injustices of the school youth drama club and life in general. We didn't take any action, of course, that wasn't the point at all, we just wanted to moan and grumble long into the night. We had lots of dates, you and I. We went to the theatre and films and exhibitions and concerts, where we became unfeasibly harsh critics. We performed onstage together, we learned lines together, we wrote sketches together. Probably the first bit of comedy writing I ever did was with you. I think it was a piss-take of a Pinter play, with jokes galore about pauses and dot dot dots. But the most wonderful, inventive and thrilling part of it all was the letters. At least once or twice a week, do you remember? You wrote to me as many different

140

characters, inviting responses from me in the character you had addressed your letter to. So, it was my mission to reply in kind, becoming one of these many people, inventing a whole life around them and a situation in which the two may be corresponding. Sometimes they were engaged in a torrid affair, or in the midst of a petty row, or a communication about a lost dog, or they might be gossiping about the news of their time. It might be present day, or Edwardian, or Elizabethan, or anything. The joy of these letters and my eagerness to reply filled many a long evening of boarding school life, and often entirely replaced prep. When I look back at it now, I probably gained more from writing those letters and using the skills they developed than I ever would have from the study of silt and sediment in riverbeds for Geography. I only ever wanted to make you laugh and I hungrily sought your approval. So, in a way, you were my first script editor.

Obviously, admitting this does not commit me to any form of pecuniary reimbursement. You will have the ankle bracelet, and that's that. We're quits.

May my suffocatingly enormous love for you smother you to certain death.

Your devoted hag

Dear BF,

I have always enjoyed partnerships. It's how I think and work best. A chum to bounce ideas around with, to have a career with and laugh your tits off with, like Jennifer. A chum to trust and to go into business with, someone who inspires and motivates you, like Helen Teague. A chum to dress up in bridesmaid gear with and share dreams of hairdos and bouquets, like Sarah. A chum to guide and listen, to share home truths and teenage wrangling tips with, to be continually delighted with their direct-from-heaven-via-nowhere-else talent, like Alla. A chum to gossip and chirrup with like Di Cracknell. I have needed every one of these important partnerships and I have greedily gorged on all of them, and felt grateful to know and care for these wonderful women. And to be cared for *by* them.

You. You have so generously encouraged me to give myself to these remarkable relationships because you know the utter joy they have given me back. The bigness of your love is astounding. You are selfless. I don't know how you are able to be the phenomenon you are. I don't know anyone else like you and I never will, it's too tall an order for any other human to emulate the beauty you have. If there is such a thing as reincarnation, I reckon you are the result of several astonishing souls merged together. If I had to put the ingredients together, I'd say you consist of varying degrees of the following (apologies to those still alive!):

Bessie Smith for raunch and heart
James Joyce for rich characterisation
Spike Milligan for wit and splendid insanity
Van Morrison for poetry
Mother Teresa for patience and selfless love
Lassie for alertness to danger
Emily Pankhurst for righteous anger
Anne Frank for bravery, dignity and hair grips
Liberace for campness and bling
Tinkerbell for fairy outfits and shoes
Giacometti for surprise and elusiveness
Howard Hughes for fiercely private
Hercules for tenacity and stamina
Mary Magdalene for sauciness and forgiveness
    in equal measure
Tiny Tim for fun and silly singing in a high
    voice
Garbo for style and class
Dusty Springfield for song and soul
Edith Piaf for heartache
Marilyn Monroe for ditz
St Joan for dedication and commitment
Cher for chutzpah
Joyce Grenfell for pure funny
Archangel Gabriel for heavenliness
Jung for philosophy and method
Mike Yarwood for mimicry
Confucius for wisdom

Marianne Faithfull for hair and make-up
Lilith for earthy rootyness
Your mum and dad for everything else

Meeting you at college was my saving grace. I arrived late for the start of term, and I didn't really fit in. The groups had forged themselves and I was a sort of lost puppy bounding hopefully between them, looking for a way in. My dad had committed suicide a matter of weeks before and I was dripping with sadness. But of course grief is invisible and suicide is tricky to introduce as an ice-breaker, so I kept it to myself until I knew and trusted people more. You have an extrasensory superpower, and it wasn't long before you sniffed me out as the walking wounded, which was remarkable considering you weren't even in my year. Central School of Screech and Trauma was run under a regime of separation. The actors didn't speak to the lowly teachers (who were, in their opinion, people who had failed to make it onto the acting course), the speech therapists were distinctly aloof, so only those on the stage-management course were friendly with everyone else, and that's because they were too knackered to put up any resistance. On reflection, I can't understand why the staff allowed or even encouraged these damaging segregations. Except, of course, that they themselves were divided. Anyway, it was unusual to mix with folk from other years and you were someone who refused to be limited by that. I remember very early on, you required of me a proper, formal commitment to this new friendship. I think you must have been subconsciously searching for a 'bestie' forever, and when we set our sights on each other there was, frankly, no other avenue open except total devotion. I knew instantly that I would know and cherish you till my dying breath, or yours. I would truly lay my life down for you, give you my kidneys, my eyes, my teeth, my tits, whatever you ask for. That's the key though, isn't it? You never do ask, for anything really, which is why I belong to you. Our friendship is a labour of love, a pledge to keep watch over each other and to stay constant. It is a quiet arrangement. Deep calling to deep. I will never leave my post, I will remain vigilant, I will not falter, I will always forgive. These are our unspoken vows and I respect them. The massive anchoring stability of my love for you, and vice versa, means that I can float about quite carefree in the surety of it all. You know any secrets I have, you know my fears, my demons and my delights, and I yours. I feel honoured to have obligations to you. You make a mirror for me in which I used to seek out my shortcomings, but with your ceaseless support I have learned to recognise my strengths. What a very grown-up thing to do.

Being grown up isn't exactly a mainstay of our partnership though, is it?

Do you remember when Billie was about to arrive? We only had a week or so's notice and I had to somehow get every bit of baby kit together in one day, without rousing any suspicion. It was essential that her arrival was calm and unannounced by the press. We wanted her to come home without any fuss and to nest in with her away from any noisy publicity. It was the most important thing we had ever done and we were very serious and protective. Fatty swung into action, like a superhero, helping me to suddenly walk out on a *French and Saunders* series that was in production by taking over the crew, the studios, the whole obligation and plonking her new sitcom idea *Absolutely Fabulous* right down on it instead. It fitted well. She has since said that she needed that kick up the bum to force her to develop the idea we had written together in a single sketch on our show a year or so before. She was thrown in at the deep end and swam easily along with her brilliant new project to buoy her up.

On the day in question, Len and your chap Barrie remained at home putting up shelves and trying to navigate their way around the construction of a cot. Potentially disastrous. We drove the 40-odd miles into London and parked behind Mothercare in Hammersmith. Your mission, which you boldly chose to accept, was to pose as the heavily pregnant first-time mother, and I was there as your mate, helping you to select all your baby kit. I nearly peed with glee when you shoved our sofa cushion up your front and rearranged it under your top to look convincing. We went into the store and you were immediately offered seating and a glass of water, which you graciously accepted. You stumbled about a bit when a young assistant asked 'how far on' you were and when the 'little one' was due. You had to do some quick mental maths

— never your strong point. With my hasty calculations you were confidently informing her the baby was going to be eleven months in gestation . . .

Our elaborate system of coded winks and blinks and coughs meant that you could be seen to be choosing everything you wanted for your baby, whereas in reality I was making every choice. The downside of you being up the duff was that I had to load up the car while you looked on smugly from the comfort of your chair in the shop, nursing your 'swollen' ankles. With the car now full of baby stuffing we went home, where you gave birth to your baby cushion in a hilarious display of torturous labour. That cushion slept in that cot until that real bundle turned up. You were a great decoy.

We go back a long way, you and I. Thirty years or so, I reckon. We have witnessed the big stuff of each other's lives haven't we? The loves, successful and disastrous, the weddings, the IVF, the miscarriages, the births, the adoption, the kids, the families, the deaths, the birthdays, the meals, the New Years, the houses, the schools, the pets, the shoes, the choices, the phases and the fads. The friends and the enemies. We steer each other on with unfaltering concern. We keep each other safe and steady, and because of that, we can take the chances we do.

Big respec' to the BF.

Dear Val Doonican,

Hello, my name is Dawn French and I'm 14 years old and your biggest fan. We are doing a project at school about investigating song lyrics and looking for the subtext behind them. I love and therefore have chosen your song 'Paddy McGinty's Goat'. A lot of people probably think it's about a goat. I know you are a kind, handsome, wise man who wouldn't just simply sing about a goat for goodness' sake, so I know it must have a more deeper meaning. So I went looking for that meaning, rooting around in the lyrics for what you really meant to say.

The first verse concerns Patrick from the title, and his buying of the goat. He claims that 'I mean to have me fill' of goat's milk, he's obviously very excited. But of course, when he

148

gets it home, he discovers the Nanny goat is in fact a Bill, or Billy goat, meaning a male. Is this some kind of representation of the disappointment Patrick feels about his life? Or are you trying to say something important about what we call 'the troubles' in your fair Emerald Isle of Ireland, maybe? Or not? Or yes?

In the second verse, you refer to 'all the young ladies who live in Killaloo', and you sing, rather daringly I suspect for you, about their many undergarments. After you have described their petticoats you say, 'leave the rest to Providence and Paddy McGinty's goat'. Now, I looked up the word 'providence' in the dictionary and it says 'the foresight and benevolent care of God', so I'm wondering whether, for you, the goat is some kind of Holy Spirit? Like a fourth member of the great celestial trinity? Am I close? Or could it be very different? After all, Satan, who is the opposite of God, is often depicted as a goat, isn't he? That is certainly food for thought.

Later on in the song, you mention that the goat munches on Norah McCarthy's trousseau, which was hanging on the line. You say he 'chewed up all her falderals, and on her wedding night'. Are you trying to make a comment about marriage and the sacred commitment people make to each other? Or the lack of it or something? What exactly are falderals, I wonder?

Actually, I've just had another listen to the song and I have a creeping feeling that perhaps it *is* just about a goat, which would be

149

a shame, but I still like the song. Especially the way you sing it, so jauntily. I also really love your jumpers and your rocking chair, which make you seem like you are such a friendly man. I really mega love it when you are singing your lilty love songs, which I stupidly sometimes think are mainly just for me. Ha ha! . . . Are they?

On a finishing note, if 'Paddy McGinty's Goat' *is* just about a goat, does that therefore mean that 'Delaney's Donkey' is about a donkey? Which would be awful because I'd worked out it was mainly about love.

With all my very best hugs to you, my special favourite singer.

Moo French

↗

(just a nickname, don't worry)

Dear Fatty,

I love that you are good at horses. You've got the lingo and the gear and the confidence, and you know what you are talking about. I think your mum knows stuff, doesn't she, and you have absorbed a lot of knowledge over time and now you have a full and valid passport for Planet Equine. You are unafraid, for instance, to own a yardful of beautiful horses, and I admire that spirit in you.

Let me tell you *my* experience of horses: I always wanted a horse. I read *Black Beauty*. I watched *Follyfoot Farm* and *National Velvet*. I sang along with *The Lightning Trees* and Jackie Lee's 'White Horses' till my head hurt. I pleaded with my dad to buy me a horse, but RAF quarters only have tiny gardens as you know, so I had to settle for lessons, which I took eagerly, everywhere we lived. All the while, I continued to fantasise about owning my own ONE day, please GOD, one day.

The first time we lived off camp was around 1971–3 when my dad was posted close to home at St Mawgan in Cornwall. My parents rented a farmhouse called Roskear Farm in St Breock near Wadebridge. At last, we had a couple of meadows and a barn. There was NO excuse now. My dad would have to have a heart of ice to

151

deny me the pony-love I craved. Imagine my total joy when one day he told me there would be a horse in the barn when I returned from school that coming Friday night. For me. A horse, for me. Actually, not just one horse, but two! Oh my actual God, at last, all of my clippy-cloppy dreams had come true. I had to endure four more sleeps before I could meet them, and each one of the sleeps was full of pony dreams, where I was astride a powerful thoroughbred, cantering bareback along the seashore with my hair fluttering in the wind, like a Timotei advert.

Imagine, then, my surprise when I was introduced to a little fat chestnut pony and her wall-eyed foal. It transpired that my dad had come across these two abandoned dobbins on a garage forecourt, left in lieu of a debt, and my dad, feeling sorry for them and seeing a chance to fulfil my dream, had struck some curious deal. I don't mean to sound ungrateful and, actually, I was devoted to them both, but it was a typical example of the Frenchies not getting it quite right. I renamed the pony Shula, after a character on *The Archers*, and her unbroken, uncontrollable foal Marty, after Marty Feldman, who was one of my favourite funnymen and who also had wonky eyes. Shula hadn't been ridden for ages and was quite unwilling, initially, to have a tubby sack of potatoes like me clambering all over her. Her saddle didn't fit her properly and neither did her bridle. We couldn't afford to replace them, so my dad set to with his toolkit, did a bit of tack tailoring, and somehow we made do. Shula was just beginning to get used to me riding her each weekend, when the spring came — and to my horror her entire mane fell out and so did her tail, leaving cracked skin and festering sores everywhere. We called the vet and found out that this was a disease called 'sweet itch', which only shows up when ponies who suffer from it eat the spring grass. Of course there was no sign of it when Dad brought them home. We had to bring her in and keep the flies from her, cover her in greasy white antibiotic cream and put her on a strict diet of garlic and nettles. We even sought advice from the local witch, recommended by the farmer next door, who vouched for her traditional potions which had cured many of his cattle's various illnesses. She made up a cream from God knows what mixed with what the hell's that, and we tried that for a while but to no avail. Gradually, as the months went by, Shula started to heal up a bit but the hair didn't grow back. So there I was, at the local county show, having brought my precious pony to take part in the prestigious gymkhana. All the pony-club girls were turned out like new pennies in their correct gear, with their shiny hair in nets, their shiny buffed-up boots, and their shiny tack, mounted on their shiny, muscly big horses. Then there was me, in one of my dad's old gardening jackets and my welly boots, wobbling about on a scuffed old saddle atop a scabby, bald, fat pony with zero interest in completing the course. We were straight out of a Thelwell cartoon. However, I held my head high and we finished the course with no panache whatsoever. As we romped home, with Shula farting on every stride, in last place in the gymkhana games, the final humiliation happened, and the saddle, which had never fitted properly and which had gradually worked its way up to Shula's shoulders where it was utterly loose, just slid slowly all the way round, with me still attached. For a brief second before I hit the grass I was actually riding my pony upside down. No one could accuse us of unoriginality!

So, you see, Shula was essentially pretty much pants at all the classic pony stuff, but I tell you what she was great for — hugging. I used to spend ages in that barn with my brush and currycomb and hoof pick, just grooming and primping her. I would have liked to plait her mane and tail but sadly the baldness prevented it. So I would put my arms about her neck and hug her. We would stand in this quiet loving embrace for hours, just hugging and breathing.

I settled happily for that sweetness. As is so often the case with me. I know I won't get most things exactly right, so I seek the parts I *can* do, and love, and enjoy those, in the full knowledge that someone is doing the other, perfect stuff confidently elsewhere. Just not me. Hey-ho.

Dear Nick,

I haven't seen you or heard anything about you
for a lot of years now. Whenever I was visiting
Plymouth or Cornwall, I used to get little
snippets of information about you. Sightings of
you in various places, or stories about what
you'd been up to, the jobs you had, the people
you hung around with. Such was the residual
strength of our adolescent relationship in the
minds of others, they felt the need to update me
about you. I didn't mind at all. It was good to be
still aware of you, still interested in you. I haven't
heard anything for some time now, though, so I
hope you're all right. I suddenly feel concerned
for you, and that concern is very familiar. I was
always worried for and about you. Your life
seemed so stormy and often very difficult.

I was 16. You were the first boy I felt the right,
or right *about*, to call 'my boyfriend' in public.
Plenty of boys disliked this kind of proprietorial
display, but you were cool about it. I liked that.
We were included in each other. I was part of
you, and you were part of me. Quite often our
couplenicity was camouflaged by the busy
groups we hung around in. We would hold hands
proudly, but the intimacy and exclusivity I so
enjoyed were inevitably diluted by the distraction
of so many others. We sat endlessly in sweaty

clusters in pubs trying to be, and for the most part succeeding in being, served alcohol when we were so obviously underage. Dubonnet and lemonade. Lager and lime. Rum and Coke. Always something AND something. Never just something. Never just wine, or just cider. The AND something helped the drink to be sweeter, more like pop, which was what I really wanted to drink all along.

Rather than boisterous evenings in big gangs, I preferred the quieter times, because in you I found probably the first boy I could talk to properly, about virtually anything. We were easy in each other's company and I was so very impressed with you, with everything you thought and said. I was consumed with thinking about you all week at school. Images of you, constantly pulsing through me, and I couldn't wait till Friday afternoons when we could be together again. I loved how funny you were, and how utterly irreverant. You were without doubt the cheekiest chap in Cheekyville.

My friend Jane was dating your friend John and a considerable amount of time was spent sneaking off to a flat somewhere in Mutley that John had keys to. Do you remember? We took boxes of cheap Spanish wine-inspired liquid, and got bladdered and laughed A LOT. The booze helped with any shyness or awkwardness. It was fabulous to be in a proper flat, pretending we all lived there, slobbing about, drinking and listening to Thin Lizzy, T. Rex and The Sweet. Eventually the laughing and flirting would dwindle and in our separate partnerships and on opposite sofas, we got down to the serious business of petting. Light petting, heavy petting, moderate to heavy petting and a healthy dose of extreme and nearly dangerous petting. Hours and hours of mutual, delightful exploration. I can still remember the excitement of going practically all the way but stopping just inches this side of trouble, pulling in to the temptation lay-by for refreshments and a cool-down. All blood returning from groin to brain, momentarily. Lovely. Safe . . . And then we'd be at it again, just to test if we dared go further each time. It's amazing how inventive you can be when you are both aware of the limitations. The constraints demand creativity. In fact, I would definitely say that once you have crossed the line of propriety into the full penetrative mode, I'm not sure you can ever reclaim the bliss that was those endless hours of innocent twiddling.

I remember you lived in Modbury, an impossibly pretty town built on a huge hill. When I first knew you, your mum ran the cafe called The Teapot, I think, which stood at a 45-degree angle to the steep gradient of the high street. I liked your mum Mary very much, she seemed liberal and exciting to me. You and your brothers and your cool, handsome dad could so easily have run any mum ragged but she seemed to revel in the testosterone-charged energy in that house. It was a loud, muscular, masculine environment, but she was the feisty feminine buoy you all tethered your roaring adolescent engines to. Lots of men and then Mary, running her tea shop with great panache, and with *great* scones. Oh Lord, those scones were the utmost in tip-topness, they were sublime tasty treats, they looked good enough to eat. Oh, that's right, they *were* good enough to eat. So we did. Plenty. Plenty. Heaving with home-made strawberry jam and lashings of crusty clotted cream. Probably travelling directly from mouth to arteries, but hey, they were young arteries, and anyway, what price Elysium? Yum-yum in my tum.

It seemed pretty much perfect, our tender, young relationship. Somewhere in the midst of the perfectness, you arranged a party. Was it a birthday party? Maybe not — your parents were chilled out and would, I think, have let you have a party for no particular reason so long as it was well organised. The excitement of it all was massive. I remember lots of frantic phone calls (not easy or cheap from boarding school where the queue for the phone was constant and achingly slow) to discuss everything. Who should come? What music should there be? How would we all get there? What to drink? Eat? Wear? We were determined that we should all get a bit drunk, but the skill was to be drunk enough to party but not so bladdered that anyone was sick all over your nice house thereby compromising any future parties.

The day of the party came and I remember we spent quite a lot of time and effort making the house ready. Your mum and dad had agreed they would stay out of the way and watch telly upstairs. Close enough to help in a crisis but far enough away so's not to interfere or cramp anyone's style. We had the rum AND the Coke,

158

the lager AND the lime. We had home-edited tapes made with meticulous care by recording particular songs directly from the radio during the Sunday-evening chart show. *All* our favourite music! — one song after another! — on the *same* tape! Omigod. Modern state of the art technology.

Contrary to your typical party-thrower's last-minute paranoia, our mates actually turned up and the party started. It was just right. People got drunk quite quickly and unexpected couplings started to happen, which is the stuff of a great party. Various abandoned partners were in various states of despair on various front steps in the street. You were in your element as the host, chiefly finding interesting new mixes of alcohol. I'm not sure vodka and lager were ever going to be happy bedfellows but I was glad to be part of their inaugural outing. The atmosphere was loud with the tapes blaring out and the clamouring of teenagers trying to be heard above the music. There was laughing and sobbing and singing in equal measure. We were sweaty from snogging and dancing, and we were hoarse from shouting and crying. The room oozed that fantastic funk of hot hormones and alcohol, and we couldn't have been happier. Teenage kicks all through the night . . .

The next thing I remember was your mum shrieking for you. The kind of shrieking that pierced the din like a pin through a balloon. I heard her. You heard her. It was a painful sound to hear. It was an urgent and frightened cry. The party lumbered on but through the swaying bodies I saw you stumbling towards your mum and I saw fear in her eyes. What was going on? You disappeared upstairs with her and my memories of the following hour or so are a jagged blurry collage of strangeness and horror. I waited a while, then I started to climb the stairs to find you. One of your brothers stopped me and said something was wrong. Your dad. He had passed out. Call an ambulance. Don't go up there. Don't call an ambulance. Someone had already done that. Get everyone out. Stop the party. Send them all home. Your mum crying. Turn off the music. Drunken complaints. You shouting and telling everyone to go home. Tears in your eyes. People staggering about, drunk and confused. You darting out to the front door to check for the ambulance. Teenagers on the dark street. They expected to crash on the floor tonight. How were they to get home? Plymouth was twelve miles away. What's happened? Shock and fear. A creeping dread. Still your mum crying. Your brothers shaking. You pacing like an angry animal, ashen and anxious. A taut and strange stillness. The ambulance arriving. The rush of fresh air coming in with the paramedics. The urgency of action. Some quiet mumbling from the upstairs room. The muffled calling of your dad's name. Heavy footfalls on the stairs. Your dad on a stretcher. An awkward descent. A glimpse of his pallid face. I knew. I knew. Random puzzled party kids colliding with the stretcher by mistake. Apologies. Sirens. You were gone. All your family were suddenly gone. Only the chaotic debris of a broken party was left.

160

I can't remember what happened next. How did I get home? Where and how did we all go? Who locked up? Did we clear up? I don't know.

My next memory is the following day at home, sobbing into my dad's chest and feeling the hard buttons of his shirt making marks on my face. He held me so tight and stroked my head and tried to comfort me through the shock. It was the first time I ever dared to imagine a death in the family or what it might be like to lose my own father. How unbearably painful that would be. How were you, Nick, going to cope with it? I knew I would be devastated if it was him, my precious father. I would be lost. The sorrow would surely melt me away. It was unthinkable. Then my dad spoke to me about you properly for the first time. How one of the things he liked about you was your irrepressible cheek. He said it took some courage to be so cheeky, that it was a risky strategy to adopt in life because it could backfire so easily. That your pluck and wit combined to make you a person of substance. He told me that you would feel bereft but that you were a reinforced person, a survivor, whose close-knit family would sustain you through your grief, and prop up your courage. I knew he was right. I knew you would have to be brave about it eventually but at that very moment I was apart from you and had no concept of how you could still be breathing. How could you be doing anything normal, that other people whose fathers HADN'T just died were doing? How were you functioning? At all?

My dad spoke very softly to me about how

161

your life would have to change now. How, as the eldest son, you would probably have to grow up very quickly, prematurely, in order to support your darling mum and brothers. He also told me that I had a role in this, to support you if that's what you wanted. He said you might attempt to live your life right, as a tribute to your dad. I could see a purpose in that. Suddenly there was some sense in the muddle.

I went back to school for another week of boarding the next morning, feeling exhausted and aimless. Everything was topsyturvy. I didn't want to call you because I was aware you were in the tight centre of your family and it seemed wrong, but I longed to speak to you, to know how you were. I was also a bit scared to call your home lest your mum should answer. Try as I might, I couldn't concoct anything that felt right to say. I hadn't been around death before and it felt massively difficult. I was 16. What does a 16-year-old say to a woman who's just lost her husband? 'Sorry'? 'How are you'? 'Hope you're not too sad'? 'Can I speak to Nick please'? Nothing felt right so I kept quiet and I kept my distance.

I was surprised when later that week I was told to report to the headmistress's study, to find my mum sitting there. This was highly unusual. I didn't normally see my mum during the school week. It transpired that *your* mum had phoned *my* mum to say that you were refusing to leave your bedroom at home and she was extremely worried. Mary thought it might help if I came to see you and so here was my mum to collect me.

162

We drove to your place in Modbury and the minute I saw your mum I started to blub and stammer some kind of rubbish condolence. Mary immediately released me from that hell by saying she was so glad I had come, that I really COULD be of some use if I would go and spend time with you and see if I could persuade you to come out of your room.

So it was that I climbed up those same stairs I'd seen your dad being carted down a few days before. It felt utterly unreal, and for the first time ever, I felt nervous about seeing you. As I approached your room I heard the sound of you thumping eight kinds of hell out of the drum kit you kept in there. This wasn't practice, this was fury. I knocked. Silence. I said it was me. A more silent silence. Then you opened the door and there you were, wide-eyed, shirtless and crazy with the madness of it all. The room was humming. It smelt of stale sweat and tears and agony. It seemed a violent and volatile place. I wasn't sure at first whether you wanted me there. Was your grief an intensely private matter? Was I an intruder? You let me in and I shut the door behind us.

I didn't leave that room for three days, other than trips to the loo on the landing outside. Your mum pushed trays of food in sporadically. I think we both grew up quite a lot in those three days, don't you? It's not for me to say what happened in there. It would be disrespectful to you. I just want you to know that I'm glad I was there, I felt privileged that you would let me weather that storm with you. I learned a lot about profound sadness and extreme hurt. It was raw and loud and honest. Then it was tender and careful. In the end I think we were flushed out by the sheer rankness of ourselves. We were pretty feral and strangely euphoric. You can never know, Nick, just how useful that time was for me later. It gave me permission to flex every muscle of my own grief when it came. By then I knew that anything goes when you are deranged with sorrow. Of course, I didn't know then that my time would come all too soon . . .

Our relationship fizzled out naturally some months later and I remember feeling a sense of shuddering injustice for you when I heard that your mum died also. That's not fair. That's really not fair.

Do you remember when we met briefly on the sea tractor going over to Burgh Island? Blimey, it must have been 15 years ago or something. Len was with me and it was a bit surreal. Impossible really, to encapsulate so much, so many important memories in the briefest of moments. I'm pretty sure we were both remembering an extraordinary time together. Both the delights and the difficulties. I truly learned a lot from you, Nick.

Dear Parents of everyone I ever babysat for,

SORRY. Here are some things I did in your houses:

1. I did drink a 'sitter's privilege', which is a cocktail consisting of a tiny slurp of every single bottle in your drinks cabinet. Including Angostura bitters and advocaat. Rest assured it wasn't really stealing, more like renting, because virtually everything ended up back in your loo.
2. I did let my boyfriend in five minutes after you left and he left five minutes before you came home. On one occasion he hid in the garden when you returned unexpectedly to collect a bottle of wine. Incidentally, he also drank a pint of 'sitter's privilege'.
3. I did try on quite a lot of your clothes.
4. I did try on quite a lot of your shoes.
5. I did try on quite a lot of your make-up.
6. I did smoke your Sobranie cocktail cigarettes out of your kitchen window.
7. I did read your *Joy of Sex*. I drew extra genitalia on the hairy people in it.
8. I did leaf through your photo albums, occasionally removing photos of unsavoury-looking relatives and writing

165

'bum' or 'tit' or 'flaps' on the back and replacing them with no trace.

9. I did find a sealed warehouse box of fifty Cadbury's Dairy Milk bars in the cupboard under your stairs. I removed the staples from the bottom of the box with your carving knife. I removed four bars. I replaced the staples (considerable skill required). I ate all the chocolate. I felt no guilt whatsoever.

10. I did read some of your letters.

11. I did wash my laundry in your machine.

12. I did graze in areas of your fridge and cupboards that I wasn't invited to graze in.

13. Sometimes bogeys did go on your carpet under the sofa. This was rare.

14. Sometimes I did take your restless children for a walk up to the local shop and we did buy flavoured milk and dunk KitKats in it, instead of the food you left out for them, which I took home for my flatmates.

15. I did rifle through your contraceptive-hiding area and study your preferred methods. During this procedure I often found other, more thrilling and sometimes sinister contraptions . . .

16. I did once swear at your eight-year-old son who kept running in to the room to display his frankly unimpressive erection.

17. I did once start a call on your phone when you went out at 8pm and finish it at 11.55pm just before you returned.

18. I did teach some new rude made-up words

to your children, e.g. 'arselooker', 'cock-dandy' and 'boobhead'.

19. I did have a small bit of sex with my boyfriend on your sofa.
20. I did tell some people who called up that you had gone to a swingers party.
21. I did take cuttings from your plants.
22. I did do your daughter's homework with my left hand to make it look like her writing, so that she could play.
23. I did lock your scabby old cat into a separate room for most of the evening.
24. I did accidentally let a spoon fall into your waste disposal unit which then made a terrible grinding noise and stopped working. I did *not* report this to you on your return.
25. I did let your two children get dressed and we went to the pictures instead of staying indoors.
26. I did find some money down the back of a big chair, which I kept. That was definitely stealing and I regret it, but I was a student and I was broke.
27. I did not return to your house again after your husband put his hand on my leg when he dropped me home.
28. I did lick a tub of solid home-made sorbet in your freezer.
29. I did bake a secret cake with your depressed six-year-old son to give to his estranged dad on his birthday even though you had forbidden it. We hid a small toy in the centre of the cake, which melted.

The toy not the cake.
30. I did let your dog on the sofa.

Thank you all for trusting me with your kids. I always kept watch over them and they taught me heaps of good and bad things. The cash you gave me went straight to where it was most needed. Absolutely nothing was spent on administrative costs.
Cheers!

Dear Madonna,

What the cock is happenin'? I is lookin' at you on the tellybox cheeky teen channel, with many musics by pimps and 'hos, and here you is, poppin' up with the new song and the new face! I is wonderin', have you had a go at the face-tuggin'? Or have you by mistake gone to a chair-upholstery place instead? Why did you get it so tight? Is you plannin' on playin' the bongos on it? I think you would get a pretty good noise. Is it possible to loosen it by turning knobs behind ears? Maybe even just for sleepin' or cryin' purposes? The new face is good in the way that I can still see it is you inside it, but more like a you what has been ironed. With spray starch added on.

I is feelin' annoyed about it coz up till this bit I was believin' that the way you is lookin' good was the jumpin' and jiggin' stuff for tonin' with some extra upside-down yogurt lotus positions stuff. Plus the eatin' of the good-for-you foods with macrobiotic wonder and fibre things in it, and the constant sexuals with the gangsta posh boy Ritchie. And, of course, the inside exercises of the soulhead with the kosher red string vests and bracelets, etc. I know that is importantin' for you. So, on top of all that busy stuff, what in the name of fanny repossessed you to go and get your face swapped? It might look a bit tidier for a few months, but what will you be doin' for gestures when you need people to know what mood you is in? You isn't possible to do the angry (which you will need when the teen Lady of Lourdes does bad homework) or the surprised (for when the baby David poos in the bath by mistake) or joy (for when the Rocco Forte asks if he can have a pair of kitten heels) or even the loved-up mama (for when the husband Lionel Ritchie is in horn). What a big fat sorry you is gonna be then.

Did you know you is 50? Or is it a secret? You was one of the best 50s I ever saw, and now you've gone and messed on it. Is there any way you could get the old face back? Is the upholsterer keeping it in a jar with vinegar to preserve? Could I help? I is quite nifty with the needle and wool and have done plenty of lettin' out on all slacks I buy since I was ten. Could I bring *my* face round to your house to show you the other option, with flaps and neck gobble? It doesn't look so clean in pictures but it does do movin' and smilin' and grumpy looks. No one has been too scared of it yet in my knowin'.

On a high note, good to see you back in the slutty bosoms basque separatists again. That underpantie look is good on you, specially since you is allergic to clothes. I like the bit where we can see your arms what is so muscly and veiny like a drawing of a body with no skin on like you get on the side of headache tablets boxes. Is you tryin' to wear your limbs inside out like an octopus so we can see all the lovely, raw tendons?

If so, it is workin'. And also, I need to give you respec' for the teeth what is shinin' brighter than a nuclear blast from a toxic bomb. Are they painted on, or your originals with facades? I want to copy it myself please, if you don't mind. Perhaps you can send me one to give as a sample to my builder for comparin' to a wall chart? I love the Dulux old-fashioned sheepdog puppy, don't you? He gets all the toilet roll round his neck, it's so sweet.

Anyway, let me know if you is needin' my help with any new renovations, interior or exterior. No job too small.

Lard buckets of love.

Dear Big Nikki, Little Nicky, Angie, Jane and Patsy,

The six years I spent at St Dunstan's were very important, and remain tinging clear in my memory, and I couldn't move on from thinking about that time without writing to you, my beloved school friends, who I still know and still love. Perhaps because I was a boarder, school chums became as close as family, more like sisters than friends really. It's impossible to chart those years in detail in one letter, so I want to try and concoct a sort of mnemonic scrapbook to celebrate our time there together. I'm looking at a photo of us all, and I'm going to pluck moments as they occur to me. Here goes:

First of all, it was always unjust to label Nikki R as 'big' Nikki. She wasn't at all big in the lumbering sense of that word — it's just there was the other Nicky to distinguish her from, who was about an inch and a half shorter. Ironically, Big Nikki drew the short straw . . . I'm going to refer to her as Nikki R instead, as we always *should* have done.

Like many other 'belated' occasions in my life, I arrived at school a bit after everyone else, in the second rather than the first year. Yet again, I had to navigate my way carefully through the treacherous waters of the established friendship groups. Again, I had to put on quite a display of personality fireworks in a desperate attempt to attract your attention, and be accepted. Look how funny I can be! I can fall over! I can pull faces! I can dance! I can clown! I can mimic! Roll up, roll up! Book early for disappointment! It worked. I was in. Phew! Another audition over, I could relax. In actual fact, all of you were incredibly welcoming to me straight away, and for that — cheers!

I remember dormitories, with huge, high arched windows, iron beds and one little locker in between. There were about ten or twelve beds in each big dorm and as we grew older, we shared smaller rooms in twos and threes and then finally in the sixth form we had our own hallowed room. Mine was between the chemistry and physics lab and smelt of Bunsen burner gas. I didn't care that it was potentially lethal. It was *my own* potentially lethal room.

A regular entertainment in our dorm was to leave a mysterious object, a note or a piece of jewellery perhaps, on someone's bed, then hide under your own bed till that person came in and discovered it. The utter joy of eavesdropping on their confusion and being invisible was bliss. I found it *so* funny (much funnier than it actually ever was) that I would often wet my pants with the effort of keeping my hysterical laughter as silent as possible. I would sometimes be under the bed for *ages*, having failed to note that my intended eavesdroppee was, say, taking part in an 'away' hockey match. It wasn't unusual for me to be stranded under the bed, motionless and soundless, for three hours! Meanwhile, I enjoyed the general comings and goings of a dorm full of people who didn't know I was there — hidden, secret and naughty.

I remember my mum's anguish when her worst fear came true, and I started my period the *first week* I went away to boarding school! She had given me a good informative briefing about it all, making only one tiny mistake: she had laid out all forms of 'feminine sanitation' apparatus in a row on her bed at home, like some kind of zealous, gynaecological saleswoman, showing me the difference between pads and tampons etc. and she explained that losing this particular type of blood didn't mean you would die, which was a blessed relief, because I was convinced otherwise. Unfortunately, among the array of equipment she had forgotten to take the wrapper off the Tampax, so I was certain from the off that I wouldn't be allowing that six-inch monster cotton stick anywhere near *my* toilet parts. Later, of course, I realised that two-thirds of that alarming package was the applicator. Something which I wish I'd known on that first day when I disappeared into the loo at the end of our dorm for over an hour trying to work out what to put where, too embarrassed to ask for help. In a panicked attempt to use a Lil-let correctly, I fumbled about in my own lady-garden for aeons, trying to hold the instruction leaflet with one hand and insert the tampon with the other. I'm sure most women will recognise the pickle I found myself in when, after slumping against the door in a giddy tizz, and jabbing about hopelessly, I finally managed to invade myself correctly. Or so I thought. It hurt. It really hurt. I could hardly stand up. I certainly couldn't walk without my legs wide apart, as if astride an invisible horse. This was AGONY — how did women do this? I very nearly fainted twice in the first five minutes and hobbled back to the loo for another go. Extracting the enemy tampon was almost as bad as putting it in. Where was the string? Where was the tampon? Had it disappeared up into my intestines somehow? Or my lungs? Would I cough it up at supper? Did I need an air ambulance immediately? Was I dying? After more frenzied furtling, all was well, the tampon was retrieved and I realised that it had somehow bent over on entry, and I had been valiantly stuffing it in *sideways*, forcing a very junior fanny to accommodate a very senior-sized intruder. When, eventually, I managed the manoeuvre successfully, I realised just how mightily wrong the first attempt had gone. I was, frankly, lucky to be alive . . .

I remember loathing the new matron who had come to fill in temporarily for our beloved kind matron, Mrs Coombes. This new beast very quickly alienated all of us with her strict rules and loud handbells in the morning. I appointed myself nomenclator and bestowed the title 'Hitler' upon her. We goose-stepped and Nazi-saluted her — do you remember? — but still she remained. She was ash grey and made entirely of granite, not dissimilar to the school,

175

and seemed impervious to our efforts to oust her. In the end, we were forced to take serious action. Little Nicky and I decided to sneak into her room and sprinkle her bed with mice droppings or, even better, rat droppings if we could find them. We thought we ought to be able to — there were plenty of them darting through the shadows around the school grounds. But try as we might, we couldn't find ANYTHING revolting at school, so I was determined to bring some form of odious poo from home at the weekend. After a fruitless search around our cottage in North Petherwin, I had to resort to the guinea-pig cage. I smuggled in half a shoeboxful of guinea-pig-poo missiles, which Nicky and I spread over and in Hitler's bed on the Thursday night. Obviously we weren't there when they were discovered but, suffice to say, she didn't return on the Monday. Rentokil came though, and were sent into her room. I presume they cited a serious case of guinea-pig infestation in their report to the head.

I remember turning our radios on early in the morning and Noel Edmonds would wake us up with lots of gags and silly voices and tunes from Mungo Jerry and Slade and Diana Ross and Benny Hill. It was perfect, because that first moment when we opened our eyes was the very instant we missed our mums the most, so badly, and he helped us get past that bit.

I remember working out that French was taught precisely the same to each year, day for day. Therefore, Patsy's prep on a certain day would be EXACTLY the same for me, the year

176

below her, on the same day the following year. So I could copy her prep from her previous year's book, word for word. It helped that you were clever, Patsy, and your prep was usually right. I got away with it for about a month, getting better marks than I ever had before! Then two bad things happened: 1. Mrs Whitfeld (who I loved and respected) totally knew and didn't even punish me, just whispered in my ear that it was most disappointing, and 2. I didn't learn any French. A huge regret. Bugger. On both counts.

Do you remember the night we clambered up to the high windows in the dorm in our nighties and flirted with some boys down in the street on North Road? We were giving it plenty of flutter and cheek when all of a sudden they started climbing up the walls! In a trice they were over the Bishops Garden wall and into our dorm. BOYS! IN OUR DORM! AT NIGHT!! This was both thrilling and threatening. A heady mixture. We tried to shush them but they were loud and boisterous. Oh God, I wish they could have stayed longer. We were starving for them. I know we only had to last till the weekend, but nevertheless, we were ravenous . . . In no time at all, Mrs Coombes heard them and they bolted. The police were called and the boys were rounded up and paraded in front of us. We had to identify them so's they could be charged with breaking and entering. As one, we refused to do this and, even under threat of parents getting involved and expulsions, we kept our quiet. A small nobility but an important one, a tiny moral victory. Miss Abley was fuming. We didn't do it again.

I once put Julie Searle's head in a suitcase and sat on it. I couldn't help it. She was really whining. On and on and on. I don't think she minded too much. She was laughing. Eventually. I'm a bit sorry about it now. A bit.

I recall the anxious moments in the morning, when the post was handed out, and how vital it was to get some, any. Valentine's Day was especially horrendous, but every day mattered. Thank God for my regular correspondence with Nigel. Our many letters written under pseudonyms were probably the germ of sketch writing. All letters, however, from parents, brother, boyfriends, girlfriend were — are — so welcome. A proper personal connection, an intimacy and a gift. I have never ceased to feel the same joy every time a proper letter arrives. My nearly 100-year-old grandma has written to me every few weeks for the best part of 40 years. Our shared history is invaluable, our connection is strong and continually nurtured through those hundreds of wonderful letters.

I remember the staunch, tough facade you presented, Nikki R. You were my first experience of a person my age with a strong moral centre. An unshakable sense of justice and left-ness. Being a day girl, you brought in a fresh breath every morning, the astringency of your big, loving, boisterous family. Others, (idiots), mistook you for grumpy and severe, but I knew and know you to be a fierce protector and an insanely loyal advocate. And you were so physically fit

178

and determined. I remember your supreme dignity in the gym competition when you chose to do a routine to Gladys Knight's version of 'The Way We Were'. You settled yourself into position on the floor in the middle of the hall, arms aloft, waiting for the music to start. There was a hush. Whichever twit was operating the sound system took ages to switch it on, and then stupidly spooled right back to the beginning of the track where Gladys blethers on about 'the good ol' days', and 'try to remember . . . the kind of September . . . ' and 'the skies were bluer . . . ' on and on for a good two minutes of solid cheesy chat. All the while you maintained your ready position and didn't flinch a muscle. After what seemed like years of waiting the song eventually started, and even that had its own internal introduction before finally Gladys sang, 'Memories, like the corners of my mind . . . ' And you started your graceful, winning routine. I'm not sure many other teenagers would have had such composure. That's you all over, quiet, patient, dignified. Until the music, started of course, because it was you who introduced me to soul music, to blues, to Motown and all those fab girl groups. You had your mojo workin', maid, and still do.

And you, Nicky V, 'little' Nicky Twobells. Always dodging and diving, nervous but keen, sporty and sensitive. A girl so desperately in need of approval from parents who, inexplicably, seemed to withhold it. So you sought it elsewhere, making sure you were appreciated by many, and you were. Always canny you stayed on the right side of the more dangerous girls. The queen of malapropisms, inventing a whole new language of not-quite-the-right-but-sort-of-much-better words. Your cheek and your beauty enabled you to pilfer our boyfriends from right under our noses but somehow I never minded because you deserved them, and they adored you. I remember our kissing technique practice with pillows, backs of hands and even each other when measures were desperate! I remember chapel every night and how sentimental and virginally obsessed we were with Jesus for a while. I remember how kind you were to some of the very young boarders, flexing your maternal muscles and discovering how lovely it was to be needed. I remember our chambermaiding exploits together down in Salcombe, to make money in the summer holidays. The endless disgusting sheets, the sticky rooms, the trolley laden with individually wrapped biscuits too delish to resist, taking photos of each other's bums on residents' cameras for them to discover in Boots when they returned from their holidays. Fighting off randy chefs and barmen, far too old for us. Sharing a bedroom in the attic of the hotel, for protection. I was eventually seconded to the laundry by the housekeeper, to keep me out of the trouble I was always in. For instance, one time I knocked and walked in on a shirtless man doing press-ups behind the sofa in his room. I chatted away inanely while I tidied up until I realised he wasn't alone, and he wasn't doing press-ups. Yep, that was me then demoted and safely ensconced in the bowels of the

(Above) Me being a baby.

(Above right) Bath time in French household. Uncle Owen restrains Gary.

(Right) Dad as a nipper.

Mum pushing me in a pram on windy Anglesey. Gary as outrider.

(Above left) Gt. Grandma, Auntie Win, Grandma, Gary and me (unhappy).

(Above) With my best friend Carlo.

(Left) The fabulous Marjorie and Leslie French giving us their old time dancing.

(Below left) With Gary and Hunni. He refused to let her wear a bonnet for this shot.

(Below) It's Gary's gang – I'm not going to challenge him.

I bow to you, 'Spam'. Look, see the quality of the cloth.

Who's nicked the ruddy crown?

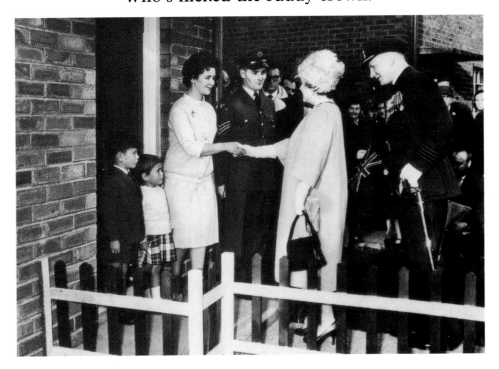

Jaw set, on bed in Akrotiri, Cyprus. Determined to conquer the world of ballet despite shortness and roundness of stature.

Cyprus. Whole family
drowning a lilo.

(Above) Dad in
Cyprus as a
Reservoir Dog.

(Left) Ballet class.
Me as a dying
cygnet. Note the
fabulous
floor/chin work.

(Above) Another riding lesson,
dreaming of having my very
own magnificent steed.
(Right) A rare moment where
we are all clean. Gary has
Mum's spit on his hair.

(Above) Sarah
Walton and me in
puppy heaven.
(Right) I must, I
will upstage those
bridesmaids.

(Above) Outside Tussauds. The beginning of monkey love.

(Right) At last! Me and Heather. The sinister glint is, in
fact, triumph.

(Left) With cousin Karen and mini skirts.

(Below) With chums on RAF base.

(Above) My first car, 'The Bomb', at Pillaton.

(Above right) My first love, Nick Brentford, both sporting the same mullet.

(Right) With Jane Veale, writing songs of love and loss.

St. Dunstans Abbey
School, 4th Year.
Front row (circled):
Me, Little Nicky,
Mrs Whitfield,
Angie, Jane. Back
row: Nikki R.

Sixth Form. I am
squeezing Nikki R's
bottom.

Me 'n the two
Nickys.
The dreaded
boaters.

Trying to attract males on beach at
St. Mawes. On holiday with Angie.

(Above) I take the two Nickys
along as bait for David's
friends. My friends don't
really like his friends.

(Right) The blue net curtain
tent dress and the officer and
a gentleman.

The Venue.

Moody and
recently sexed.

A study in denim
and Fair Isle.

(Above) On a Circle Line
cruise around Manhattan.
Age 18.

(Left) A couple made entirely
of denim.

(Above) Spence School Graduation Day: me as a vestal virgin in Auntie May's emergency frock.

(Below) Uncle Dr. Mike comes to support me. We go to see Stan Getz to celebrate.

(Right) Lizzie, Wendy and me at 25th reunion.

(Below) Same three amigos on Graduation Day.

My care is like my shadow in the sun — follows me flying,
— flys when I pursue it.
— Elizabeth 1, Queen of England

Life isn't all beer and skittles; but beer and skittles, or
something better of the same sort, must form a good part
of every Englishman's education
— Thomas Hughes,
Tom Brown Schooldays

Devise, wit; write, pen; for I am whole volumes in folio.
— Shakespeare.
Love's Labours' Lost

Dawn Roma French

Moo, Mou, Mu . . . Darn, Dahn, Dane,
. . get it right it's Dawn, ok? . . . What's
a gene, anyway? . . . save it . . . mail
. . so what's wrong with the British econo-
my? . . . 'Mathecaire' . . . parties on 101
. . Spaghetti at 4:00 a.m. . . . badminton
. . how come Dr. Heuston keeps inventing
'famous' British authors I've never heard of!?
. . . the best goddam squash player . . . the
Royal Navy . . . photography . . . Why
does everyone at Spence hate Elton John?
. .

17

1977. N. York. My page in the Spence School Yearbook.

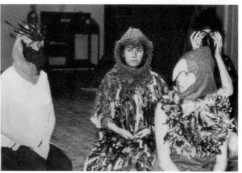

(Above) Dad, on my return to the UK.

(Above right) First year at college.

(Right) College. As an owl in Aristophanes' *The Birds*. Not happy.

(Right) Me and Fatty outside 15 Steeles Rd.

My 21st birthday in a Greek restaurant in Camden, singing with Fatty. I have come as a Stepford wife.

(Above) First official sketch together at college.

(Left) Peter, Jobo, Fatty and me. Theatre in education. A dreadful 'devised piece' about trains.

(Below) Scottie with me and Fatty.
Right) T.80 at a 'wedding'.

Being a teacher, with my class. I am one minute older than some of my students.

(Below) Some favourite kids we taught.

(Above right) Me and the B.F. outside the drama studio/toilets at Parly.

(Right) The B.F. on Charles and Di's wedding day.

(Left) Onstage at the Comic Strip. I am believing Tartan is 'it'...

(Above right) Punishing others with Ralph McTell songs in Comic Strip dressing room.

(Below) Comic Strip tour. Backstage at gig (porn cinema) in Sachiehall St.

(Right) First Comic Strip film directed by Julien Temple. Have come as bin bag.

C Strip on tour. Dangerous
comedians in children's
playground. Fatty must be
taking photo.

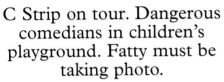

(Left) The first
dip in pool at
Oberoi in
Adelaide.
I am last due to
disability of
natural
buoyancy aids.

(Below left)
Me 'n Fatty.

(Below right)
Fatty 'n Me.

(Above) A Fistful of Traveller's Cheques. Ade, John (sound), Keith and Rik.

(Above right) Nige is saying something disgusting.

(Right) Famous Five with Licky Timmy.

(Below) Len visits the *Famous Five* set.

(Below) In bed with Ade, filming *The Beat Generation.*

(Below right) At Edinburgh Castle with Nige and Ade.

(Above) Ill-advised first publicity shot.

(Above right) In N.Y. Len as Statue of Liberty.

(Above) Us and our mums.

(Left) On holiday in Sicily.

(Left) The Menopatzi Sisters.

(Below) F+S Live at Shaftesbury Theatre.

(Below) The 'romantic' holiday in railway carriage at Gwithian.

(Left) Len in sheepskin coat. He didn't remove it once.

(Right) Our wedding invite.

(Below) The Frenchies are on a step. The Henrys are not.

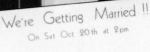

We're Getting Married !!
On Sat Oct 20th at 2pm

We'd love you to be there

St. Pauls Church
Bedford Street
London WC2

and afterwards at

The Savoy Hotel
189 Strand
London WC2

please use "River Entrance" on the Embankment

(Below left) My hen night. Many beloveds in towels at 'The Sanctuary'.

(Below) The reception. With Ade and Jen. Again, tartan.

(Right) On tour.

(Below) Filming *Slags* written by Fatty.

(Below left) Day out whilst filming Ben Elton's *Happy Families*. Me, Helen Lederer, Hugh Laurie and Fatty.

(Below) With Len in Jamaica at his cousins' shop.

(Left) The Fat Men.

(Below) Girls on Top: me, Tracey, Jen, Ruby and Joan.

(Above) 'Whispering Your Name' video with Alla.

(Right) Filming *Murder Most Horrid*.

(Above) We 'come out' in a *Hello* mag shoot at home with tiny Billie. This gets rid of eight paparazzi camped outside front door.

(Right) Len and Bill.

(Below) Bill improvising at piano, a daily occurrence.

(Above left) Bjork.

(Above) Frodo.

(Left) Well, if she refuses to come on our show, we'll just have to 'be' her!

(Below left) Country Ladies, who are basically The Fat Men with lipstick.

(Below) Exorcist. Feeling pretty as a picture.

(Left) At something
with Len.

(Left) Unidentified
Susans at a 'conference'
in Mustique.

(Below left) Susans in
uniform.

(Below) Nigel and me,
forever.

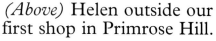

(*Left*) Me and the B.F. in *A Midsummer Night's Dream*. *Not* the B.F.'s own teeth.

(*Above*) Helen outside our first shop in Primrose Hill.

(*Above*) With Natalie and Juan Diego in *La Fille du Regiment*. I have come as a giant ice cream.

(*Right*) Prima Ballerina, ready to meet Princess Margaret.

The Diblets.

(Left) With Gary Waldhorn as Easter Bunnies.

(Right) The puddle. The second time.

Mum visits the set.

(Above) On Dartmoor filming *Jam and Jerusalem*.

(Right) Wild West with Catherine as my lesbian lover. Yum Yum.

(Below) Len gets to be Commander.

(Below right) Gary, Bill, Jack, Hannah and Grandma French on her back step.

Me 'n Fatty. Big love.

Salcombe Hotel, washing, drying and ironing on a huge industrial roller thousands and thousands of mounds of dirty white sheets. As every chambermaid finished her duty, in she would come and dump another mountain of sheets. If there had been any unsightly accident in the sheets or they were particularly soiled, the chambermaid would shout 'Thunder!' as a warning, and leave me to it, to bleach and wash the offensive linen on an extra-hot boil wash. I was surrounded by piles of sheets that looked like the tips of icebergs. Sheet icebergs. The floor was never, *ever* clear of them. I used to sweat a lot and drink pints of Vimto to replenish my fluids, and I smelt of bleach and starch, but to this day, I appreciate the feel of a well-ironed crisp sheet because I know the effort that made it so.

I remember the endless rows about the school uniform, among all of us. In the sixth form we were finally allowed to ditch the dreaded stripy blazer with blue serge kilt and heavy jumper. Each new sixth form were allowed to choose their own uniform, a chance to be unique and expressive. How, then, in the name of cock, did we end up with brown and mustard as our palette? What were we *thinking?*!

I remember Miss Abbott, our drama teacher, with her beautiful clear diction and her twinkly eyes. I begged my mum to let me have extra lessons after school with her, where we sat in a tiny musty room above the bow arch at the main entrance to the school. I knew that paying for these lessons was a stretch for my parents but I

181

decided I would rather die than miss them. We discussed plays and writers, new and classic. We worked on voice and we prepared pieces for exams. When I think back now, I was behaving much like an aspiring young actress, but actually I didn't have any desire to act at that point, I just wanted to spend time with Miss Abbott. More than that, I wanted to *be* Miss Abbott, and if I couldn't be her, I wanted to be *like* her. She had trained at the Central School of Speech and Drama in London, and she told me all about that. Very early on I decided it must be a fine school, if Miss Abbott went there. So I would go there. And I did. I would be a drama teacher. And I was . . . briefly. All because of my crush on the fabulous Miss Abbott.

I remember you, Angie. The Cornish rebel, by far the most defiant of us all. Where we were cautious or wary or even a bit pious, you were reckless and bold and wild. You were the first with the boys, unafraid to experiment and full of confidence, which was *so* appealing. You knew how to scrub up and play the ravishing siren, which was singularly irresistible for everyone who met you. How many times did I cover for you with little white lies to your mum and dad about staying with me, when in fact you were on another of your wildcat adventures? I used to worry that you might slip up, or be disappointed somewhere inside the anarchy, but you were too astute for that. As has been proven all along, you have a strong survival instinct and have always manoeuvred your way out of a sticky situation with great aplomb. With all this firebrandery bubbling inside you, I was amazed that you were able to conceal it at will with the flip side of your nature, the no less real nurturing, motherly and astonishingly upright character you also are. A woman of fascinating and fabulous contradictions, you are one of the most enthusiastic and energetic people I know. So much of this came to bear when later in our twenties we shared a room together in a flat in London. I had no hesitation jumping in to that adventure with you because where you are, there is thrill . . .

Jane. Janey. Or 'Sausage' for some reason I've forgotten . . . The stylish, clever one among us. If we were in *Sex and the City*, you would be elements of all the characters mixed together with the largest part being Miranda, the contained and ferociously intelligent one. You always played your cards close to your chest and I had an abiding feeling that you were finding most of our school life highly amusing in a very internal and sophisticated way. You were quick-witted and observant, and I loved sharing jokes with you. If my memory serves me well, we did quite a bit of double-dating so saw a lot of each other outside school on dates with Nick and John, our gorgeous mullet-haired boyfriends. I have pictures of you and I outside our house, Forder Cottage, near Launceston, in Cornwall. We are writing songs and strumming guitars. The songs were *very important* tortured songs about love and loss, neither of which we had experienced at that stage, but about which we were experts. We used to go to a folk club called Friars and believed that we were genuinely much better than everyone who performed there. Except Ralph McTell of course, who we idolised because he sang of *exactly* our pains and joys, right? Yeah. The other man who was singing just to us, although not at Friars club sadly, was Jim Morrison. He was, sort of, our boyfriend. You and I fancied we were very like Ali MacGraw in *Love Story* except we weren't American or dying of cancer. We didn't have hockey-champion preppie boyfriends either, but otherwise, we were *so* like her. We favoured the long, dark, parted-in-the-middle-and-worn-in-bunches-or-plaits-like-a-squaw-type hairstyle that Ali did and we thought it looked pretty good. I'm looking at the photos. It didn't. Since your dad was the housemaster of Mannamead House at Plymouth College Boys School (where my brother went though he was in a different boarding house), I spent some time staying with you there. Which meant staying inside a boarding house. Full of boys. Your room was literally one wall away from about SIXTY boys. I could smell them! No, seriously, I really could smell them . . . I could hardly contain myself when I was there with you. You were so cool about it, it was second nature, you could ignore it, them. I spent the whole time pathetically squirting teenage oestrogen from every pore, but I was desperate to hide my so uncool excitement in order that you didn't feel compromised or think that I was your friend only in order to gain such privileged access to so many captive chaps. However, I can't deny that it was a fab bonus . . .

184

I remember Goodbodies coffee shop just off Mutley Plain, where we would go on a Friday after school. The preparations for it would begin around lunchtime, when we would sneak into the loos and start the makeover. It was of the utmost importance that the teachers should *not* notice any added make-up or change of clothes etc., so all was executed with great subtlety. Tiny but effective measures were taken, e.g. the yanking up of bra straps to force teen bosoms into a more upright position, the rolling over of the waistband of the school kilt incrementally raising the hemline of the skirt, loosening of a button or two on the blouse, the careful arranging of a special magician's-secret-type knot in the school tie which could be hoiked off in an instant without wasting the precious extra three seconds it would otherwise take to get it off at the end of the day. A *tiny* imperceptible amount of orangey Avon spot-cover and foundation and perhaps the merest hint of pale lipstick. The afternoon lessons were pointless on those days. We could not possibly concentrate. All we could think of was the imminence of boy time. We clock-watched and fidgeted our way through French and bloody vile double maths until, like New Year's Eve, but silently, internally, we counted down the seconds to the end-of-the-day bell. Then, and only then, could we race to the loo, hastily slap on the full orange grouting and many, many, many layers of thick gloopy mascara, eyeshadow, blusher, roll-on deodorant, breath freshener, brush teeth, brush hair and let hang loose, roll up skirt even further, put on jewellery, spray Aquamanda perfume behind ears, on wrists, on crotch, whisk off tie — hey presto! — pop in some gum and off. Being a weekly boarder, I was always dragging my suitcase but I didn't mind. A 30-minute brisk lug up North Road, past the train station, over the top of Pennycomequick, on to the bottom of Mutley Plain and into the cafe. There they were, the pantheon of prized Plymouth College sixth-formers all sitting at one table huddled around hot chocolates. Bliss. The key was to make it seem coincidence that we were all there together. We couldn't let on that we had come with the sole intent of being near them, so we walked past their table and totally ignored them. We purchased one Nescafé or one Coca-Cola and we sat at the furthest table. Oh boy, did we ignore them. It was delicious to turn our backs on those boys. Our plan seemed to work. They also ignored us. We took this to mean they were gagging for it. Neither table made any eye contact and we certainly didn't speak. We were often in there for three hours, not communicating at all. Eventually the time came when one group had to leave, and would slope off without so much as a grunt to the other. Result! Once outside we would burst into skittish fever pitch, twittering about how amazing it all was. The debrief after such prolonged, intense, mind-blowing, complex flirting was essential. We were over-intoxicated with arousal. Fit to burst. Nobody at Goodbodies had said a word. Excellent. What a trip. Phew. Let's do it again next Friday. Christ. Hope I'm not pregnant!

I vividly remember roundly loathing maths, until one day Mrs Cooper decided to teach us about longitude and latitude. She brought out a globe to explain time zones, degrees, etc. It was as if she had given the class a sedative. When she observed some of us (myself included) slipping into a listless coma of disinterest, she took evasive action and pulled an arithmetical rabbit out of her geometric hat by producing, of all things, a Terrys' Chocolate Orange. Now she had our attention. We didn't see much chocolate during the week. There *was* a tuck shop but it was expensive, and now here in our classroom, during MATHS, was a small perfect orange sphere of delicious tastiness. We gathered round as she likened it to a globe and explained the lines around its girth would be latitude. Then she unpeeled it — oh joy — and pointed out the lines from top to bottom which marked the segments — the longitude. Then, she tapped it and it fell perfectly into its open leaves like a beautiful chocolate lotus flower. We had one piece each and I virtually swooned with satisfaction. Thus began a lifelong love for Terrys' Chocolate Oranges. Little did I realise one day somebody would offer me a fortune Croesus would envy to eat them.

I remember quoting *Monty Python* sketches word for word, and retelling Dave Allen gags and copying endless Pan's People dances with solemn and supreme accuracy.

I remember us all going to Nikki R's family beach house at Gwithian after our A levels in '76 and running into the sea as a triumphant cleansing rite of passage, a marker of the end of study FOR EVER! It wasn't, but it felt like it then. There was a drought and the country was baking, but we were eating Fab 208 ice creams and listening to our Marc Bolan records so we didn't care. We lolled about in bikinis getting nutty brown and fanning each other, simultaneously loving and hating the sizzling heat.

So, that was school as I remember it. I wonder if you remember it the same way?

One last thing — I know that segregating children into 'houses' at school is divisive and potentially dangerous because it can create hierarchy and dissension. It can cause unnecessary competition. Yes, I know that, but all of you need to face one irrefutable fact. Downton House *is* best. Sorry, but it's true, and you know it, you losers!

Dear pioneering all-female US rock band FANNY,

Hello! My name is Moo French. I'm 16 and I saw you play at the Guildhall in Plymouth last week! I am truly four of your greatest heroines! Christ allbloodymighty, you chicks really know how to rock on! The evening was just amazing and I'm so glad you came to Plymouth! Lots of bands just don't seem to care about us down here! They think we eat turnips and babies or something! Well, we simply don't! We eat pasties like everyone else, after all, at the bottom of it, we *are* human beings, yeah?! Even if we do have accents! Plymouth is an important city, it's where Francis Drake (you might not know about him, he was one of our greatest sailors in the 1500s; he wrote the poem 'Drake's Drum' if you want to learn about him. It's quite interesting because he was playing croquet on the Hoe when he saw some Spanish Armada ships pulling in to the marina so he halted his game to go and fight them off. He was incredibly brave and saved our country from Spain and there's a statue of him) comes from!

Boy oh boy, you play those axes and drum kit and piano keyboard like crazy and I can't believe how good you are at singing simultaneously at the same time! I myself play a Framus bass guitar! I got it because the fretboard is very narrow and my hands are mega small! I'm getting better at it all the time! I used to practise by playing along with your album, but I found that a bit difficult so I swapped to copying Status Quo, which helps a lot since there are only three chords on that! I would one day like to put my own chick rock band together! Not sure what a good name would be! You've stolen the best one! In our country, I hope someone has bothered to tell you, fanny is quite a rude word for a woman's minky! I believe that in your fair land of America it means bum! But not here, sisters, so watch out, mamas! Don't invite anyone to pinch or slap your fanny cos you will regret it! I was thinking of what a good name could be for my band, following after you with such a strong female name! I've decided 'Quim' would be good! Like it? Hey, maybe when Quim are playing near you in California or Sacramento or wherever you live you could drop in an' jam wiv us! Quim is always open to the godmothers of chick rock, the legendary Fanny! I love you so much! Thanks for being so ace! Rock on, you rock dolls!

Fanny rules forevva!

Moo French

↗

(Nickname from childhood, don't worry!)

Beloved Billie,

It is Mother's Day. I am on the last ever French and Saunders tour and I am in Manchester, so I am not with you. You are not with your mother and I am not with mine. That's pretty much wrong. Three generations of wrong. I woke up this morning and thought it might potentially be a truly grim day but then I remembered that when your dad visited briefly to watch our first night in Blackpool on Friday, he stuffed a big brown envelope in my case and said, 'Open that on Sunday.' So I did. A card from you. A handmade card. Honestly my uttermost favourit-est gift I ever get. Your dad does the same, always makes cards himself. You both have that fabulous desire to personalise. Top. I can tell you had little time to make this one, and I understand that, because you have just recently fallen in love and I know that is quite simply all-consuming. What a delicious distraction! I am astounded you remembered at all, considering everything that's going on for you at the moment, during the maelstrom that is this strange age of 16. The words in your card are simple, 'I couldn't ask for a better mum. I love you so much . . . ' You cannot begin to know how gladly I read those words because I know what it costs you to write that.

I have had to stop writing here to have a little self-indulgent weep, as I allow the significance of your easy forgiveness for my absence, and the sheer warmth of your appreciation, to flood through me. I should be with you today. I don't feel guilt about it, I just feel the pain of separation, which confirms for me how connected we are. That in itself is a kind of miracle considering what you and I regularly go through together, especially at the moment. Apparently it is quite usual for mums and daughters to war when the daughters are rampaging through their teens with all guns blazing. I suppose I knew that, but actually, I don't remember much in the way of big shouting at my mum. Plenty of sulking and violent inner thoughts, but not outright raging. That's what you do. You roar. You blast us with your bellowing. You insist that you are heard, and y'know what, Bill? Good for you. Be heard. Be loud. Get it out, whatever it is. I would far rather have eardrum-replacement surgery than have you bottling up all this boiling fury till you erupt like an emotional volcano in your adulthood.

You have a lot to feel furious about, so your anger is justified. Anybody who is adopted as a baby has the right to a fierce hurt. There is no more tragic and painful a rejection imaginable than by a mother to her newborn baby. You will probably wonder how on earth she could have looked at you, at the perfect beautiful tiny new you, and still make the decision to give you up. Surely any mother is so connected to the baby she has grown inside her for nine months, that to

make that horrific decision would be impossible? Do you think perhaps you just *weren't* perfect enough or beautiful enough for her to instantly adore you? Or maybe she was a dreadful, selfish or mad person who would never know how to show you love? Perhaps, worst of all, you are not lovable? How unthinkable.

The truth is, Billie, none of the above suppositions are real. Quite the opposite. The details of your adoption are private to you, and you know all about it as far as we know anything. There is nothing hidden from you, but there is part of it that will be hard for you to imagine at this point. This much I know: your birth mother *did* love you. Undeniably, enormously, as much as any mother has ever loved any baby. Or more, even. To infinity and beyond. Her heart is connected to your heart for ever and no one can cut that properly sacred thread. The pictures we have of you as a newborn are palpable proof of how hard that decision must have been for her, because you were the most wondrous baby. Fact.

It is a sort of unwritten law among kind humans to praise babies even when they look like shrivelled-up old constipated rhesus monkeys, because we all know a mammoth effort has just been made by a scared mum to push this big sack of potatoes out through a hole only big enough to accommodate a chip. She has nearly died in the effort, and we all want to be kind in respect of that, so we tell her that the fruit of her labours, her ugly baby, is gorgeous and bonny when quite often it is genuinely breath-takingly hideous!

194

This was not the case with you. The pictures show a bright-eyed beaming little face, with wide, open features and flawless caramel skin. Your mouth was a perfect, kissable little O with full, plumptious lips. The kind of 'O' that an Austen heroine exclaims when she's feigning a prudish rejection of her suitor's advances . . . Like 'Oh, Mr Darcy — no, please refrain, oh oh'. Divine. Your dear little face was round and irresistibly cute with a ready grin and a winning twinkle from the off. You were marvellous, a perfect tiny wriggling example of one of God's own masterpieces. A rare thing, an exquisite baby with unparalleled beauty. Your mother *must* have been instantly besotted. Everyone who ever saw you was. It was even a bit disconcerting how people were drawn to you. We often had a hard time reclaiming you from overzealous, cooing, smitten adorers. THAT'S how gorgeous you were. So, Bill, try to imagine how hard it was for her to look at you, at this splendid little shining thing, and to know she had to make what was probably the hardest choice of her life. The choice to give you a better life than she might have been able to, to put *your* interests before her own powerful maternal urges. Personally, I think that she did a mighty thing that day. She prized you above herself, above her own desires. That is a feat of love, Billie. Big, powerful, priceless love. Selfless love. LOVE.

I will always be thankful to her for having the enormous courage to make that decision because otherwise we would never have known you. We wouldn't have had you, that splendid little spudling, in our lives. And although I often think about her grieving and how that must continue, I thank God daily for her choice. She is our link to you and we don't forget that. Our little triangle has an invisible, important fourth side, which is constantly in my thoughts. I'm sure she must be in yours too. Especially on Mother's Day. We are related to each other, all of us. In the spirit of that bond, I accept this card to a mother on her behalf too, because as a testament of her love for you, she gave you to me, to my keeping, and thus I am truly blessed. There *is* no greater love than that. You say, 'I couldn't ask for a better mum.' And in the truest sense, you're right. You couldn't.

Thanks, Bill.

Dear Mum,

It was 1973 and I was 16. As you know, I was obsessed with horror films and the most scary horror film *ever*, *The Exorcist*, was released that year. What a stir it caused! Do you remember watching the local news and seeing reports about the protests taking place outside the cinema where it was showing in Plymouth? I thought people had gone doobonkerslally. The St John Ambulance had set up there to deal with the potential hordes of people who would no doubt faint, or at the very least vomit, in response to this 'truly evil' film. There were representatives from many different religions objecting to it, local councillors, mothers' groups, all manner of moral defenders. It was crazy and of course served to make me all the more determined to see the film. Sorry to tell you, Mum, but I *had* managed to sneak under the radar into a few X-rated films before then; still I knew this one was going to be especially tough since so many people were keeping an eye on who came and went, and I didn't have much faith in my sad attempts to look 18, which mainly consisted of wearing lipstick and slouching. You gave in quite early on when I begged you to take me. I think you knew I would go anyway come hell or high water, but Mum, I also know how little you would have wanted to see that film yourself. You worked such long hours and always had a long drive home down into Cornwall, so I appreciate the effort you made. Thing is, Mum, you see, I *had* to go. I HAD to see it! Maybe you thought that accompanying me was a lesser punishment than death by nagging. Anyway, we went together and because I was with an adult, in we swanned, past the barracking and jeering. You were, apparently, sacrificing your daughter to Satan's power. Wow. Great. Lucifer, here I come, your willing handmaiden!

The tension was high inside the cinema and I was bursting with excitement and anticipation about the film. All the reports about it had been phenomenal. It was gruesome, vile and down-right black, which was perfect.

I don't think you and I had been to the pictures together since I was a little kid when we went to see Jerry Lewis or Elvis Presley or Disney films. I experienced the strange juxtaposition of feeling very grown up because I was about to witness an X-rated film, but also feeling decidedly junior because I was with you, my mum. My discomfort was exacerbated by the fact that the couple directly in front of us decided to eat each other's faces off, and you started to mutter your disapproval of that. Then, the man next to them, in front of me, seemed to lose control of his head, it was lolling everywhere as if it were was attached to his shoulders with a Slinky. He was obviously off his cake in readiness for a truly trippy experience of this supposedly shocking and heinous movie. Your grumbling

198

was now building from a low hum to an audible steady rant with occasional snaps at the man to 'pull yourself together' and 'stop being so silly'. Drug addicts *love* being told off, don't they . . . ? By the time the lights went down, I was a strong beetroot hue, and wanted to be almost anywhere else. It didn't help that the folk behind started to crinkle their sweet wrappers for which further admonishment from you was apparently necessary. Just when I thought the torture of mum-next-to-you-in-a-cinema-ness was over, there was fresh hell. Before the main film, there was a suitable short B movie. You *must* remember this?! Which buffoon was it that sat down and thought, 'OK, the main film is a sinister and distressing voyage to the dark side, what shall we give them as a warm-up? Oh, I know, nude hippy dancing. Ideal.' So here I was, in the dark, surrounded by freaks with you, annoyed and pumping away on the verbals, and we are presented with three naked hairy rejects from *The Joy of Sex* via Woodstock, who jumped about, wobbling their genitals for our delight and entertainment. By now the extent of your distaste was clear to the entire auditorium. I know you were embarrassed, both for yourself and for me, but times your embarrassment by infinity and that's how I felt. Mercifully, the naked jangling was relatively short and at last the haranguing stopped, and we could relax into an hour and a half of soothing evil as we witnessed the noxious possession of an innocent child. Which was lovely.

As we left the cinema you picked up where

you'd left off with plenty of 'Well, honestly, what a load of old rubbish that was. Really. I can't begin to understand why you like this sort of nonsense. It was just silly. Utterly unbelievable. Pointless', all the way back up to school where you dropped me off with a kiss and 'See you on Friday, Moo, night'.

You would think the running commentary and the damning review would help to dilute any fear that film might have instilled in me, but no, frankly. I had nightmares about it for months afterwards, which were unfortunate souvenirs. Nightmares to remind me of the nightmare that evening was.

I love you, Mum, but I'm not going to the pictures with you again. So there.

Dear David,

Thank goodness we didn't get married. I thought we were a perfect match, a couple who complemented each other, like yin and yang, or Little and Large, or Jack Sprat and his missus, but on reflection, that was wishful thinking. Really, we were, and are, like chalk and cheese, and if we're honest, they don't go together, do they? I've never had a successful chalk-and-cheese sandwich, for instance.

This difference was all too evident when we met that afternoon a couple of years ago, for the first time in, ooh, nearly 30 years. We went for tea at what is, in my opinion, simply the best place to take tea in London, the conservatory in the Lanesborough Hotel at Hyde Park Corner, or, as I prefer to call it, my London office. I chose that place to meet because, firstly, they pride themselves in their amazing choice of fine teas and since you are a tea man by trade, I hoped you would feel comfortable with that. Secondly, the cakes are sublime. What better way to ease the awkwardness of a difficult reunion than with cake? 'Cake is life's great moderator. Cake is Kofi Annan.' Who said that? Oh yes, me. Boy, did we need the mediatory benefits of cake that day. The purpose of our meeting was an apology, from you to me, for making the fundamental error of speaking to a hack about me. No friend or lover or family member had ever done that before, and I was truly shocked that you were so easily tricked by her artifice. She had failed to dupe any other beloved, but I guess you have little cause to be wary of sneaky press. Lucky you. Most people around me recognise the warning signs because I have endeavoured to advise people of the depths to which desperate journos of a particularly slimy ilk are prepared to plummet. Here was a woman writing about me, having never met me, resorting to intrusive tactics with, among others, the ladies who run the flower shop over the road from my house, and pestering the staff at my local salon where I get my legs de-fuzzed and used for mattress stuffing. Desperate measures really. All these people, however, took offence at her nosiness and didn't cooperate. But for some reason I still don't entirely understand, you decided to talk to her at length, giving her details of some particularly private moments between us. How very ungentlemanly of you. Were you caught off guard? Or were you flattered? Or what?! I was keen to hear why you had made this rather uncharacteristic choice. Within ten minutes of sitting down with you, I was reminded of a key aspect of your personality. You were *annoyed* that your accounts of our time together were so ill reported. You weren't *sorry* at all. So, the fault lay entirely with the greedy, opportunist lout who apparently tricked you, not with you. Innocent ol' loose-lips you. In the end, you didn't apologise at all really. Yes, you were sorry, but sorry for yourself. Hmmmm. You were one part blameless to two parts patronising. As I say, thank goodness we didn't get married . . .

The telling aspect about your account of our relationship is how very favourably you depict yourself. I'm not entirely surprised at your bending of the truth. I guess we *all* do this to some extent, remember our past selves with a rosy glow. Woe betide we should reflect on any decisions or actions and recognise moments of true cowardice or dismal failure or even regret. That would be something; to own up to and face our mistakes and shortcomings. I include myself in this department of flattering self-delusion. Writing this here book is, in itself, an exercise in trying to remember the *truth* of a moment rather than the edited highlights where I figure as the heroine. It's so tempting and easy to cast oneself as a tad splendid, but ultimately that would be daft. Since it is so clearly not accurate.

It's a pity that our reunion reminded me of a tricky aspect of our relationship because I remember so much of it with utter happiness. I *think* we met at a party in Liskeard, is that right? I must have been about 17 or 18 and you were about 21, 22. I was instantly attracted to you. Oh yes, that's for picking cotton sure. You are a handsome man, David. Properly handsome. Flawless skin, twinkly pale eyes, a strong masculine jaw and the most heavenly mouth. The hands were a crucial factor — could they cup a 38DD? Yes, with ease. Then there was also your easy manner and soft Irish brogue. All systems go! Back then, you were a navy sub-lieutenant. You were recently out of Dartmouth and on HMS *Hermes*, if my memory serves me well. Being a Plymouth girl, I had heard plenty of racy stories about navy chaps, or 'fish-heads' as we called you. The navy regularly swarmed the streets of Plymouth on a Saturday night. I would avoid Union Street where the nightlife was a bit explosive, but I sometimes used to go to a club called, I think, the Yacht Club, down on the Barbican. The reason I can't remember the name so well is that we gave it the nickname 'GX' — which stood for 'Groin Exchange' . . . Dashing young navy officers like you frequented this club and so, when us local girls went there, we knew we would be batting away a fair amount of overeager groin activity. Plus, you guys were that bit older than the boys we usually dated, you were exotic visitors, and you had jobs and MG sports cars. We LOVED that!

You and I fell for each other pretty heavily and pretty quickly. You introduced me to your brother Ian and took me on my first visit to Ireland, to your home town, Belturbet in County Cavan, to meet your ma and pa. A tiny clue to our mismatch became evident even way back then. You insisted on buying me an outfit to meet your folks in. I suppressed my hurt and attempted to find the right thing. So, none of my clothes were suitable for the kind of girl your parents should meet, then? I suppose you wished I was a bit more sophisticated or something? My flares and cheese-cloth tops weren't right. So, for the love of you, I went shopping. It's hard to shop for clothes when you don't know who you're supposed to be. I have had similar experiences since, when trying to choose costumes for a character I'm playing. The clothes provide vital clues to the person and it's important to get it right. The mission back then was to find clothes that would earn me the parents' approval. What *are* those clothes? Well, I look at the photos now, and apparently the perfect parent-meeting clothes are a white blouse with a Princess Di lacy collar, an A-line flowery skirt, matching bolero with trim and bows in the same floral fabric, tan tights and a good low court shoe. Or two. It seemed to work. Your parents were delightful and I *think* they sort of approved of me. Well, not really me, because they weren't actually meeting me, they were meeting some strange clothes with a person inside trying desperately to be like the person who was wearing those strange clothes.

Clothes were important on various occasions with you. Being a navy officer meant lots of formal 'dos' where everyone dressed up to try and look as grown up as their job suggested. Little boys and girls in grown-up uniforms and long dresses being allowed to play like the adults. I have to admit, the uniforms were pretty spunky. I liked yours most of all when it was hung on a chair at the bottom of the bed . . . You guys were lucky to *have* uniforms and clear rules about what *you* should wear to those endless balls and dinner dances. They may have been a bit uncomfortable, especially about the neck, but they were regulation and mandatory, so no agonising choices had to be made. As for me, well, it wasn't as if I had a wardrobe full of long floaty evening dresses. I had one cheap navy-blue empire-line maxi-dress that I wore with beads galore to look hippy and bohemian, but which could, just about, look formal at a push. That one, the 'Josephine' which always smelt a bit of the joss sticks from the shop I bought it in however often I washed it, came out a few times on those occasions. However, there was one ball, I think it was actually on board the ship, where a different, special dress was necessary. I couldn't afford a new one, besides which I'd be unlikely to find anything nice in my bigger-than-deemed-normal size anywhere in Plymouth. Being an absolute devotee of Pan's People, I had seen my favourite dancer, the perky and petite Cherry, in the most fabulous minidress with floaty gossamer-wing-sleeves and I sorely coveted it. I drew a picture of it, in a maxi version, and begged my Auntie May to make it for me in time for the ball. I hunted for the material and although I couldn't locate *exactly* the same type I found something pretty close in a beautiful lilac-blue net-curtain fabric. Auntie May was a great seamstress, but she was also my auntie (or my great-auntie to be precise), so she altered the design of the dress here and there for the sake of modesty. She censored it at will. Where Cherry's dress had been plunging and funky and daring, mine was virtually Amish. Where Cherry's sleeves had been sheer and light, mine were double-layered and extra long. It was a virtuous frock. In yet another stupendous example of the

Frenchies getting everything ever so slightly wrong, I took your arm on the night of that important ball in my demure, floor-length, decent-necked net-curtain tent, looking for all the world like Nana Mouskouri's prim sister. You must surely have been horrified. Sorry about that. Auntie May made me many more similar horrors in her time, like homemade jeans for instance, but she came up trumps one day, much later on, when I needed a graduation dress quickly . . .

You were always a natty dresser, with classic, conservative taste. A proper young man. I guess the navy expected a certain standard. I quite liked it actually, you always appeared to be a man of reckoning, definitely in charge, with ambition and a plan. I don't think I did it on purpose, but I do remember constantly trying to puncture the air of slightly smug confidence you exuded. To reach in and find the exciting, impetuous you I felt sure you were hiding. In fact, I think on reflection, I was plainly attempting to just change you into a more suitable boyfriend. At one stage I even persuaded you to wear dungarees and sandals and, bless you, however much you must have loathed it, you did! If I was you, I wouldn't forgive me for that, ever.

Costumes notwithstanding, we managed to have a lovely time together. I have such happy memories of driving trips in England and Ireland, staying at funny little B&Bs and enjoying calling ourselves Mr and Mrs Smyth. Because that's who you properly are. Mr Smyth.

I remember lots of romantic suppers and robust political debates (another clue!) while we both worked out who we were, and what we thought. I remember skinny-dipping at night, on Slapton Sands, in Devon. Oh, and thinking about beaches and the sea, of course I remember the most important moment of all . . .

I was 18 when you and I were planning to go camping in Cornwall, by the sea. I told my mother you were supplying the tent. She was silent for a moment, then she said, 'Don't you mean tentS?' And I said, 'No, tenT.' And that was it, I was telling my mum what was about to happen, giving her a warning shot across the bows. She didn't like it. Back then she was quite strict about such matters and would often tell me: 'Under my roof, it's my rules.' Fair dos. But this wasn't going to be under her roof, this was going to be under your canvas. The canvas of one, single, naughty tent, giving grown-up privacy and delicious cover to two randy young people fit to burst with desire for each other. A young man who had waited patiently, with great restraint and respect, and an anxious, excited young woman finally ready to be cherry-picked!

We drove down to the beach in your car, with the venue for the main event, the tent, packed in the boot. I had waited for this day, I had imagined it and dreamt it. Now it was here and we were en route to it. To 'it'. 'It' was going to happen. Tonight. In that tent. I wanted it to. We had decided. You were calm and masterful about the whole thing — after all, you'd done it before. I sat and watched you put petrol in the car at the garage. I couldn't believe you could be so casual and normal on such a momentous day. After all, SEX was going to happen. Within hours. Y'know, *SEX*. With genitals and everything! I was going to have proper sex for the first time ever, and you were putting petrol in the car, your hand on the pump, *filling up* the car. The imagery made me giddy. The excitement of it all was too much for me, and instead of erotically enjoying the palpable anticipation, I decided to counteract it, to dissipate the tension, as I always have done and always do, by talking. Happy talk. Non-stop. Industrial-strength talking. Jokes, stories, anecdotes, more jokes, other people's anecdotes, items in the news, family gossip, football scores, list of favourite names, pop-chart info . . . ANYTHING. I didn't stop talking for the two-hour journey. I didn't stop talking while we put the tent up, in fact I talked more, faster, when I saw it, the *actual* arena, the scene of the imminent crime, the pleasure pavilion, the sinning site. Oh Christ, I was going to be doing sex in *that*, very soon. In that tent. We decided to go to the pub. Well, you decided. I don't think it was for Dutch courage. It was for sedation, for me. By now I was in a total spin, chattering chattering away, a hundred to the dozen. Keep talking. Lots of inane jokes. Don't draw breath. Keep fluttering and twittering and sputtering. I had St Vitus's dance of the mouth, I did not miss a beat, I was utterly hysterical with apprehension. I effervesced myself into a manic, frothy, verbal vortex until, finally, the effects of the several gin and tonics started to take control. It didn't stop me babbling, but at least I was also breathing now. Slowing down from a yapping gallop to a gentle verbal trot. And breathe. And relax . . . Nope, I can't. We walked back to the tent. I was still jabbering. We undressed. Still blethering, ha ha, 'Here's another funny thing, anyway! . . . ' You laid me down . . . ha ha — here we go — it's going to happen — oh God — I kept making jokes, 'We've made it to the foothills, sir, shall we rest at base camp one?' Ha ha, 'Ready, steady, GO!' Ha ha, 'God bless her and all who sail in her!' Ha ha, 'Houston, we have liftoff . . . ' Ha ha, 'Is it in yet?' Ha! Ha!

You took my face in your hands and said, 'Just . . . please . . . Dawn . . . It's time to shush now.' 'Yes but, ha ha . . . ' 'No, shush.' And then you shut me up with a kiss, and you opened me up with a touch so exquisite and gentle and careful, I felt myself actually swell and bloom.

The next morning we woke and, still sleepy, we clambered out of the fuggy tent and silently walked hand in hand over the dunes and into the sea. Oh, the beautiful beauty of it. I was finally quietened by it, by the bigness of it all. We laughed and shared muted intimate mutterings. We played in the sea. I was new and definitely different. I felt sort of glossy. Loved. I hope you remember it this same way — it's so clear in my head. The noise and then the quiet. Splendid.

Soon after this in September 1976, and while I was still utterly besotted with you, I went to America for a year and you went off to sea on your bloody big huge big boat. I won a scholarship with the English-Speaking Union, through all the debating and public-speaking competitions Miss Abbott had encouraged me to take part in at school. In the final round of the competition, our local politician, Michael Foot, seconded my attempt and voted for me to win. As you know, I did, and winning meant an exchange year. Twelve American students were going to come from the US to study in British schools and I was to be one of the twelve British students going to America. You and I were to be separated, for quite some time, and I dreaded that part. The American scholarship part, however, was AMAZING. When the application form came through for me to fill out my choices of where I would ideally like to be placed in the States, I chose locations like Texas (got huge burgers) and Colorado (might meet John Denver) and Montana (horse riding on Western saddles and more horse kissing). Stunning open country, that's what I wanted. Fresh air. Of course, *my* placement, when it came through, was New York. Manhattan. At that point in my life I had not yet lived in a city and had absolutely no desire to. I couldn't think of anything *worse* than Manhattan, which, to me, was surely the set of *Kojak*? A place where you would DEFINITELY get murdered. On a regular basis. It was going to be all concrete and crowds and cabs and I didn't like any of that. I was furious that I had been sent to the most exciting city in the world . . .

My year in New York was, of course, unbelievably fab. I missed you very much and wrote to you every other day and I still have your letters back to me. They chart our relationship during that thrilling year. They come from many different ports and navy bases and they are a gauge of how your attitude to navy life was rapidly changing. You speak of getting out, of getting a job, of us being together more. I sense a rather concerned interest in the experiences I was having that year. Perhaps you were a little anxious that we might grow apart, that I was having too good a time? Well, yes, I WAS having too good a time . . .

For the first time ever, I was alone in a different country. I was nervous about how I was going to cope in this big bustling city and so I employed a technique which still serves me well today. I imagined myself as someone who relished new exciting opportunities, who was utterly unafraid and perpetually optimistic. It was a kind of reinvention. Everyone I met was new. These people didn't know me, there was no shared history, so I could be anything or anyone I wanted to be. My theory was that if I *behaved* like a confident, cheerful person, eventually I would buy it myself, and become that. I always had traces of strength somewhere inside me, it wasn't fake, it was just a way of summoning my courage to the fore and not letting any creeping self-doubt hinder my adventures. This method worked then, and it works now. I tell myself that I am the sort of person who can open a one-woman play in the West End, so I do. I am the sort of person who has several companies, so I do. I am the sort of person who WRITES A BOOK! So I do. It's a process of having faith in the self you don't quite know you are yet, if you see what I mean. Believing that you will find the strength, the means somehow, and trusting in that, although your legs are like jelly. You can still walk on them and you will find the bones as you walk. Yes, that's it. The further I walk, the stronger I become. So unlike the real lived life, where the further you walk the more your hips hurt.

When I first arrived in New York that September, the heat was blistering. I hadn't anticipated that at all, and I was sweating in my new bought-specially-for-the-trip red mohair polo neck. The first family who had agreed to put me up were the O'Neils, who had a daughter about my age — she'd just gone to college so they had a spare room in their apartment and were kind enough to let me stay. I had never been inside an apartment or even a flat before, let alone on the posh Upper East Side. There was a doorman, six heavy locks on the door and I had a compact little bedroom looking in on the central well of the block, which was mainly a pigeon toilet. I had *my own bathroom* for the first time ever. It was tiny, but it was perfect, and the family were kind and welcoming. They had a son, Martin, who was a couple of years younger than me and delightfully shy. He blushed every time we spoke, but we persevered and eventually we could speak without any awkwardness or redness whatsoever and he became a good pal. On the first night, hot in my woolly jumper and fazed by the jet lag, I sat down for supper with my new family and was shocked to be served, as a starter, *SALAD*. This wasn't salad as I knew it. Salad, according to my mum's way, was a huge plate with two tiny lettuce leaves entirely masked by heaps of chicken, boiled eggs, coleslaw, tomatoes, cheese, beetroot, onions, spring onions, corned beef, any other onions and onions. With lashings of salad cream. But here, in America, a salad was some green leaves, with vinegar (?) and oil (??) drizzled on top, and on a small plate, on its own! After successfully disguising my salad shock, we ate our main meal, a tasty hotpot thing, and chatted. Soon, it was time for bed and as I left the table, I remarked that I had an early start at my new school in the morning and no alarm clock so I wondered if it might be possible for Mr O'Neil to knock me up in the morning? He practically fell off his chair sputtering into his coffee. Apparently 'knock me up' meant something entirely different in the States, and he was more than a little surprised by the request. Luckily we all had a good laugh and thus began my year in New York, with a customary faux pas.

I attended the Spence School, a highly academic private girls' school on the East Side, and, in effect, repeated my last year of school again, but in the American system. It was *so* different to my recent experience of A levels. Instead of taking three quite focused and advanced subjects, I was taking five different subjects each term, including American literature and anthropology and art history and photography. It was bloody amazing! The facilities at the school were breathtaking and the staff were funny and friendly. The canteen was phenomenal — no more one choice, eat it or starve, oh no, this was a buffet where you could *choose*! Wow! That canteen gave me the first of many satisfying encounters with the wonder that is tuna mayonnaise. And bagels. And pizza in single slices. And pastrami. And pickled gherkins. And potato salad. And . . . Well, basically, food. I got fat very quickly in New York. There was something new and remarkable to taste EVERY DAY! Plus Reese's Peanut Butter Cups. Invented surely by angels?!

Anyway, apart from food, the best thing about that year was the people who looked out for me and let me live in their homes. The Butler family and the Slussers, and the Wallers whose daughters were at school with me and who made it their priority to give me a great time. They took me *everywhere*. We went on boat trips and sightseeing tours to art galleries, shops, museums, the theatre, movies, skiing trips in Vermont, and holidays by lakes to see the fall in New England. There were parties and Halloween and Thanksgiving and Independence Day and St Patrick's Day celebrations. All new, all exciting. I went to Yale with Winnie, a girl in my class, on a three-day college visit to see if this was where she wanted to study. For the first time ever, I was the only white person in a hall full of hundreds of black students going through the process of positive discrimination and minority admissions. I was brought up to speed very quickly about the situation for black students in Ivy League colleges, which was both shocking and hopeful. I had a week in Washington DC living with a clever writer who made it her mission to familiarise me with US politics and culture. A crash course I was so privileged to have. Back in New York, I heard opera, I saw ballet, I skated on ice under the magnificent Rockefeller Center, I window-shopped at Tiffany's, I went to delis, and Saks, and ball games and I wore a baseball cap. It couldn't have been more Yank.

Some of the best fun was had when my Uncle Mike, who was a professor of American history at the University of Michigan in Ann Arbor, came to visit me in NY. He took me down to the Village to hear Stan Getz in a smoky jazz club, and to see the Andrew Wyeth exhibition and out to Ellis Island to see the Statue of Liberty and to understand how New York had evolved, with all the tired immigrants arriving by boat with one suitcase each. He explained how families were divided and quarantined and how so many didn't survive the port authorities' strict process. He knew it was important for me to understand America a bit and not just eat pizza. He conceded that pizza, however, is an important factor . . . After all, as Thomas Hughes tells us in *Tom Brown's Schooldays*, 'Life isn't all beer and skittles; but beer and skittles, or something better of the same sort [pizza, surely?], must form a good part of every Englishman's education.' Hear, hear.

Of course, my entire year in the States was spent longing for your visits and you did come to see me as often as you could, whenever your ship was in a port nearby, like Puerto Rico, I think, one time. On your first visit, you came to spend Christmas with me, do you remember? You arrived on 19 December and my diary reports that I woke up with 'butterflies in my heart'. (Well I was still a teenager after all.) On 20 December you took me out for supper to a restaurant on West 48th Street called 'A La Fourchette', which I think is French for 'don't make any hasty decisions', and you asked me to marry you. I was overjoyed. I wanted so much to be Mrs Smyth. Mrs Dawn Smyth, wife of David Smyth. Lovely.

We spent Christmas in snowy Ann Arbor with Uncle Mike and Auntie Pat. It was so cold that our tears froze on our faces and we could pick them off. I loved the little solitaire diamond on my left hand. I looked and looked at it. I looked at it in the mirror, I looked at it flopping off the side of the sofa in repose, I looked at it when my fingers were linked with yours. Yep, it looked right. It looked really almost . . . well, nearly married. We spoke to our families on the phone on Christmas Day, and told them we were engaged. They were a bit surprised but they seemed pleased for us. We spent the holiday making snow angels and kissing a lot. It was very romantic. Except for one evening when Auntie Pat read our tarot cards and told us we wouldn't end up together. Party-pooper . . .

When you went back to work, I went back to school and showed off my ring to my American chums, who were utterly baffled and couldn't work out why anyone would want to be married at 19 years old. No matter — I skipped along, continuing my American adventure, studying hard and playing hard. By this time I was included in the goings-on of an off-off-Broadway theatre company whose home was at the Church of the Heavenly Rest, close to the school. The school secretary, Molly Grose, was part of it and asked me to come along and help out. So, for the best part of a year, I was tea girl, lighting assistant, runner and general factotum for this company. It was not amateur, it was professional. The actors weren't paid much, but they were good actors doing good work, serious plays and musicals alike. The hours were long but I loved being part of it and I had a proper apprenticeship, watching and learning how a play comes together, and being part of a backstage team.

Sometimes, when I was in New York, I would be overcome with powerful, aching homesickness. My lovely friend Liz was good at noticing this and would quickly jump in with suggestions of a game of squash, or a swim, to have something physical to take my mind off it. One time we went swimming at a gym I hadn't been to before. It was so typical of New York. The journey on the street offers a viewpoint that is impressive with all the grandeur of those mighty grey imposing buildings, but what you see outside belies the veritable hive of seething activity on the inside of every building. Like a honeycomb, each gigantic building holds thousands of other, smaller cells, where masses of people are doing masses of things. They are working and playing and shagging and sleeping and typing and getting their teeth fixed and getting their psyches fixed and getting hair plugs and cooking and eating and flower arranging and reading and . . . and everything people do. All manner of human stuff going on inside one mammoth skyscraper. Liz and I walked into the elevator and went up to something like the 34th floor. Out we trotted into the reception of the gym. We played squash, thwacking the ball about and sweating, more than 30 floors up from the earth. Then we went swimming. The pool was built to the very edges of the building, so that, in effect, the windows formed a see-through wall on two sides of the pool. I jumped in and swam underwater to the edge. Here I was, underwater with my hands on the glass, looking down on Manhattan from 34 floors up in the sky. For me that was a revelation. My brain couldn't make sense of it, couldn't understand it in any elemental way whatsoever, but my soul utterly devoured the moment, and the sense-memory is for ever etched on my mind. My world at that point was strange and wonderful and I wanted it to stay that way — I was determined to be open to many more of these inspiring moments.

I ran out of money when I was in New York. I didn't want to ask you for any, or my parents who really didn't have any, so I had to come up with a plan. I decided to utilise the misguided American impression of a young Englishwoman travelling abroad. Friends of the families I stayed with often used to say that well-spoken young Englishwomen reminded them of Mary Poppins. So, I put an ad up on the staffroom noticeboard and sent word about that I would be willing to do some childcare at the weekends or babysitting in the evenings. The wording indicated that I was of the English-nanny variety by offering: 'English nanny available for weekend childcare or babysitting.' Not subtle. The response was amazing, and some weeks I would babysit *every* night. This was fine by me — it meant playing, watching TV, having free food, reading stories and getting paid. Just what I needed to survive beyond my meagre allowance. I looked after kids called Chandler Bigelow III, and Zorro, and Clymer, and Nancy. They were very different to English kids, more relaxed and proper little city dwellers. I earned tons of lolly and that meant I could complete my American trip by spending the last few months in LA, where I stayed with a crazy nurse on the ocean in Santa Monica.

Just before I went there, though, was graduation day in New York, which was a big deal at Spence. All the girls had to attend, looking like virgins, in big white dresses. A quick call to Auntie May resulted in a simple V-neck (not too low!) cotton frock by return of post, thank God. Some of the girls had spent thousands on theirs. I suspect mine was made from whatever was on the floor of Auntie May's cutting table, but it did the trick and we sat for our photo, pretty maids all in a row.

At the end of that summer I returned home. I had missed my mum and dad very much and couldn't wait to see them. They came to collect me at the airport and I was shocked by my dad's appearance. He looked haggard and drawn. I knew he had been through the mill a bit since he'd had a nervous breakdown the year before. They were living in Saltash and I knew his business wasn't going very well. He was also sporting a huge beard and moustache, which totally wrong-footed me. I had never seen him look so different. I'm so glad you met him, David. It was very important to me later, that you knew him and he knew you. I think my family were a bit concerned about our future together, especially my brother, who unlike me, blinded by pure love, knew that you and I were basically too incompatible. He knew me as a bit wild and he could see that you were much more strait-laced, so he worried. My dad, however, never expressed any specific doubts to me but did say that I should always follow my gut instincts and he advised me to take things slowly, which, of course, I didn't. He liked you well enough though. I think he knew I was safe with you, which was true. I *was* safe. You would never be cruel to me or intentionally hurt me in any way. Safe isn't *it*, though, for the long run, is it? Not for you, or me.

I remember after Dad died, when I went to college in London and lived in a cramped room in a flat in Kensal Green, you left the navy. We wanted to be together more. We couldn't bear the separation that navy life was always going to mean. I was bereft after my dad's death and you were incredibly comforting. Then you landed that job with Lipton's as a new young tea-taster with great future potential for rising up through the company. A proper company man. I think

221

the headquarters were in Chertsey or somewhere and you were living in digs out there, so at last we were close by. Then they sent you to Calcutta. Of course they did. Duh. Tea comes from India.

So I went to college and started to work out who I was, a sort of leftie hippy, and you went to work and discovered that you were a company man with right-wing tendencies. I was red and you were blue. It was doomed really. A hopeless mixture. In love and doomed.

Dear Fatty,

I've often told you how fabulous the big beaches are in Cornwall. Not to say the little ones don't also have their rock-pooly charms, but the big ones that stretch as far as the eye can see, like Polzeath or Watergate Bay, are awesome, with the spray hurtling off the massive crashing waves, and the sheer vastness of it all making you feel so small. I love it when I take very deep breaths till my lungs are bursting with salty, thick-as-clotted-cream air and I feel like I am half Dawn and half Cornwall. You must come and walk on the beach with me and we'll take the dogs. The north coast is, of course, the wilder, with its strong Atlantic attack dragging along high winds and huge rolling waves for surfers. I spent quite a lot of my youth gazing out at the beautiful surfers, so distant they looked like toys tossed about in the swell. Even up close though, when they finally strode back up the beach, surfers are immensely attractive. Even the ugliest of fellows is quite dreamy when a summer of sun and salt have scrubbed him up.

Anyway, anyway, anyway, a friend of mine, a young surfer in Newlyn, told me that he had an unfortunate incident last summer, when his cousin from Milton Keynes came to visit. The cousin hadn't been out in the sun at all and certainly not on the beach, so he was as white as a milk bottle and rather shy and unconfident in his brand new Speedo swimming trunks. My friend told him that he needed to strut up and down the beach to attract the attentions of young ladies, and that it would really help if he were to put a potato in his Speedos, that this would undoubtedly rouse their interest. The cousin thought this was a *bit* strange. I think I would have concurred with that: I've never heard of that technique before. It must be a modern thing, among the youth. Anyway, anyway, anyway, the cousin *did* want to attract young ladies so he apparently slipped a potato, a King Edward I think, not a new one, that would be silly, into his Speedos and off he went to the beach. It was a little bit cumbersome, as I'm sure you can imagine, but eventually he got the hang of it, and started parading up and down for all the pretty ladies to see. However, not one of them seemed at all interested and when the cousin returned to my friend, he said, 'Sorry, mate, but this potato down the Speedos idea isn't working, the girls aren't remotely interested, in fact they seem repulsed.' To which my friend was forced to retort, 'I think you'll find it will work much better, mate, if you put the potato down the FRONT of your Speedos.' Can you believe that?

Dear Mum,

When I was about eight, I bought you a present from an antique shop. It was a brass wall plaque. The man in the shop said it was original (yes, originally someone else's). But anyway, it had a picture of an ancient granny in a rocking chair doing her knitting, and below that was a verse I still remember:

> Who is the one who ne'er finds fault,
> Who never seeks to blame?
> To whom you go when troubles come,
> Whose love remains the same?
>   — Your mother.

How ridiculously sentimental. How archaic and cheesy. How revolting. How true.

Something I've always admired about you, Mum, is your ferocious independence. Only recently have you allowed any of us to properly do things for you. Perhaps retirement has given you permission to be more vulnerable? I don't know, but I certainly do remember all the remarkable things you have managed to pull off on your own. I remember once returning home to Stoke in Plymouth to find a giant wardrobe in a different room. How had you moved it alone? Impossible. I think you've always regarded difficult and seemingly insurmountable problems as challenges, daring you to solve them. And you usually do, somehow.

One day, about 12 or so years ago, you were due to arrive at our house in Berkshire because you had signed up to start a reflexology course you'd booked and paid for in London the next morning. When you arrived, I was surprised to see there were no side windows in your car. Someone had vandalised it the night before, and you hadn't had an opportunity to get the windows replaced before your extremely windy journey up to us, on the motorway. You said that you had cleared the seat of shards of glass as best you could and sat on a newspaper for extra safety for the duration of the drive, intending to get the windows replaced when you reached ours.

Once you'd had a cuppa and a chance to thaw out, you voiced a concern to me, and I could tell by the serious tone of voice that what you were about to say was difficult for you. I soon found out why. You told me you thought a splinter of glass might have, somehow, found its way into your fanny. You said you felt pain there, that you'd tried to find it, but you couldn't see well enough to know how serious it was. You were worried, that if, indeed, it was serious, we ought to call the doc. If not, you could just apply some antiseptic cream and be done with it. You wanted to make it to your course first thing in the morning and you didn't want any stupid shard of glass up your wazoo to prevent you going . . . stuff and nonsense . . . So, you explained,

226

quite matter-of-factly, 'I'm sorry, Moo, to have to ask you, you are the only one I *can* ask, but could you please have a quick peek and see if it's anything to worry about? C'mon, let's get it over with. No fussing. We're all animals after all . . . come on.' Throughout this whole exchange I fixed a wide, understanding smile on my face so as to appear sympathetic to your plight. Indeed, I genuinely *was* sympathetic, right up to the moment I realised what you were asking me. I kept smiling compassionately though, because I knew how very embarrassed you were, and I didn't want to embarrass you further by showing my true feelings and screaming out loud in shuddering horror. The walk upstairs to the bathroom behind you took at least five years. You were quite spry, but I was slowly climbing the steps to the guillotine, smiling ever more weakly all the while. Once in the bathroom with the door safely locked, you whipped down your tights and pants in a trice, and quick as a flash, which it actually *was*, chattering all the time, as normally as a normal chatty thing, you bent over. What took place next was an exercise in the utmost trust, willing, intimacy, fear and pure love. I didn't in a million years imagine that I would *ever* be required to furtle around in my own mother's ladygarden and I can't say that I enjoyed it, Mum, but d'you know what? — to my surprise I didn't mind it either. There was something very civilised about it, about realising that all women are the same, really, gynaecologically. I thought I might be queasy or squeamish (y'know, a bit like you're feeling right now), but

NO. I found it comforting that I could be of use in such a practical way. Don't get me wrong, I wouldn't recommend it as a hobby, but it dawned on me that, after all, I'd been there before, hadn't I? — and it was all strangely familiar and perfunctory. Easy, really. We found the splinter, didn't we? Removed it, dabbed on the cream and now you are a fully qualified reflexologist. Done and dusted.

The second time you took my breath away with a suggestion was when I had been very ill with hepatitis A, remember, in about 1994 or so? I knew nothing about hepatitis until I contracted this vile version of it, and turned bright yellow and felt like my skin was on inside out, I was so raw. The sheets hurt me in the bed. It was awful. The local health-and-safety bods came to visit me with their clipboards to check what I'd eaten in the previous two weeks, since hepatitis A usually involves someone unhygienic preparing food without washing their hands. A better question would have been what *hadn't* I eaten?! I'd been to restaurants, had sandwiches, eaten at home. It was impossible to identify a culprit and I was too weak to bother, I just wanted to be well again. I knew I was ill because I didn't eat and that never, *ever* happens otherwise. I was just starting to feel a tiny bit stronger when you came to stay and nurse me better. I clearly remember the familiar smell of your lovely stew cooking downstairs and feeling hungry for the first time. I knew it would give me strength. You brought me a bowl and I struggled to sit upright in the bed. As I slurped away greedily at it, you plonked

228

yourself down on the bed and said, very seriously, 'Right, madam. Now you're feeling a bit better, I want to know how you got hep A in the first place. Don't shilly-shally about, tell me the truth, come on.' First of all, I was shocked to hear you describing it as hep A, in such a knowing streetwise sort of fashion, but of course by this time you were working with a lot of drug addicts and you were quite au fait with street talk. Nevertheless, it was odd to hear it trip off your tongue so casually. I tried to explain about it being a kind of food poisoning but you were having none of it. 'Oh come on, admit what you've been doing, we're all grown-ups here. I know how you catch this, Dawn. Just say it.' Say what? I didn't know what you were referring to. Did you think I was a crack whore or using dirty needles or something? What?! And then you said it, the most remarkable thing you've ever said, and which I cannot ever forget. 'You've been rimming, haven't you? Admit it. Yes, you've been rimming. Rimming your own partner is bad enough Dawn, and very dangerous, but rimming strangers can lead to exactly this. A massive dose of hep A. You've only got yourself to blame. So, be sensible and just stop rimming in future. Now eat up your stew and I'll rub your back for you.' Oh. My. Actual. God.

My favourite faux pas of yours (sorry, Mum, but you *are* hilarious sometimes, and long may you continue to be!!) was when I managed to get great tickets to see Elton John perform on the Argyle ground at Home Park in Plymouth. Argyle hadn't hosted a rock event before and the

229

city was abuzz. I'd bought tickets for eight or so of us in the family and you were due to babysit for Jack, who was too young to go. Only as the hours crept by did I realise you were a bit put out about it. I saw the ol' lemon lips setting in and asked you what was wrong, remember? You told me that you were sad not to be going, that you adored Elton John, that he was one of your favourite singers ever, that you would've loved to go. Cousin Keiren stepped up and heroically sacrificed his ticket for you in favour of an evening of fun with Jack instead, and a chance to show his auntie Roma how much he loved her. What a guy! I apologised for my oversight. 'I didn't know how much you loved Elton's music,' I ventured. 'Yes,' you replied, 'he's wonderful. My absolute favourite song of his is 'Ben'. I love that one.'

After we'd all changed our pants from laugh damage, we explained that song was in fact Michael Jackson's and we giggled all the way to the stadium. Just before the show we popped in to say hi to Elton, who is always the most genial of geniuses. I felt a daft amount of pride that he'd come to our stadium, and I wanted to show our support as a family. Sorry if I embarrassed you, Mum, but I just *had* to tell him what you'd said. It was worth the bruise on my ankle when you kicked me for doing it! When he was halfway through his blisteringly great set, Elton said loudly into his mike, 'This one is for Dawn's mum, Roma. Sorry it isn't your favourite but maybe this will do instead. It's 'BEN . . . NIE AND THE JETS'!' The song boomed out over our hallowed stadium, we winked at each other and sat back to lap it up. Thanks for all the laughs, Mum. I know they weren't intentional but they were delightsome all the same.

'Whose love remains the same? Your mother.'

Yay, yay and thrice yay to that . . .

Dear Liza Tarbuck,

Please find below my completed application form to become a lifelong friend and loyal admirer of Liza Tarbuck. I hope my application meets with a favourable response. I await your reply with anticipation and a small bout of the belly flutters.

About me

SURNAME: *French* FORENAME: *Dawn Twat* MALE/FEMALE: *Yes*

Position applied for: *Friend of Liza Tarbuck (platonic)*

What type of friend are you looking to be?

TEMPORARY ☐ PERMANENT ✓

PLEASE INDICATE BELOW THE DAYS AND TIMES YOU ARE AVAILABLE FOR THE POST

	MONDAY	TUESDAY	WEDNESDAY	THURSDAY	FRIDAY	SATURDAY	SUNDAY
MORNING	✓	✓	✓	✓	✓	✓	✓
AFTERNOON	✓	✓	✓	✓	✓	✓	✓
EVENING	✓	✓	✓	✓	✗	✓	✓

can't, sorry, Big Brother evictions

How did you hear about the opportunity?

1. NEWSPAPER
2. JOB CENTRE
3. FRIENDS AND FAMILY REFERRAL SCHEME
4. SAW ON TV ✓
5. HEARD ON RADIO ✓
6. KNOWN ABOUT HER FOR SOME TIME AND LIKE THE CUT OF HER JIB ✓

Criminal convictions? *None to very few. Low-level pilfering. No incarceration.*

User of alcohol? *Yes please. A pint of cider. Thanks.*

User of drugs? *Yes, long-term Calpol abuser. Partial to a bottle of Dr Collis Brown linctus.*

232

Ethnic origin

WHITE ☐	ASIAN ☐	PINK ☐	CARIBBEAN ☐
BLUE ☐	AFRICAN ☐	MOTTLED ☐	ASIAN/BLUE ☐
TARTAN ☐	CARIBBEAN/PINK ☐	EAU DE NIL ☐	AFRICAN/TARTAN ✓
OTHER ☐	MARTIAN ☐		

Previous friendships

NAME: *B.F. (Best Friend)*   NAME: *Fatty*

DURATION: *30 years*   DURATION: *30 years*
and it don't seem   *and counting*
a day too long

Do you have any demands on your time which could affect your ability for regular attendance?

Yes. Husband, daughter and Big Brother commitments. The latter can be shared. The former cannot.

What skills can you offer?

Clean driving licence. Tennis. Punctuality. Book Club membership. Rudimentary grounding in Hair Care and associated products. Nosy parking. Juicy gossiping. Dunkin Ducklings elementary swimming certificate (5 yards or less). Talking without listening. Some listening without talking. Access to Gok Wan. West Country accents (various). Good manners. Good diction. Can behave in company of parents. Willing to go Dutch (not in relation to money, but to actually become a Netherlander). Good at arsing about. Good bladder control. Can swear proficiently

List what it is about Liza you like

Excellent taste in skirts, shirts and shoes. Good personal hygiene. Big brain. Good with ears. Dog lover. D.I.Y. skills. Abundant beauty. Courage. Humility. Selflessness. Satan worshipper.

SIGNED
D.T. French (light entertainment)

233

Dear Dad,

I knew you were ill. I knew that. I didn't know *how* ill. It turns out you and Mum were very clever at concealing any trouble from Gary and me. We have spoken about it, he and I, trying to think back and work out if we'd ever noticed anything amiss while we were growing up. Here's what I know: I know you suffered dreadfully with migraines and often had to lie in a quiet dark room until you could see properly again, or until the punishing headaches and sickness had abated. I know that leaving the RAF and rejoining civvy street was extremely stressful for you. You'd been in the air force since you were a teenager, and forces life is so singularly regimented and controlled. You knew exactly what was expected of you there. You knew your projected career path and all its opportunities for promotion. Civilian life was full of uncertainties and responsibilities you weren't used to. I think, as well, that you missed the camaraderie of the air force.

As the eldest son, you were expected to take over from Grandad at the newsagent in Ernesettle. I don't know if you ever really wanted to; it didn't occur to me to ask you. I know you adopted some more forward-thinking procedures in your running of the business, possibly changes

234

that didn't pan out quite the way you might have hoped. I know the constant barracking from customers about late papers (not your fault — there were endless train strikes back then) was difficult for you. You were used to being in charge in the air force, where your men didn't answer back, where the only barracking came from higher ranks whose job it was to command you. Here you were, being taken to task over situations you could not affect or control. It seems that you spent a great deal of time and effort trying to implement standards of fairness and motivation among your staff and the paper boys, which of course in the RAF had been routine, taken care of and expected. But when you work for yourself the buck always stops with you, and only you. On top of this, you had the shadow of Grandad at your shoulder with whom this business had been so clearly identified, for so long. Everyone in Ernesettle knew him, they called him 'Father', and his stamp on that shop was indisputable. You were the new blood. Gentler and quieter. Traits that are often mistaken for weakness in business. I think it was difficult for you to pick up the baton and very difficult for him to relinquish it.

The grinding erosion of your energy, working those slavishly long hours, was evident. You aged a lot in a relatively short time. I remember you regularly leaving the house at around four in the morning and not returning until nine or ten at night. It didn't help that, for a large chunk of your time at the shop, we lived 40 miles away in Cornwall and the long drive back and forth was wearing. On days when the whole family made the journey, say a Monday morning, the rest of us would sleep through the trip in sleeping bags on the floor in the back of the van, while you fought your exhaustion to stay awake and get us all there safely. That part of the stress was lessened when we moved to Old Ferry Road, in Saltash, closer to Plymouth, but the work hours were still ludicrously long.

There were issues with debt too. When you left the RAF you assumed the entire costs of the school fees and mortgage, which I know were beyond our means. I also know that, despite the money problems inside our own family, you were supporting other people, specifically your brother-in-law who needed help with his own newsagent's in Devonport. I know that after a lot of agonising you eventually sold the Ernesettle shop, which must have been difficult for lots of reasons, and I know you started a business breeding rabbits! Why or how I *don't* know, because I was in the States when most of this change took place. As always, I knew very little of the difficulties for two reasons: you were skilled at hiding them, and I was far too wrapped up in my own exciting world, utterly ignorant of any signs of your depression, which, I'm sure, is just as you would have wished.

Mum knew the financial situation was bad and had taken steps to avert a crisis. Mum is a problem solver, and made of strong stuff. You know that, you married her. Much as she would hate to admit it, I do think that when it comes to survival she is a chip off the old Grandma Lil block. Unlike Lil though, she would do anything to protect her nest and everything in it. When money was tight, Mum knew she had to find something other than the shop to sustain us. So, ever-resourceful, she did a bit of research and took herself off on a course to train to become a 'canine beautician'. For a woman whose skill-base was in bookkeeping, this might have seemed a surprising choice. Not really. She loved and understood dogs, she was a hard worker, she was prepared to learn and she knew there was a gap in the market. While Mum was on her course to learn this bizarre trade, I remember you, Dad, locating and procuring a shop on Market Street in Plymouth — I think it was an 'adult' shop when you leased it — and turned it into 'Felicity's Pet Parlour'. Porn to poodles in one fell swoop! I remember how bloody furious Mum was when she found out what name you had registered it under. Felicity is her proper, Christian name but she absolutely hates it. She hates how pretentiously posh she thinks it sounds and how much it doesn't suit her. She says it was an act of sadism by Lil. She *hates* it. So, of course we have always teased her by using it and for you to put the parlour in that name was a great gag, though perhaps a step too far. Phenomenal courage on your part there.

Once she recovered from the Felicity horror, she set about making the shop a success. Downstairs was a pet shop, selling all kinds of pet supplies; from the necessary, like food, to the novelty, like jewel-studded collars and leads for the more barking of the pooches and their

237

owners. There was cat-wormer and budgie seed and flea powder and pigs' ears and, of course, there was the livestock. We had parrots, some fish, occasional kittens, but mostly small rodents like gerbils and hamsters. I remember working in the shop in the holidays with Nicky or Nikki and having to sex the hamsters. Not *have* sex with them, that would just be silly and complicated, but rather, decide which gender they were when they were chosen by customers. Some little kids would spend all day choosing, with their noses pressed up against the cages, then rejecting, then rechoosing the perfect rodent chum. Of course, even though Mum had shown us how to do it (it seemed like it was the difference of one small flap of skin. Just like humans, really), we often did it wrong and sold Hattie Hamster to a little boy who called her Thor or Steve Austin or Hercules or Stan.

Upstairs, Mum had her parlour. 'Parlour' conjures up images of poofy striped pink chairs and beehive hairdos, ruched curtains and fluffy handbag dogs. It wasn't like that at all, was it? There was a row of kennels, some big sinks and a central table where the drying and snipping took place. It was hot and smelly, and dangerous. Dogs generally don't enjoy this process, so they try to kill you lest you dare to apply shampoo. I think they find it vaguely humiliating to stand in a sink, looking drenched and bedraggled. When they're not wet, they are convinced their coats make them look big and tough, especially the chippy little ones, but when the water reveals

238

their ratty scraggyness, all bravado and self-esteem swirl down the plug'ole along with the dirty doggy water. They become shivering wrecks trembling in fear of the imminent torture that is the dreaded hairdryer, and the worse torture that is the mockery they must endure when their doggy homies rib them about their visit to Felicity's.

Mum had so many dodgy moments in that place. On the whole, she loved the dogs and would give them all a chance not to bite her, but if they persisted in objecting she would have to muzzle them to get the job done. Only loose muzzles of course, the kind greyhounds wear before the race that make them look like famished Hannibal Lecters. She had little poodles who needed new pompoms to show off, and big English sheepdogs who hadn't been brushed in years and had maggots growing in their matted hair. She had airhead Afghan hounds who were so snooty they couldn't look her in the eye, and feisty little Westies who looked like skirted clouds as they trotted out giving her a beady sideways glance and a snuffle with the triangle of black dots that was their eyes and nose. She dealt with droolers and farters and nibblers and panic wee-ers. And that was just the staff! Once, a big black poodle got his head stuck in between the bars of the kennel and the fire brigade had to come and saw him out while the owner waited, unaware, downstairs. Not only was he a poodle, he was called Bunty *and* he'd got his head stuck at Felicity's. Quite a dollop of cringing canine shame to deal with, poor mutt. I remember some old dogs simply found the whole experience too overwhelming and would faint. Or, even worse, die! Mum was known to have administered mouth-to-mouth on more than one occasion to resuscitate a pooch that had passed. After all, there's no tinkle in the till if the dog is delivered back in a carrier bag stiff and cold. She would proudly hand the panting, resurrected creature back to its grateful owner, having kissed it back from the brink of death five minutes before.

Mum took all comers, from cheeky Heinz 57 variety mongrels to aloof pedigrees, and endeavoured to send them out perky and clean. Our own dogs, a couple of dirty-grey West Highlands, looked on with great amusement. As is so often the case in any trade, they were the last to be plonked in the sink, too much of a busman's holiday. Sometimes Christmas would warrant a spruce-up, if they were unlucky.

I remember how tired Mum was after a day of such labour-intensive work. I remember how hot and dirty she used to get, how the dog hairs would stick into her pores — she said they felt like a thousand tiny jabbing needles — and how they would sometimes get infected, just like the endless bites she sustained. She was constantly boosting her tetanus levels, in order to give the dogs another chance. And in order to give us another chance. This second income was crucial at this time, so she had to make her business pay.

I expect it didn't help your self-respect to realise that, conversely, things were sinking your end. Nobody in our family would have echoed that feeling but you were an old-fashioned man, believing that the head of the household, the man, ought to be the one bringing home the bacon. I see now that must have been hard for you but I also see that everyone was just trying to do what they could to get by.

I have written fondly in my diary about a time, before I went away to the States, when I was off school for a couple of weeks and so I could be at home with you. Mum had to keep working, Gary was away at uni, and it was obviously deemed necessary for someone to be with you, watching you, watching over you. Did people fear then that you might take drastic action? I write that you'd had a nervous breakdown and were feeling 'poorly'. You were in bed for a few days but then I write that you are up and about, laying a floor in our bathroom and we are laughing a lot together, drinking coffee in the garden. I like to think that I was unknowingly part of your recovery on that occasion, maybe serving to remind you how much your family loved you.

Then I went away for the year in America, where we all kept in touch by letters and phone calls. I came back to find you bearded and gaunt. There's no doubt that you had a haunted look about you. You told me things were a bit rough with work but that it would all be OK and not to worry. Despite my concern for you, it was difficult to be anything other than euphoric on my return home. I'd had an amazing year in the States but I was ready to be back with you, with my family, and you made it clear you were so happy to have me home. On the long drive back

241

to the West Country from Heathrow, we babbled on, hardly stopping to draw breath, catching up on all the stories, all the gossip. Yes, we had spoken on the phone while I was away, but only in that 'well, I won't keep you, it must be costing a fortune' sort of way that we all did then, ever-fearful of the costs — and of the phone itself for some reason! Of course, I was now a 'fiancée'. You hadn't laid eyes on me since I had become a 'fiancée'. I fancied that I looked entirely different, more mature and desired and mysteriously unattainable. No, you assured me, I just looked more American. Back in Saltash, I made contact with all my pals and family, rushing about recounting details of my exchange-year experience, boring them all with tons of photos. David was due back from a long trip on his ship and I was beside myself with excitement to see him. You liked him, I think, yes? Obviously it took a bit of time to get used to the idea that I was dating someone in the NAVY, but you knew he was decent and that he looked after me. I imagine the handover from dads to son-in-laws is always a bit fraught, but overall I think you approved.

I can't remember much about this period except that I was so happy to be home. I knew that you had a horrible bout of piles, which had been a regular ailment, and that, to avoid waking Mum in the night, you were sleeping on the sofa or in the spare room. You'd long suffered with this affliction, but I could see that this time, more than before, it was difficult for you to move about easily, and that you were tired from lack of sleep. I didn't know that this discomfort was just the tip of the iceberg, that underneath, inside, you were in hell.

On 10 September 1977, I waltzed off with a casual farewell to you and Mum. I was going to stay with David at the home of a friend of his and the friend's wife who lived in navy quarters in Devonport. It was one of those nights where I was playing at being a grown-up. Let's have dinner with our grown-up married friends and stay in their grown-up married house and sleep in the same bed as if we were grown-up and married, for soon, my love, we shall be grown-up and married. Well, I grew up fast the next day.

How did it start? Was there a phone call? I can't remember, but suddenly, early in the morning, David and I were dressing hurriedly and racing back to Saltash in his car. When I arrived home, Mum was sitting, ashen-faced. Gary looked like it was raining inside him, grim and beaten. Oh God. What? Where's Dad? What's happened? Who told me? Mum, I think. Yes. It was Mum, because she said you had been suffering badly all day, and that last thing you went upstairs together, with quite a struggle due to your discomfort. You kissed her goodnight. You told her you loved her. You shuffled out to the other room. So as not to disturb her sleep.

When she woke the next morning, she said she had a strong sense of disconnection immediately. Something felt wrong. She called out to you and there was no answer. Then there was a panicky frantic bit where she and Gary searched for you, shouted for you in the garden. The car was missing. I don't know how or why he looked there, but Gary drove, on his motorbike I think, up to the field where you kept some of the rabbits near Pillaton. He found you. God. That must have been dire, sickening. You had planned it. A hose on the exhaust, fitted carefully, fed through the window of the car. A bottle of sherry, so that a teetotal man might drink himself into the oblivion necessary to start the engine and lie back. And sleep. For ever. No more hell. Did it feel lovely? Like the grasp of anaesthetic? Did you feel giddy from the sherry? Was your head swimming? Or were you howling in agony, raging in your depression? Did you go out still fighting? Or did you surrender to the stillness, willing it to take you? Did you weep? Did we cross your mind? Did flashes of our life together show inside your head like a splendid movie? Or did you have to extinguish any thought of us so that you could do it? Did you say goodbye? To what? To whom? To the night sky, or the inside of the car, or the life lived? Did you sputter and drown? Did you choke? Struggle? Did you just float away? Did you see a light? Did you hear a voice? Did dead beloveds hold their arms out and welcome you to their dead place? Is that where you are? I've lost you. Where are you? Can you see me? I'm in fucking agony, you selfish bastard, don't you care? How could you do this to us? How dare you steal our happiness? Why didn't you say? Why didn't you give us a chance to stop you? Was it our fault for not noticing? Did you want us to stop you? Did you pray that someone would knock on the car window at the very last moment and drag you out? Did you consider that we couldn't — can't — live properly without you? So, you lied when you told me you would always be there for me? Were you so very alone with your hopelessness? Did you think we would be better off without you? Did you think you didn't matter? Did you think you had failed? Failed us? Did you feel ashamed? Did you suppress your sadness so much that it started to eat you from inside? Did you decide not to drag any of us into your black pit with you? Did you think this was the most selfless thing you could do? Did you think it was the *only* thing you could do? Did you think about it many times before and battle against yourself to stay alive? Did you just need to go? To find any sort of quiet? Away from the clanging racket of your mistakes, reminding you constantly that you have spoilt everything? Were you racked with wretchedness and unable to see light, anywhere? Was it dark and terrifying in your head? Did you want to be in a light place, to be hushed and tranquil? What did you hope it would be like? Like a lazy hot sunny day on the moors, or like a walk on the beach in Rock, or like bobbing about on the ocean? Like going home, maybe? Or did you just want it to be *anywhere* but here? The unbearable place where you felt savaged. The misery was too much. Maybe our happiness was too strong a contrast to bear? You wanted us to be happy but it tore you apart to not be able to include yourself in it any more. Your torment was a monster, and to kill it, you felt you had to kill you. That was the only way it would die. The only way for you, and us, to be free of it. You were slaying the monster so that life could continue for those who deserved to live it. You were being the dad. Protecting your family. From you. I understand. At least, I understand that I don't fully understand. But if I love you, I have to try to understand. And I do love you. So much. And I miss you. Profoundly miss you. And I do forgive you. Because what do I have to stay angry about? That you have found your peace? That you did what you needed to do, however heartbreaking that is? I feel no regrets for you, no shame. Just awfully, awfully sad. For myself. For a 19-year-old with your skin, your eyes, who felt strangely responsible until I worked out your illness wasn't my fault. And even *that* I worked out by tapping into a synergy I always had with you. By thinking, 'What would you wish for me now, in this pitiful grief?' and, of course, you would wish me to live my life to the full, and not waste a single second or a single chance at happiness. You would want me to relish those chances, and I do, Dad. I live my life fully, as a tribute to you and in the full knowledge that you couldn't so I will, for both of us. I carry you with me, not as a heavy weight or some kind of sorrowful burden, but as my energy and my engine. You are around me and part of me, my father, my dad. My darling dad. Denys Vernon French.

We were utterly broken, Gary, Mum and I. All of us just kept on breathing, but we weren't really living. We were numb with grief. Mum tried to be strong and distracted herself with getting on and organising stuff. I offered to stay at home for a year, to defer my place at college, and stay with her. There was no altruism in this — I was in pain and wanted the comfort of home. Mum was stunning — she refused outright to let me stay. She said that we had to work through it and be busy, that she couldn't endure any pity heaped on top of the harrowing heartache.

The house was full of family, my clearest memory being of Mum's three brothers, Terry, Owen and Mike, the triumvirate gathering around her. She had cared for and looked out for all three in their lives and now it was time for them to look after her. They helped with everything, the funeral, the money, the planning. You had been a mixture of father and brother to all three and they too were devastated by what happened.

I also clearly remember when one particularly insensitive (different) uncle, the brother-in-law who had been at the centre of so many of the troubles leading up to your death, made a very big mistake by walking into the midst of the sorrow in our home and demanding the return of the tools he'd recently lent you. Gary literally flew from one side of the room to the other, where this dolt was, and put his hands round his throat and started to throttle him. If the triad of uncles hadn't been there to pull him off, I genuinely think we would have witnessed a murder. I had never seen Gary so incensed with rage. His grief and fury combined to make a combustible force he couldn't contain. He became the man of the house the day he found you, Dad, and it was hard for him, but he took his role seriously and has been there to watch out for Mum and me ever since.

I couldn't go to see your body. Everyone encouraged me to, to know that you weren't here with us any more, and to say goodbye. I hadn't seen you since that night when I casually breezed out the door, same as always, chucking goodbyes over my shoulder in my haste. I can't even remember what you said, what your last words were. It could so easily have been 'I love you', you said it so often. Was it that? Did you know that what you were saying to the back of my head as I rushed out was the last thing you would ever say to me? No matter really. It just crosses my mind sometimes. I only pray it wasn't 'Don't go'. I didn't want to see you because I was afraid I would have that final lifeless image of you etched on my brain instead of all the vital happy memories that were and are so clear. Mum said you looked like you were having a nap. So that's good.

Mum became very quiet and soft in the days leading up to the funeral. I think she was girding herself for it and trying not to die of the misery which was threatening to swallow her whole. She told me that David could sleep in my room. I was gobsmacked! Under her roof it was her rules, and this was a definite no-no ordinarily. But this wasn't ordinary and she wanted us to have all the comfort we could. So, for the first time, David and I slept wrapped up in each other in my tiny single bed in my teenage bedroom surrounded by my dolls and my posters of Steve McQueen and Steve Harley. I cried a lot and woke up startled in the night many times, reliving again and again the shock of what had happened. David was there and he held me close through each night.

The funeral was excruciating. It was in the church where you and Mum were married in St Budeaux, behind the old Blue Monkey pub which has gone now. We always called it the Blue Monkey church. Following the hearse was harrowing, Gary and I on either side of Mum, all clinging on to each other for dear life. Yes, dear life. I was so touched when we pulled up outside the church, and I saw so many of my friends there, who had all loved you, Dad, who wanted to say goodbye, or 'chio' as we say in Plymouth. I can't remember the service except being fixated on that box where you were — but I do remember getting back in the awful big black cars and, again, following the coffin, with you inside it, up to Weston Mill Crematorium. Up, up the hill, and into that little chapel where there was more pointless blether. More platitudes and clichés and metaphors. Blah blah. Shut up! You didn't know him. Then, it happened. That woeful moment when the vicar is saying something about committing you to God and suddenly a buzzing starts and the curtains begin to close around your coffin like a macabre matinee finale. Curtains closing, obstructing my view of you, of where you lay, of where you were. This was suddenly a palpable, final, finite moment. I wasn't ready for it, it was too much and I started to sob uncontrollably with Mum and Gary. I have never before or since felt such aching despair.

We couldn't face a 'do' after the whole dreadful thing was over. The family were probably perplexed by this, but we preferred instead to go home, get the dogs and go for a long walk on the beach at Rock. We were closer to you there, where we had often walked, where we had laughed and loved each other as a family. Looking out at the sea that day, the significance was overwhelming. I realised that your suicide was the wave crashing on the shore. The wave was sinking back into the ocean, and I was left standing on the shoreline without you, utterly lost.

The next week, bruised and broken, I left home and went to college in London . . .

Dear Dad,

Mum was right, as always. It made sense to go to college straight away, and not to delay. I was distracted from my big you-grief by the thousands of new things that were suddenly happening.

A friend of a friend's daughter had a room to let in a flat she shared in Leighton Gardens, Kensal Rise. I didn't know London at all really, except for the few times I'd been there with you and Mum when I was little, to do tourist stuff like visit Madame Tussauds — outside which a man placed a monkey in my arms and another in Gary's and we had our photo taken. One of the more surreal memories I have of childhood and marking the day my monkey-love began. After that, I nagged you to get me a pet monkey about twice a week, till I was 16. That's a lot of nagging that resulted in no monkey. It's OK though. I've forgiven you for not getting me a simian best friend, ever since I found out they try to hump your earholes whenever they can. How very impolite. I'm glad I didn't have a monkey. I hate them now, I reject them and their ear buggery.

So, anyway, the flat in Kensal Rise. Yes. Well, I didn't really have a bedroom — it was one of those awkward half-rooms where you might store an exercise bike or perhaps a Hoover. Just large enough to fit a single bed if the last six inches were sawn off. Large enough for that, but nothing else other than that. Just the mini-sized single bed touching the walls on three sides, that's all that fitted in there. Well, no, maybe I should take my foot off the exaggerator, there was also room for a cup of tea on the floor, so long as you were inside and the door was shut. I did, very briefly, consider kipping on a chair instead, which would free up a couple of square feet for a chest of drawers, but decided against it in the end in favour of sleep.

I didn't know my flatmates very well and when I discovered that one of them, a guy, was taking copious amounts of drugs, I retreated further and further into my little cubbyhole. I should have been living in the new, exciting, huge buzzing city, but in reality I was living in a cupboard. I couldn't afford to venture out much, I was gobsmacked at how much everything in London cost, especially travel — the flat was a long way from the college in Swiss Cottage and practically all of my grant was spent on travel. The grant itself was another problem. The amount was calculated by the local authority at home, who took into account the income of you and Mum. The figure they gave me for the year was supposed to include support from both of you. Of course, you weren't around any more, Dad, on top of which Mum was dealing with a bankful of enormous debt. She was already having to sell the house and buy a flat in Plymouth on Mutley Plain, she was broke, I couldn't ask her to stump up more. I went to the bank and organised a small loan, but no spotty student was allowed much, and luckily one of the hero trio of uncles stepped up to help out a bit. Uncle Terry lent me enough to get through the first year, on the strict understanding that the loan would be paid back by such-and-such a time with such-and-such interest. I know he was teaching me a lesson about borrowing, he was trying to be a substitute for you, Dad, helping me to manage a budget. Once all the books and equipment for the course were bought and my rent and travel was paid, I was left with less than two pounds a week to buy toothpaste and other essentials. Like food. Of course, I should have bought vegetables and pasta and made big hearty soups that would sustain me and last all week, but I chose a different, edgier route. This was the first time I had ever lived on my own, away from any adult guidance. No one could tell me what to do, so I did what I ruddy well liked thank you and went cocking crazy and spent all of the two pounds on chocolate milk and crisps. Every day. For a year. Wild. Sometimes I even left the bloody fridge door open and I very rarely made my mini-sized bed. Honestly, dude, I was out of control . . .

My journey to college each day found me at Finchley Road station with a long walk to Central, which was great for exercise but added hours on to my day, and was a bit scary when, as was often the case, we finished late at night. It was odd that I had just come from living in New York, widely regarded as one of the most dangerous cities in the world, and yet I was more

253

afraid walking home in the dark in Kensal Rise.

My first day at Central was a shock. I was a couple of days late because of the funeral, so I was nervous that I hadn't been part of those crucial first few moments where everyone is in the same boat. By the time I arrived they were already on their boat, it had left harbour and I was rowing furiously behind in my little dinghy to catch up. (A bit like you and me, Dad, in that awful fibreglass home-made kit boat we nearly died in on the River Camel, remember?) The first class of the day was Movement. I had no idea why something was called 'movement'. I knew how to do movement. I did it all day, didn't I? That's how I got about generally, by moving. I had the same confusion about classes on the timetable labelled 'Breathing' or 'Voice'. For a misguided instant, I imagined that perhaps only West Country people knew how to move, breathe and speak. Perhaps these natural skills weren't as widely practised as I had taken for granted. Wow. I was an advanced mover, breather and speaker already, without even trying because, frankly, I'd been doing all three my whole life! These other suckers better catch up.

Oh, how very wrong I was. I clambered into the regulation black leotard and tights with added ugly jazz shoes and slunk into the movement studio. A terrifying space with huge mirrors and barres. Terrifying because we could see the full horror of what we looked like in the black all-in-ones. Leotards don't look good on ANYONE. Even Madonna. And she looks better than everyone else who's ever worn one.

So there we were, the teachers' course class of 1977–1980, known as 'T80'. A sorrier bunch of stooped, bewildered, crushingly embarrassed subhumans you have never seen. This was the environment in which I first laid eyes on Jennifer, my beloved Fatty. Her disdain for the whole leotard experience was obvious. She barely made an effort with the shake-out and warm-up, and the leg-swinging was an affront. Somehow, in this torture chamber of lycra lunacy, she maintained an air of cool. She was as lumpy as the rest of us but she refused (publicly at least) to acknowledge the humiliation of the leotard, so her controlled demeanour remained intact. No nylon nightmare was going to ruffle her. I noticed this seeming self-assurance immediately and chalked her up as unattainable, out of my league, too sophisticated. Again, utterly wrong. She didn't make much eye contact with me, but then again, outside the class I *did* wear beige corduroy A-line skirts and a back-to-front baseball cap and I did call biscuits 'cookies' and think everything was 'neat'. That's what happens when you have no taste and you live in America for a year when you're 19 years old. I mistook Jen's lack of connection with me as low-level loathing. I now know how shy she can be, which is an explanation for her sometime coolness, alongside the equally likely probability that she was mostly distracted by thinking about what she might have for her tea. Fatty is a consummate daydreamer. Unlike most of us amateur daydreamers though, she doesn't visit woolly, blurry places where your mind can have a little dance and a rest, or if she does, it's only for a short time. No, her mind whisks her off to vivid, fresh places where she can live at the pace her brain is constantly working at, which is quite a lot quicker than most mortals. She is constantly running a cynical, internal parallel tape of her real life, what she sees, hears, reads, eats, loves and hates, and it never ceases to amuse her. It's this sharp skill of observation that gives her the comedy spurs she uses to jolt her mind on from a trot to a canter when she is improvising or writing. On the surface, though, all is calm. Calm to the point of catatonia, while she floats in a warm sea of procrastination until the moment the urgency kicks in. It's usually a deadline that provides the fear and that is the cue for her to switch to shark mode. It's as if she has smelt the blood in the water, her eyes focus and she swims very fast, very skilfully towards the target, using all the muscle of a new idea that's been slow-cooking during her reveries, as the power to thrust her forward. It's an awesome talent to witness. Back then, though, I thought she was a snobby git.

After a year of Kensal Rise and only seeing David on the odd weekend only, he was sent to India to work for Lipton's. It was ironic really, one of the reasons he had left the navy for the tea trade was that we didn't want to have so much time apart and now here he was, off to abroad. I didn't want to stay in the pot-reeking flat any more and I was overjoyed when one of my favourite college mates, Gilly, mentioned that her boyfriend Malcolm, who owned some properties, had a new conversion available for eight flatmates to share in Steele's Road, Chalk Farm. This meant only a ten-minute walk to college and a spanking new flat. The rent was more expensive than I had been paying so I knew I would have to share my room. No problem, my fiancé was away in Calcutta, it wasn't as if I was going to need privacy. I knew my old schoolfriend Angie was looking for accommodation, and I knew we would get on sharing a room together, so that was that. Gilly was putting together a group of us to share the flat, some people from college, an American student called Cici, one single guy called Tom, and she said that Jennifer Saunders from our course was also interested. I was definitely underjoyed by the prospect of that. It wasn't that we actively disliked each other, not at all, just that we had been on the same course for a whole year by this point and not really found each other, not really bothered, both assuming that the other wasn't our type. I thought she might be the only one in the flat I wouldn't be able to relate to . . .

Then we moved in and, of course, within days we were walking to college together and getting to know the virtual strangers we were to each other. She made me laugh so much, she was bright, and leagues and layers deep. She was, and is, incredibly attractive in lots of ways I didn't expect. She is a bit mysterious and it takes an effort to know her well, but once in her orbit it's a very cockle-warming place to be. We could subvert any seriousness about our college course by finding it all a bit ludicrous, and taking the piss. We equally sought out chances to puncture any pomposity or pretension we saw around us. This meant that, by very early on in our friendship, the only point of each day was to make each other laugh. In fact on one memorable occasion we decided to see what it would be like to laugh heartily out loud, non-stop, from the second we stepped out of our flat till we reached the steps of college. Of course, loud laughter is pretty funny and contagious so by the time we reached college we were uncontrollably lost in genuine laughter, exhausted, and suitably damp of crotch.

It was so good to find a buddy to laugh with like that. I needed to laugh — there hadn't been much to laugh about for a year or so. In fact, probably the last time was with you, Dad. Laughing with you remains a powerful memory for me. I remember how much John Cleese made us laugh in *Fawlty Towers*, helpless, falling-off-the-sofa laughing till we were begging him on the TV to show mercy and stop being so funny. Cracks and gags and affectionate teasing were a mainstay of our life together. To share a sense of humour is such a privilege, such an intimacy and such a love. I wasn't at all surprised to find, then, that this was the same for Fatty and her dad. I went to her home in Cheshire that November because her parents were having a bonfire party. Their house was big and rambling and friendly. I suppose she must have told her parents about my situation having just lost you, and from the moment I met her dad, he took great care to ladle me with lots of love. I suppose it's unthinkable for another loving dad to imagine his own daughter left fatherless, so he always winked me into his little gags and asides so as to include me. I will never forget his kindness at a time I was starved of dadness.

College was a bit disorganised. The degree as a three-year course was new for the staff, and they hadn't quite sorted it out. I vividly remember the disquiet, especially from the more mature element among us. By mature, I mean about eight years older in most cases; nevertheless, there were several people at Central for whom getting there had been an ordeal. They had worked to save for it, or taken other jobs till they could get in, and they were furious that the course was such a shambles, so they formed quite a militant force and made complaints. The complaints were justified, but most of us in T80 were very young and having a ball just being in London. We weren't that bothered about learning, we wanted to have fun, and magically have a degree by the end of it. I remember one particular exam — was it theatre history? We all filed in, sat down and turned over the question paper. I didn't know ANY of the answers and immediately assumed it was because I was thick or had revised entirely the wrong subject (not unusual). Pretty soon it became obvious that no one could answer anything because we simply hadn't been taught it. The grown-ups of T80 took a stand — literally — and we all followed, marching out of the exam room in revolt. It was quite handy having eloquent and assertive people to represent us, to lead the mutiny when necessary and to shake up the college, which was a bit sleepy. Further education is often the time when we formulate our political leanings and it was fantastic to be in such a lefty environment, listening and learning. And for the last year and a half of our course, we had Margaret Hilda Thatcher the milk snatcher as our foe, so boy didn't *that* unite us under a common enemy. Nothing like a spitting, spouting monster to bring even the loiteringest sluggards out from the back of the cave to stand their ground. Even me.

We were required to do some twatty things during our time there. There was one exercise where we had to wrap each other in newspaper with Sellotape to form human eggs. The lights were dimmed in the studio and we were instructed to stay inside our 'eggs' for as long as we needed until it was time to slowly break out, reborn into an entirely different world where we had to invent a new language and find a new, utopian way to live together. You can imagine how seriously I took this. I figured outright giggling wouldn't go down well so I opted instead for a little snooze inside my hot paper egg. When I woke up, I had no idea how long I'd been asleep, so I thought I'd better break out pretty sharpish in case they were all waiting for me, imagining I was being introspective and interesting. I pierced the paper with my finger and made a hole just big enough to peer through. In the gloaming, I could just make out that everyone else was still inside their eggs. I

must have only nodded off for a few seconds. Drat. The teacher saw me peering out and gestured encouragement to give birth to myself and come out into the brave new world. I was buggered. So, very slowly, I ripped my shell open and crawled out, muttering my 'new' language, which I had decided would be a slowed-down, slurred version of Elvis's 'Can't Help Falling in Love'. So, I was shuffling across the floor, spreading like a lumpy puddle, gurgling, 'Wahse — meen — saay — ooonleee — foolz — ruuuhsh — eeen — ' This went on for an eternity. I was alone in the nightmare until some other sucker finally joined me. The minute I saw Fatty pop out of hers, that was it. I couldn't control the laughter any longer, and was eventually asked to gather myself outside. Honestly, hard-working folks were paying taxes for us to arse about like this! Of course, there was the flipside where we did serious classes which, had I bothered to concentrate, would have come in very handy later on. Voice, for instance. By the time I left I didn't know the difference between a uvula, a vulva and a Volvo but, astonishingly, I somehow had the qualification to teach it! Phonetics would have been another good one to have had under my belt, the language of language. Phonetics would have helped me to write down accents and nuances in shorthand and replicate them later. I have needed this skill a thousand times and, stupidly, I haven't been equipped, because back then I was too busy doing laughing to focus on anything important. How I achieved the degree at all I have no idea.

One particular exercise has returned to haunt me over and over again. In the first year, we were all instructed to go to the zoo, choose an animal, draw it, study it and bring notes back to class for further work. A trip to the zoo! For free! Hurrah! Of course, my day consisted of ice cream, gorilla impersonations, a ride on a camel and some colouring in of parrots on a kiddie drawing pad. It was a fun-packed day out, just grand, a day at London Zoo. When it came to the tutorial, I hurriedly sketched a sloth — a creature I hadn't even visited on the day — improvising the picture using a sort of koala bear mixed with a huge slug as my starting point. I thought that even the tutor might be a little bit amused by my choice of the laziest creature on earth. Little did I know that these choices would dog us for three years, that it was some kind of psychological trick. In the many months that followed, I had to pretend to *be* a sloth, think like one, invent a human like one, improvise like one, make costumes for one. And why? Because apparently, I *was* a sloth. My choice indicated the animal I most identified with, supposedly. But I was mostly identifying with ice cream on the zoo day! No matter, I was labelled a sloth from that day on — even when I went to see my tutor for my final farewell tutorial, he greeted me with, 'Ah, the sloth. Come in!' I am NOT a sloth . . . am I?

Meanwhile, life in the flat was peachy. Angie and I loved sharing, except for the not infrequent occasions she had a gentleman caller, whereby the form was that I would vacate our shared room for the night and kip on the sofa. On one

of my sofa nights, I woke up suddenly to Angie screaming for help. It transpired that her beau had somehow split his foreskin doin' the dirty, and she was useless at the merest sight of blood, never mind when it involved genitals! So there I was, half-asleep, cradling this shocked stranger's todger in some icy water in our sink, while she called the doc. Happy days!

We had a cleaning rota and each took our turn, or not, to clean certain areas of the flat, which inevitably led to hilarious arguments. We made marks on the side of milk bottles to ensure no one was illegally slugging our precious pints, we ate huge six-day-old stale pasta soups with grated cheese on top, and quiche, and mash, and bread with butter and sugar sprinkled on top. We had big, loud, themed parties, tarts and vicars, togas, rival drama colleges, all sorts. We took weekend jobs chambermaiding or in the local pub or cooking for firemen to make a few bob, which we then spent on punky clothes at Camden Market. We were pathetic punks, not properly committed, just dressing up at week-ends. We went to see *The Rocky Horror Show* again and again, we went to watch bands like the B52s and the Eurythmics and anyone who was on at Dingwalls if we could blag our way in. We had the most excellent tea parties with our classmates. I had a crashing crush on Rowan Atkinson, who lived nearby, and, much like David Cassidy and Peter Tork, I felt sure he would love me if only we could meet. I agonised over whether to drop a note through his door. Luckily, I lost my bottle, and didn't put him through it, but we *did* go to see his live show and considered him a genius only hindered by a geeky sidekick I later found out to be a man called Richard Curtis.

I loved the company of my new friends. Of Gilly, who had set the flat up for us, who drove her Mini like a madwoman while cradling hot coffee in her lap, and who had a comprehensive collection of Lladro figurines which I considered to be supremely elegant and sophisticated. She was dating Malcolm, our landlord, who was the most dashing and handsome man in Chalk Farm. That was good, it was unlikely we would be evicted while that lasted. (It has now lasted about 30 years, and provided me with the dreamboat that is Sophie, my first godchild.)

Then there was Jobo, or Yoyo Knickers as I called her. What a woman. Tall and gangly and über clever. She had just returned from Kenya, from some relationship with an exciting chap, and she was like no one I had ever met. Fatty was drawn to her and they were very close by the time I started to know her. She was an exuberant, daring minx with a love for elaborate pranks. She would do anything for a laugh or a dare. It was too irresistible not to challenge her. She would perform her tasks with enormous panache, like, for instance, shouting out her love for strangers on the street, or pretending to be blind at the wheel of her car and asking passers-by for directions while wearing two eyepatches. Getting entirely naked driving through central London and staying so for the whole journey. Wandering about in the street below our flat with our laundry basket on her head and no trousers, and on and on with the gags. She is fearless and wild and beautiful. She was unafraid to fake fits when difficult exams were due, to tell elaborate porkies to staff in order to explain the lack of essays she submitted. She lived in a fabulous crumbling old house in swanky Chelsea and no one believed her when, late once again for lectures, she explained that the ceiling had collapsed at her house, when of course it had. She had fabulous long legs and occasionally did a bit of advertising work for Pretty Polly tights — or did she? Who knows! She *said* she did — anyway, she had a bit of cash and was always free with it. I will never forget when she noticed how hard up I was, and how embarrassing it was for me to completely run out of dosh by the end of the week. Somehow she obtained my bank details and anonymously put money into my empty account which saw me through a whole month. I didn't know who had done it for ages, but found out later that it was she who had been so fabulously generous.

In our last year at Central, there was a student union-organised cabaret evening. We didn't ordinarily bother with these shows at college because it seemed to us they were yet another opportunity to have to witness the actors showing off and loving themselves to bits. The courses were so divided. They didn't want us there, and we didn't want to support their ego-fest. But this time, Fatty and I were encouraged by our friends to do a sketch. By now we had been amusing ourselves for a year or so, inventing characters at home in the flat. We used to put our hated leotards on backwards, we sewed tassles onto our ladybumps and thus we launched the 'Menopatzi Sisters'. Ta-da! We decided they were the last in a long line of an Italian circus family. They were useless acrobats who performed pathetic feats of weakness and ineptitude. It was such a simple pleasure to jump about like daft dafties for the entertainment of our chums. We improvised other characters too — Americans obsessed with spiritual wellness, and punk duo the 'Menopause Sisters', and lots more. Never for one second did we think these little amusements would become more than private. When our friends encouraged us to perform at the cabaret evening, we were a bit hesitant initially, we hadn't ever done anything like this in public before and hadn't intended to, but eventually we decided to go along in order to prevent it being yet another exclusive night where the teachers were unrepresented. We had very little nerves — what did we have to lose? The evening went well, we performed our American sketch and the Menopatzis. People seemed to laugh in all the right places. I'm extra pleased that Gary happened to be there that night because on reflection I realise that it was a seminal moment, a turning point, although, of course, I didn't know it at the time. We hadn't shamed ourselves and we'd had a good laugh — and frankly that's pretty much been our yardstick ever since. I try to make her laugh, she tries to make me laugh, and if anyone else enjoys it too, then that's a bonus.

I wish you could have seen us, Dad, I think you would have liked it. You certainly would have liked her. She's dead funny, my friend Fatty.

Dear Fatty,

I think you've made the right decision to go blonder as you get older. It covers up the enemy grey better than brown hair like mine. I used to dye mine a really dark chocolaty brown but I noticed a couple of years ago that my hair didn't go with my ageing face any more. I don't know why but lighter hair suits wrinkles better, so now I am trying a lighter red colour which is OK but it means I can't wear any more of my red clothes which I'm very fond of. I don't expect you to do anything about this; I'm just outlining my dilemma, hair-wise. I can't really be all that bothered with hair, to be honest. It's just some dead *stuff* hanging off your head really, isn't it? Shame we can't grow something more useful like Mr Potato Head, who so generously and wisely grows cress out of his. I'd quite like to grow asparagus or daffodils, either of which would be preferable and beneficial. Instead, I've got these limp locks which have to be constantly fiddled with and trained to do what they're told with, naturally, the aid of light-reflecting booster technology to get the illuminating shiny finish I deserve. That's why I've kept the same style for so long; I sort of know how to do it in 13 minutes, which is 13 minutes longer than I like to devote to its care.

Anyway, anyway, anyway, I was only saying this because a particular friend of mine has blonde hair (don't worry, it's not you) and is exactly like all those girls you hear about who are not the brightest button on the shirt, y'know, not the sharpest knife in the drawer, y'know, dead thick. Anyway, anyway, anyway, she was round at my house with two of my other friends, one of whom is a redhead and one of whom is a brunette. I expect you're thinking that I just choose all my friends from a Wella colour chart — well, I don't. They are people I have met as I have woven my way through the tapestry of my life like a needle containing thread is pushed through an ancient kilim rug by a blind old Arab man with arthritic thumbs who should stop making rugs now because he's so old, but he doesn't want to, otherwise he'd have to stay at home all day listening to Jeremy Kyle making poor people hit each other when they find out they're not Lauren's real dad because her mum's a slag who dun it wiv over 30 blokes without no protection on it, for God's sake, how many more times, think about the kiddie. The blind man's wife has it on every morning in their flat in Earls Court and he hates it, so he'd rather tip-tap his way to work with his old white stick against the railings till he gets to the old musty carpet workshop where he has a cup of jasmine tea and a suck on a hubble-bubble pipe, before he sits down cross-legged and threads a special curved needle with a strong cotton of many hues, which is in fact the thread of my life made up of hundreds of tinier threads wrapped around each other which are my many friends, who are many colours, *not* just redhead, brunette and blonde.

Anyway, anyway anyway, on the day that all three were at my house, they were discussing their teenage daughters and I was fascinated to listen in because I too have a daughter of the teenage persuasion as you well know, and I thought I might pick up some tips on how to do it right. My brunette friend said that she had been in her teenage daughter's bedroom, cleaning up. I don't do that any more because it's too dangerous. Some of the stuff on the floor in my kid's bedroom is now moving of its own accord. Some of it has just turned to mulch and silage, and we are thinking of selling it to the local farmer to spread on the fields. Anyway, anyway, anyway, I would NOT enter her bedroom to clear it up, especially not without protective gloves, but my brunette friend was doing exactly that, when she found a bottle of vodka under her daughter's bed. She was gutted because, as she said, 'I didn't know my daughter drank.' My redhead friend then piped up that it was an amazing coincidence because she had also been in *her* daughter's bedroom cleaning up. What's wrong with these women? Have they no health-and-safety survival instincts at all? Anyway anyway, anyway, turns out she came across a packet of cigarettes and was so very upset because, as she said, 'I didn't know my daughter smoked.'

Unbelievably, my blonde friend then admitted that she, too, had been clearing out *her* daughter's bedroom and had been utterly shocked and dismayed to discover a packet of condoms because, as she said, 'I didn't know my daughter had a cock . . . ' Can you believe that?

Dear Dad,

My last year at Central was a bit crazy. I was
aware that David and I were growing apart but I
wasn't ready to face it full on because I still loved
him very much. Isn't it mad the way we
postpone the most important stuff? I was living a
liberated life in London, free of the immediate
restraints of a big relationship because my chap
was thousands of miles away. I missed him a lot,
and I was always utterly faithful to him, but I
was also having a great time discovering who I
really was, which turned out to be *not* somebody
who should marry David, or who David should
marry. As you know, David was quite a forceful
personality and liked to be in charge. Surprise,
surprise, that's who I was becoming too,
someone quite assertive who knows their own
mind. At the time I still slightly reverted back
into a somewhat meeker role when I was with
him because that's how it had always been. Old
dynamics die hard. Plus, to be honest, there's a
big part of me, like a lot of people, that loves to
be looked after, protected and sheltered inside a
partner's love. I didn't realise then, as I so clearly
do now, that it was all possible on a much more
equal footing. On reflection, all the signs were
there but I was blind. And reluctant to let go. In
fact, I took the polar opposite action and

charged ahead with arrangements for the wedding. Fatty was to be a bridesmaid, the Blue Monkey church was booked and we were investigating various venues for the reception. Oh what a circus, oh what a show.

It was the Easter holiday 1980 and the last time I would visit David before we were to be married. It was an important trip because I was going to stay in the house where we would live together afterwards, the marital home. By now he had moved from Calcutta and was living in Colombo, Sri Lanka. I had visited him several times in the previous two years when he lived in Calcutta, and I found my trips there most odd. I loved India — the colours, the sounds, the smells, the incredible, mystical difference of it all — but I didn't really warm to ex-pat life. The exclusive clubs and the drinking and the non-working wives and the separateness from local life. Most of all, I found it difficult to stay at his flat surrounded by servants. SERVANTS! I was a 20-year-old student in dungarees and Kickers, what was this all about? I would take off my old second-hand Camden Market T-shirts, and before I could blink they'd be back on the bed washed, ironed and folded. I was expected to organise the household arrangements, order the shopping and oversee the menus. Life there was caught in amber, somewhere in the 1940s. I was addressed as Memsahib and bowed to. It was too strange. Outside, it was even stranger. Parts of Calcutta were beautiful, with a faded grandeur, but the poverty was horrific, and I was constantly confronted with situations and sights

273

direct from a Bruegel nightmare. Half-bodied people scooting along next to me on little carts, women with dead babies in their arms, pleading for money, other beggars with alarming facial disfiguring, lepers with gnarly stumps and famished, emaciated children, all tugging at me, wanting a few paise. Here I was, a fat young white woman, shopping for fruit and beads in the market while all around me was despair. The clash was revolting. I started by giving money to everyone, but of course that caused further begging, more insistent and louder, until I was forced to retreat inside in utter shock.

Meanwhile, David and I would be invited to posh dinners inside lavish homes with dozens of servants providing for our every need. Or there would be more bloody balls — Caledonian balls with only white people there, and again I never quite looked or felt or *was* the part. The part of a company wife, quietly supporting her upwardly mobile company man of a husband. Who was I? Who was he? Where was the spirited young Irish lad I had known? He was certainly highly prized by the company and I was often told by his colleagues that he was tipped for great things. I was proud of him, *for* him, but Dad, I didn't belong. So, this final unmarried visit to Sri Lanka mattered. We would arrange the teaching job I was going to take, we would hire staff together, we would hang out with all the people who would be our friends for the next couple of years. I would be a tea-taster's wife.

As always, I was very excited on the plane, I couldn't wait to see him. We were good together

274

physically and I always looked forward to that part of each reunion the most, to genuinely reconnecting in the most basic primal sense. Sorry, Dad, too much information. But honestly, each time we were apart, the lust grew stronger, it was our shared mutual need, and a big priority. When the plane landed, all the passengers headed into the airport, and as soon as I'd gone through passport control I saw him, on the other side of the glass, waving at me, while I waited for my luggage. There he was, my handsome fiancé whom I missed so much — there — at last — he was. So why was I feeling nothing? Why was my heart not pounding out of my chest as it usually did? Come on, heart, wake up! There he is, smiling and waving, we've waited for this — come on! I did the waving-back thing but something was wrong, Dad, terribly wrong.

We reached the house; it was beautiful and colourful and hot. We drank tea, amazing, well-chosen, well-mixed, top-quality tea, we chattered, and we went to bed. I felt totally numb. Nothing was right, it was all very, very wrong. Something was missing. Everything was missing. What had happened? We slept, uneasily. We went to his club the next day. He introduced me to his new buddies. Other tea men, businessmen, nurses, wives, my future friends. I felt as if I was drowning.

That evening, with two more weeks of the holiday to go, we finally talked the way we should have talked for the past year. We spoke about so much, about how different our lives

275

now were, how we had grown apart and changed into people neither of us really recognised, how we were political polar opposites, how much he loved the ex-pat life and how little I did, how much I disliked our his 'n' hers scuba-diving kit, how it made me feel 'owned'. All this was reasonable and understandable. Then, and only then, after all that, he told me he was sleeping with a nurse he'd met there. A nurse? One of the nurses he'd introduced me to at the club yesterday? Yes, he said. So, you're shagging someone else and she's allowed to inspect me? I asked if anyone else knew about it. Yes, he finally admitted. It seemed everyone knew. So he had taken me to meet a group of people who all knew my fate? It was just me, miles from home, miles from my friends, who *didn't* know? Why didn't he tell me before, stop me from coming? Was *that* what I was feeling at the airport? Did I sense then that it was over? And if so, was I just sensing that it was over for me, or for us? Did I subconsciously suspect? Or was the love just . . . gone? On both sides? I had no answers to any of this but I knew I had to get away.

I was back at the airport the very next day, and after a tearful farewell and a weepy flight home, I ran into the arms of a love I could depend upon, my brother, who took me back to his flat in London and listened to me blub on about the injustice of it all for days until he gently reminded me, mid-rant, that I had already known it wasn't going to work out. I had known, really, but refused to face it. It was better for everyone that it ended now, *before* the wedding. He was right of course. I called Fatty and she came. She was the only other one I talked to at that point, until I could work my way through it and steel myself to call the various parents to explain what had happened.

David and I met again briefly a few months later, when I returned the ring, and a few bits 'n' bobs of his old kit. I was afraid that when I opened the door to greet him I might be revisited by a rush of the familiar old love and realise we had made a huge mistake, but no. There was, instead, a rush of nostalgia, a tender remembrance of the younger, happier times, but we both knew it was right to have ended it.

So. That was over. I had been at college for three years, turning away from every possible opportunity of big sex fun with a bucketful of delish fellow students. Now I had a single term to catch up. Wahey!

Dear Dad,

Other than my friend Scottie, no one on the acting course at Central spoke to me, or to any of us teachers. They refused to make eye contact, let alone converse. I think they believed they might catch something off us. And indeed they might have. Manners for instance.

Annoyingly, their iciness made them all the more enigmatic, and there was a definite elite of blessed, golden, chosen ones. They were, on the whole, good-looking, usually blond and quite fit. Thoroughbreds really. We used to refer to them as the shampoo brigade, because their hair was always so perfect. There was one in particular who I thought was divine — I used to see him skulking about being moody and interesting. The foyer of the college was the actors' main posing arena — it was directly outside the cafeteria, thus commanding a captive audience — they would throw interesting shapes against the wall while perusing their timetables and various notices concerning chlamydia check-ups and student-union functions. My particular darling, whom I shall refer to as the 'Golden One', was quite brooding and James Dean-ish. He was a good actor, I saw him in various plays at the Embassy, the theatre at the centre of the college, a beautiful but wounded old place. For some preposterous reason, we, the teachers, were not allowed into the theatre at any time except to watch the actors performing their plays, when they actively encouraged us in because they needed an audience. All of our productions took place in the studio spaces, which were fab but just not as exciting as the proper proscenium-arch grandness of the Embassy, the forbidden Embassy. The most memorable play that I saw the Golden One in was Bill Morrison's *Flying Blind*, where he spent a deal of time naked. Yep, I saw that play several times, each night occupying a seat in the auditorium closer and closer to the front . . . I wanted to get a really good look at the . . . play.

One day, I was having coffee in Marianne's little cafeteria where I could see the goings-on in the foyer. The Golden One was there doing expert leaning against the noticeboards. He was alone. The rest of the shampoo herd were obviously grazing elsewhere. This was unusual, he was unguarded and vulnerable, so I decided to seize the moment, to pick him off. We had been attending the same college for nearly three years and as yet he hadn't even cast a glance in my direction. If I didn't take action now, college would be over and all hope gone. Plus, I was newly single and misguidedly emboldened. I wasn't entirely stupid, however; I knew I couldn't compete with the beauty of the girls at the vanguard of the shampoo brigade, but I had something else to offer. My sparkling wit, surely? In that instant, I decided to embark on Operation Flirt by winning him over with a flurry of hilarity — the romance would surely follow later. I stood up and crossed the foyer. He foolishly had his back to me, so he had no time to see me approach and consequently attempt a speedy escape. He was caught unawares. I advanced upon him in all my beige corduroy splendour, deciding that my opening gambit would be, 'Hi. Hello there. Yes it's me, I'm talking to you at last after three years. I bet you can't believe your luck, eh? You must be so frustrated that you know nothing about me. Well, that agony stops right here, right now, and you, mister, are gonna know everything you've ever wanted to know and more about me, Dawn Roma French . . . Right, I'm going to start at the very beginning, stop me when you're in love . . . ' By this time, my plan, if I had one, was that he would at least be smiling if not downright chuckling but . . . nope . . . nothing. He looked genuinely afraid and was backing up towards the wall, which meant I had to continue with the gag until he *got it*. He will get it eventually . . . won't he? So I valiantly soldiered on. 'So, um, right, I was born in Holyhead in 1957, and luckily for my mother, I was a baby . . . ' Nope, nothing. Carry on. 'I was a chunky child, bold in nature, a real rusk-taker . . . ' He's right up against the wall now and looks like he's got a bad smell in his nostrils. Don't give up, keep going. 'You will probably be keen to know exactly what inoculations I've had, well . . . ' And on. And on. Still no response except clearly utter revulsion, and the unmistakable squeaking of leather belt on wall as he tried to slide away. I *had* to

280

persevere — you know me, Dad, I'm nothing if not tenacious! I think after about six minutes of solid talking, and a tiny bit of physical restraint, I had reached as far as infants school, and was about to launch in to the junior-school years and regale him with many hilarious anecdotes about that, when suddenly the bell rang indicating the start of the next class. I was momentarily startled and the Golden One grabbed the opportunity to run, run like a hunted fox, for his life, off up the corridor to his Tumbling class and out of my life for ever.

Or so I thought. Cut to about three years later. I was in a queue at the bank in Swiss Cottage. I was still banking there although I had long since left the area. I was inching my way slowly towards the front of the queue when out of the blue I heard my name pierce the stuffy quiet. 'Dawn! God, darling, how great to see you!' I turned round and it was him, the Golden One, advancing upon me with his arms wide open, gathering me up like a precious thing and giving me a huge, effusive, loving bear hug. I found myself in a situation I would have given good money to be in just a few years earlier. Now I'm not saying that things changed so completely and so utterly because I was by then working with the Comic Strip making eight films a year and we were always casting. No, I'm not saying that. But. It was odd.

And here's *another* odd thing. The same man, who had spurned me, was, shockingly, struck by lightning. Actual, real lightning. On his head.

From God. Y'know, God, who I would later come to be the first female showbiz representative of on earth? Now, Dad, I'm not saying that it's *very* unwise for any man to ever actively resist my charms. But it *is* weird, isn't it?!

Dear BF

How the knob did we get away with calling ourselves teachers? I still see people now, grown women with children, especially in the Camden Town area, who shout after me, 'Miss French!' A clanking reminder of an extraordinary year you and I spent teaching at Parliament Hill School for Girls. 1980/81, wasn't it? Dear Lord, we were both just out of 'school' ourselves.

Parliament Hill. A big girls' comprehensive between Camden and Highgate, set in beautiful grounds backing on to fields, with William Ellis boys' school right next door. Huge and well equipped, (Parliament Hill that is, not the boys), it was a massive education machine stuffed with boisterous, confident kids and dedicated staff. I was a bit intimidated by how sprawling it was, but it helped that I'd had my final teaching practice there, so it was more of a natural progression than getting a new job in an entirely unfamiliar school. My teaching practice before that had been up the road at a big co-ed comp called Ackland Burley which had one of the most inspirational dance/drama departments in the country, so I had hoped Parly would be the same.

Well, it wasn't quite, was it? There was a small basement studio — that bit was good — but the

283

staffroom for our department was in the old toilets next door. Our cupboards were toilet stalls, with toilets still there. We balanced files on washbasins and we made a little seating area under the mirrors at the end. This attempt at cosiness was sort of futile since every uttered word pinged back at us from the mostly cracked tiles on the walls and floor. It was a cold, damp, smelly, depressing place wasn't it? I think the atmosphere had slowly eroded the head of the drama department's enthusiasm for the subject and she wasn't coping so well. She had some ill health and I was quite often thrust into her position. Me, the rookie newby twit, in charge of all the O-level, CSE and A-level drama courses, about which I knew nada. Thank God you came in part-time, to help with this frightening situation. You really helped me out Babe, and into the bargain we had an opportunity to spend more time together, cementing our friendship even further, united in fear and confusion. Quite often, I would spend the evening learning the theory I was teaching the next day from the course textbooks. I was about two pages ahead of my students at any one time. And what students! The older A-level kids were bright and inquisitive and quite a challenge — after all, I was only four or five years older than them. I spent the entire time bluffing that I was dead assured and supremely in control. For most of the time I worked with them, I was really wishing we could abandon the studying and gossip about telly and boyfriends. The O-level and CSE groups were the main ones we taught together.

What a hoot! Once we could get them *into* the studio we could have great sessions. But getting them there wasn't so easy. Parly had a culture of repeated truancy among certain groups of students. It wasn't unusual for me to go scouting about in the fields or the shops or even to their homes to herd them in like a sheepdog. I felt that if I could just gather them up, I would at least have a fair chance of persuading them to stay. I had to throw in the towel eventually when it turned out I was spending more time on the prowl than in the studio teaching. Of course, what I later realised was that if the classes could be fun, or interesting enough, word would spread and the attendance figures would rise anyway. I learned this from the completely fab PE department where I found two mad but inspirational teachers, Rosie and Gill, employing this technique: Connect with the kids properly and they will slowly come to respect you and turn up regularly. For drama classes, like PE, teamwork is crucial — there's no production if there's no cast, there are no exam pieces without groups working together, and there's no 'group' without people. Many would fail if a few let them down, so it was my dearest wish to get the full complement of kids into the studio as often as possible, and enable them to feel a sense of achievement when their group pieces were well received.

I know we both found that the actual work, when they turned up, was mindblowing. I very quickly had to put all my middle-class ideas of what would make a good dilemma for a drama

285

group to tackle away in the bottom drawer marked 'shit ideas'. These kids had real-life dilemmas to draw upon, the likes of which I couldn't begin to imagine. Issues to do with race, religion, weapons, drugs, bullying and abuse were way out of my experience, and yours. We stood agog while a kaleidoscope of their real lives was revealed to us. They put my lesson plans to shame. The biggest 'dilemma' I had written on my teaching suggestion cards was: 'The council is planning on putting a motorway through our village. What are we going to do?' What village? What motorway? Everything we planned was utter bollocks, and pretty much irrelevant. Some of the kids suggested their own dilemmas, like, 'How do you stop your mother shooting up in front of your younger brother and sister?' or, 'My dad beat me up till I passed out, but I don't want him to be taken away otherwise me and my sister will go into care.' The classes often turned into a kind of group therapy where the kids gave each other advice, and they were the ones who really knew *what* advice, much better than us. So it was proper drama, real-life drama, being talked about and acted upon right there in front of us. Slowly the drama space became a place where kids would come to hang out at lunchtime and after school; they would offer to help clear away or whatever, just as a chance to talk a bit more. It was then that I realised they were using it as a sanctuary and that we could sometimes be more useful to them as a safe place than as a drama studio. Not all the kids did this of course, but the few who needed to are the ones I remember so clearly.

The younger classes, the 11- and 12-year-olds, were my absolute favourites. They had only recently arrived at 'big' school and hadn't learned yet to be 'cool' and suppress their excitement for the subject. Their imaginations were bursting, and since there were no awful exams to stunt their enjoyment, they would trip down the stairs like a herd of happy gazelles with their new shoes clacking like hooves on the stone steps. They found it hard to keep still or listen, but when they did we had fantastic adventures, didn't we? I don't think either of us needs much encouragement to play, and in these early school years, before the tyranny of the constant assessment begins, the play aspect is what's important.

I do remember getting it wrong a couple of times, though. Once, we were doing a big improvisation about Captain Cook discovering Australia, a voyage of adventure on the high seas, on a big old ship built from chairs and tables in the studio. We had lookouts, and someone at the helm (a plastic hula hoop) and tots of rum (Vimto) and sailors cooking (chopped lettuce) in the galley and sails (sheets) being hoisted and pirates and all sorts. It was quite a project and took me some effort to keep my eye on everything that was happening. One particular kid was selected to be keel-hauled as punishment by her bosun for not coiling the ropes properly. We had talked before about what this involved, dropping her over the side and dragging her under the hull (canteen tables) at the widest part of the ship, where she could scrape off the barnacles on the way. So, we tied a rope round her middle and put her over the side, which, in effect, meant jumping off a chair and then scrabbling under the tables. I was distracted at that point by someone in the crow's nest shouting out she'd seen land ahoy! We all busied ourselves getting our galleon into port where I noticed our keel-haul victim sitting, arms and legs crossed, very cross indeed, under the table. I realised we had abandoned her at a crucial moment and tried to encourage my deckhands to 'Quick, pull her up, pull her up, me hearties!' But she sat resolutely still. 'No point,' she said glumly. 'I've drowned. And you'll have to tell my mum.'

Another time we did a term-long project about space travel, working out what we would need to bring, how long we were to be away, what our mission would be, what our spacesuits would look like, what we'd write in our farewell letters to our families, how we'd build our rocket, and so on. The last lesson of term was our lift-off day, signifying the end of the project. The kids had worked really hard on it, making costumes, painting the set, etc. The class was due after lunch and during the break I was summoned to the staffroom door where a little 11-year-old was in floods of tears. 'What's up?' I asked. 'I can't go. I just can't. I don't want to leave my mummy and daddy and my newts. Someone else can have my spacesuit. Take someone else instead . . . ' It was a good lesson for me. Kids develop their imaginary awareness at different ages. The whole class understood that what we were doing was pretend, except one little mite who was a tiny bit less mature than the others, and who had spent the whole term dreading this moment and felt guilty about bottling out of genuine space travel . . . What a bloody coward.

Another enjoyable idea that backfired on me was when I implemented the 'rule' that all students should bow to me at the start of class and repeat the following: 'We beg you, Your Majesty, to teach us, and teach us . . . NOW!' The kids loved it, and we always had a laugh doing it, it helped to focus them at the beginning of the lesson and it was a kind of unsubtle comedy message that I was in charge. The kids got it, but some of the parents didn't. I was hauled in front of the head for that when one of the parents complained that her daughter was being forced to be my 'subject'. As I say, people develop at different times and some parents' comedy development was severely stunted. Luckily the head had a twinkle in her eye when she reprimanded me.

The head was wonderful, wasn't she? You and I always had a laugh with her. Mrs McKeown. Is that the right spelling? She was a relatively new head but very popular, as I remember. She was very helpful to me when I had to make a crucial decision, and actually, on reflection, her shrewd judgement was the deciding factor in my choosing to pursue a career in comedy.

About halfway through that first teaching year, Jennifer called me up and said she had seen an advert in the *Stage* looking for women to perform at a new comedy/cabaret venue called the Comic Strip inside a strip club at the Boulevard Theatre in Soho. The audition was hilarious, mainly because we only had a couple of seconds of material, from the silly sketches we'd done at college. It wasn't as if we'd honed it into a perfect showpiece, because neither of us had intended to take it any further. I was teaching daily with you; Fatty was living on the dole and spending most of her day drinking and doing crosswords and having a lovely lazy bohemian time in shabby old Chelsea with Jobo. Her attitude to the advert was, 'Hey, why not?' So we shuffled along to the tiny red theatre in Soho, to find the auditions in progress, with a man on the stage juggling lobster pots in a comedy way. We did our Americans sketch, not very well, and lo and behold we were in! Only later did we realise that *any* women who had walked in the door on that day would have got the job. They were desperate for women in the line-up of an all-male comedy group, which consisted of Alexei Sayle, Ade Edmondson, Rik Mayall, Nigel Planer, Peter Richardson, Arnold Brown and occasional others like Keith Allen and Chris Langham. So our qualification for the job on that auspicious audition day was, basically, breasts. We had those in plentiful supply between the two of us, so — result. This meant I was teaching during the day, covering for the head of department who was ill, then moonlighting onstage in Soho, *every* night of the week, meeting a whole new gang of people and, by sheer luck, becoming part of a group at the forefront of what was mistakenly, to my mind, labelled 'alternative' comedy. The Comic Strip show gathered momentum and popularity, and became the place to be if you liked comedy. Robin Williams performed with us, and people like Jack Nicholson and Bianca Jagger were in the audience. It was sort of bonkers and I kept praying that no member of staff or parent of a kid at Parly came to see the show. I don't know now how I found the energy but then I loved being so busy with two very different jobs.

My first priority though, as you know, was the school and getting the kids I taught through their exams. It was while I was focused on this that two opportunities arose simultaneously and sent me into a maelstrom of indecision. Mrs McKeown offered me the chance to take up the post of head of department officially because the present one was leaving. I was only in my probationary year, and this kind of stroke of luck hardly EVER came along. It would mean skipping eight years of hard upward slog, and nearly doubling my salary to about £8,000 a year! Plus, I would be in control of my own little universe doing the job I'd always wanted, and had trained for. At the same time, the Comic Strip, as a group, was offered the chance to go on tour around the UK and to the Adelaide Festival in Australia. If I didn't go, Fatty probably couldn't go — we were a double act after all. Teaching or tour? Career or bit of a lark? That's how I saw it then. I discussed it with you and with my family and with Keith Allen, who I was doing a bit of jig and poke with around that time. His solemn advice was to stay with teaching 100 per cent. Twat.

I was nervous, but I felt compelled to come clean with Mrs McKeown and so I told her about the Comic Strip and my moonlighting escapades. She could have been furious, she was my employer after all, but instead she was sagacious. She considered for a moment and reasoned that, although she needed me at the school and it was a tricky transitional time for my students, they would survive it, and she could always find another, perhaps more experienced head of department. She had the foresight and generosity to say that I would probably always regret it if I didn't take the opportunity to go to Australia. She was so right about that, but y'know, if at that moment she had chosen to remind me of my obligation to those kids, emotionally blackmailing me to remain, I would have, because I was so torn and felt so guilty. It's all thanks to her savvy and her mental poise that I went off with my comedy chums Down Under, for some of the best times I'd ever know.

Dear Fatty,

I thought you might be interested to hear that a strange thing has happened in a pub near me. A couple of weeks ago, a chap walked in there, casual as you like, and asked for a pint. I don't know of what. Maybe Scruttocks Old Dirigible with twigs and bits of beak in it, as Alexei used to say, although I suspect that was just a silly beer name he made up to enhance the joke he was telling at the time. He used to do that a lot, say things that weren't quite true for comedy effect. Anyway, anyway, anyway, this chap ordered his beer and the barman went off to the cellar, to change the barrel since it had run out. To my mind, he should really have changed it before that, then he wouldn't have had to keep the customer waiting and feeling neglected. He obviously wasn't keeping his eye on the levels as closely as a good landlord oughta. Do barrels have levels? Like petrol gauges, or a dipstick? I wonder. I wouldn't have been so tolerant if I had been the customer and thirsty for my Scruttocks. I personally wouldn't actually be thirsty for that of course, because I detest beer. It is the urine of the devil with all its froth and rancid flavour. Pretty quickly, actually, it's whoever's drunk its urine, isn't it? Because boys never seem to keep it in for long. They don't buy it, they rent it, some say. I think that, possibly, boys must have very stupidly pointlessly small bladders. Perhaps it's because the exit route is a pipe with an ever-open hole at the end. Is there a sphincter or valve mechanism anywhere along that route? I've certainly not come across one, and frankly that's just bad design.

Anyway, anyway, anyway. While the barman or landlord (he could of course be both) was away from the bar, the man took the opportunity to look around and saw that there was absolutely no one else in the pub. I'm not sure why. Maybe someone, a regular perhaps, had died and everyone else was at the funeral except the barman who was furious he still had to open up because the brewery are strict about things like that? Or maybe there had been tell of a ghostly headless horseman charging through the pub which had frightened everyone off? With headless horsemen, by the way, is it the horse that's headless usually, or the man? Or perhaps it was just a Tuesday before lunch and everyone was at work? We'll never know. So anyway, anyway, anyway, the man was alone in the pub and he sat down on a tall stool at the bar. I hate those tall stools, never was there such a precarious place to perch, and *at a bar* where you will be full of alcohol for heaven's sake. The only suitable place for a tall stool is under one of Sacha Distel's lovely arse cheeks, as he lounges there with his long legs supporting him more than adequately all the way to the floor, one of them ever so slightly bent at the knee, as the heel of his snakeskin shoe effortlessly catches on the strut halfway up. He might, also, have a nice jumper on. Who knows?

Anyway, anyway, anyway, while he sat there at the bar on his own, the man inadvertently started to pick at a bowl of nuts on the counter. I wouldn't do that myself because of the statistic about every bowl of nuts containing at least 20 specimens of different wee from dirty folk who don't wash their hands after the loo. He obviously didn't know this fact, or he didn't care, or he might even have been some kind of wee connoisseur or appreciator. In which case, what a freak! Anyway, anyway, anyway, he was aimlessly popping the bar snacks into his mouth when he heard a little voice in his ear say, 'Goodness, you're handsome!' I mean, honestly, how very forward was that? He looked all around, very confused, and of course, as previously established, nobody was there. And he hadn't even had his pint yet, so we can't blame the alcohol at this point. Before you could say, 'Time, gentlemen, please! What is the time, gentlemen please?!' he heard another little voice, this time saying, 'Wow, those slacks really suit you.' Again, he was utterly confused because he couldn't work out where these little voices were coming from. Just as he heard the barman's footsteps coming back up from the cellar, there came a third and final comment: 'Mmm, you smell lovely, like limes on a summer evening in the Algarve.' Well, you can imagine what state he was in by then, really quite flummoxed, and he was glad to see the incompetent barman emerge again. Apparently he then told the barman about his bizarre experience while sitting there waiting, to which the barman responded casually, 'Oh don't worry about that. It's the peanuts. They're complimentary.' Can you believe that?

Dear Dad,

The Comic Strip was a phenomenon. Peter Richardson was the force that drove it on, and he was — still is — a very talented, determined chap. By the time Jennifer and I joined, it was already thriving. I had never seen a show like it. A repertory of eight or so regular performers with guests each night. Most people on the 'circuit' at that time had done the endless rounds of pub gigs, and back then the burgeoning Comedy Store was the hub of it all. Also based in a Soho strip club, the Comedy Store was ruled by a gong and the idea was to perform five to ten minutes without being gonged off. Considering that a large portion of the audience was drunk and thought they were there to see a strip show, the gong provided a perfect opportunity for them to be unnecessarily cruel. Some acts were gonged off as they walked onstage, even before they opened their mouths. You would have hated it there, Dad, no gentle humour or meandering understatement could survive in that boozy, gladiatorial, competitive arena. It was loud, uncouth, extremely masculine and — consequently — strangely thrilling. Fatty and I were already safely ensconced at the Comic Strip, which was much calmer — no gong, a regular income — but we knew we had to have a go at the Comedy Store for the sake of our credibility. Very few women were performing back then, unsurprisingly. The ones that did were fairly tough with confrontational political material, like Jenny Lecoat, or very dirty (good dirty, I mean!), like Jenny Eclair, or poets like Pauline Melville. We didn't fit into any of these categories. Our 'material', such as it was, was character-based and chatty. Two people talking about something, that was us. From the minute Fatty and I went onstage at the Comedy Store the very first time, oafish drunkards started shouting, 'Show us your tits!' I just couldn't abide the rudeness, Dad. I switched into teacher mode, stepped completely out of the sketch we were attempting, and ordered them to sit down and be quiet. Oddly enough, it worked and we finished our sketch with no further interruptions. However, we *did* perform it at eight times the usual speed! Maybe it was genuinely better that way.

Life at the Comic Strip was altogether more genial, though, and we were under the watchful eye of Alexei as our MC. There we could write and experiment with new material. Fatty and I were a bit green at the outset, and we used to try to perform a new sketch each night. She would come to Parly where I was teaching and we'd take advantage of the studio space to work up new material. It took us a while to realise it was the audience that changed each night, so the material didn't have to — in fact we could have a good few weeks to work on it and edit it. Doh!

Jen and I didn't have a proper name for our

act at first. We spent ages trying to come up with something vaguely amusing, for instance we seriously considered calling ourselves 'Kitch n' Tiles' . . . Oh Lord. Luckily Lexei soon tired of our indecision and eventually one night, exasperated, he introduced us with: 'Ladies and gentlemen, please welcome French and Saunders.' I though it sounded a bit like a new brand of mustard, but it seems to have stuck.

Although we had joined the group late on, we very quickly felt part of it. It was like having six older brothers who made you laugh a lot, teased you mercilessly and played a bit rough. They all operated out of one big smelly dressing room and we had the little one next door, which we shared with occasional visiting girls. The Boulevard Theatre is in Walker's Court in Soho, right at the heart of the red-light district. Every other building was an 'adult' shop or a strip joint. The Boulevard contained two theatres and a bar. One of the theatres was ours and the other was a strip club, which we passed through nightly to get to our dressing rooms. The building was owned by Paul Raymond, who was the king of Soho at the time. He often used to hang out in the bar and I clearly remember nervously asking him if he would second my and Fatty's application form to get our equity cards. He did. Paul Raymond was our sponsor, so to speak. I loved that. I loved the strange mixture of comedy and erotica in that building. On some more surreal occasions, the audiences for both shows would be thrust together in the tiny bar during the intervals. Our lot would be young people in acres of new-romantic ruffles and leather, ladles of make-up, big hair and shoulder pads, and their lot were mainly Japanese besuited men who came over all bashful when they encountered our audience. Two entirely different groups united by their common determination to be entertained. Wherever they are, comedy clubs and strip clubs have virtually the same decor and the same ambience, or so it seems to me. They are usually dark red with a small stage area and an abiding atmosphere of intensity and alcohol. They are fuggy, edgy dens where anything can and might happen. One of the most powerful sensory memories I have of the Comic Strip was the smell. Our dressing room wasn't so bad, or if it was, it was masked by a heady top note of hairspray, perfume and deodorant. The boys' room was a rank, acrid, humming place. They used to sweat a lot with nerves, then sweat more onstage, then take off their stage outfits, hang them up on the floor and never wash them. I think they thought it was unlucky to do so, or something. They might have been able to wash their armpits in the sink in their dressing room, if the sink hadn't been full of ice and lager cans. Lexei was probably the most fragrant of the smelly lot, till Ben Elton turned up as the job-sharing MC on nights Lexei didn't do. Ben was more familiar with soap and always smelt peachy!

Jennifer and I recently returned to the Boulevard to do a gig to help launch some try-out nights for the BBC Comedy Department. I was delighted to see that very funny

Miranda Hart was the MC for the night, but other than her, the line-up was, still, staunchly all-male. And the smell in the dressing room was exactly the same: eau de nervous comedian. Mmmm.

The Comic Strip tour in Australia in 1981 was fantastic. The day we travelled was just like being on a buzzy school trip. We all rejigged our seats on the plane so's we could sit together and drink and laugh for most of the very long flight. The minute we arrived at the Oberoi Hotel in Adelaide, we checked in and agreed to meet five minutes later at the swimming pool. We were in a hotel! In Australia! It had a swimming pool! So much for the supposed cool disdain of young, alternative comedians. We raced down there in our swimmers and on a count of three, jumped right in with a ferocious splash, and had a shouty freestyle race just like a gang of six-year-olds. I remember that the Pina Bausch dance troupe were also staying there, and were relaxing on their loungers, watching us scream about. There they were, all lithe and brown and elegant and slinkily nonchalant. There we were, all over-excited and goofy and fat and white. And so, *so* British.

I have rarely felt so clearly defined by my nationality as on that visit to Oz. Of course, being a Brit you're a constant joke target for the Aussies, and we had plenty of that. Australians are so full-on. It takes a bit of getting used to, but I found it really refreshing. They do, at least, like to *commit* to everything and rush at all aspects of life with a cranked-up, full thrust of brio. The energy at the festival was swirling and we enjoyed the attention our show was getting. Conversely I witnessed a couple of incidents that shocked me rigid. One such was when I took a cab. I was chatting to the driver, who seemed perfectly friendly. We pulled up at some lights, and found ourselves next to a slumped Aboriginal guy. He was obviously the worse for wear and I was worried that he might roll onto the road into the oncoming traffic. I asked the driver if we could get out and at least help him to the other side of the road. The driver yelled a definite no and told me I could catch something if I so much as touched him. He then proceeded to wind down his window, and shouted to the unfortunate man that he was a 'dirty lazy rock ape', and spat on him. A big snotty, throaty, gobby spit, right on the man's bowed head. The lights changed and we sped off. I was speechless. I couldn't believe what I'd seen. Then the driver tried to re-engage me in breezy chat, as if nothing had happened. I asked him to pull over and I got out and walked back to the hotel in a dazed state of shock. I had never before witnessed one human being relating to another in this despicable way, I didn't know how to process my reaction other than feeling sick. I tried to talk about it to work out what had happened to make relations so bad. I found that people were reluctant to say much, or if they did, I was surprised by the general dislike for the indigenous population from folk I had previously regarded as pretty liberal and broad-minded. People I expected to be humanitarian and left-thinking. People in the arts! I quickly realised that this subject was a minefield, that I was ill-equipped to wander through it until I was better educated about it. I knew the history of relations between Aboriginal Australians and white Australians was tricky but I didn't know just what a total mess it had become. People were embarrassed about it, and quite angry at my confusion, at my questions. This was evidently a big ol' can o' racist worms and I wasn't about to enter into it until I knew more. Nearly three decades later, I'm still baffled. On reflection, that was my first revolting taste of racism, which has since reared up many times in my life. I didn't know then that before too long I would be on the receiving end of it . . .

We were very much a team on that tour and my favourite memories are of the social time we spent together, after the shows, the picnic we had at Hanging Rock, the BBQs with giant prawns, burying each other in the sand on Bondi Beach and boozy trips to vineyards.

Alexei used to sing his weird hit 'Pop-Up Toaster' as the finale to the show, and it was the only time all of us were together onstage. Previously the boys had been the only ones to get together for this song but now we were invited and the finale became a girl-friendly zone. That small gesture marked a big difference in the dynamics of the group and gave us a strong springboard from which to launch into, first, the British tour and, second, the following twenty years' worth of Comic Strip films together.

Those films are quite a body of work when I think about it now. I recently did some publicity for the big DVD box set of all things Comic Strip and I realised just what a huge and influential part of my life it had all been. Oh Dad, I wish you could have been around for that. Remember all the Enid Blyton books I read as a little kid and how much I loved them? Here I was years later taking the right royal piss out of them and being part of proper ground-breaking film-making at the launch of Channel 4. Our first film went out on the opening night alongside the very first *Countdown* and an advert for a Vauxhall Cavalier 1600. It was such fortuitous timing that a new, different kind of channel started and were looking for exactly the kind of programmes we wanted to make. There were plenty of rows about what we were making and complaints galore, but we were basically left to conceive, write and produce a series of films of our own choosing. Pete Richardson and his writing partner Pete Richens wrote most of them, but we all had a go somewhere along the line. We still had the old rep company attitude to making the films. We were paid equally and we were cast equally, which avoided any squabbling. You always knew that if you only had four lines in this film, you might have the lead in the next. We spent a lot of time away together making the Comic Strip films and came to know each other very well. I knew Fatty already of course, but it was great to get closer to Ade, who is quite a dark horse, a complex and profound person, as serious as he is funny. He is a shockingly bright

304

chap, passionate about music and his family. Of all the Comic Strip boys he is the one I feel the most sisterly towards. I'm drawn to his shadows, to the hidden. He knows I love him and he loves me back in the most affectionate unlimited way. He is the most sincere supporter you could wish to have. He has come to see me in virtually every play I've ever done and has always been honest with me, for which I respect him very much. When he and Jen *eventually* got together (after no small amount of nudging, I hasten to add), I felt that they had found, in each other, a proper mate.

Rik I knew and know less. He was probably the person who made me laugh the most. I took any chance to watch him work onstage because he is a consummately funny man. There are rich comedy strata only Rik has access to and he is king of them to this day. He should be a stupendously mighty comedy star worldwide. He should be a brand called Rik. He should have shops called Rik where you can go to buy some funny. He should have an actual crown. That's how funny he is. I don't really know him, although I've known him for a very long time — y'know, that sort of person. He had a lot of attention, deservedly so, because he was not only hilarious, but also quite beautiful with the clearest, hugest eyes and the most expressive face. Other young comics copied him for a while, a bit like everyone copied Eddie Izzard later on. I also have Rik to thank for pointing out, at one particularly auspicious Comic Strip meeting, that Fatty and I were being paid half as much as the boys! He felt guilty about it and brought it up for discussion. We knew nothing of this and so were at once horrified and delighted to be awarded the pay rise. Rik is honourable in that way.

Pete Richardson, or 'Mad Pete', was our Clint Eastwood — sometimes literally. Brooding, lip-chewingly anxious and utterly committed to making films. Single-minded in the extreme. He was always astonished that anyone should want to do anything else. He had been making films with his friends and family at his mother's farm on Dartmoor since he was 12 or something. Pete is an unusual man, whose otherness is the foundation on which everything good he does is built. He didn't really seem to have watched telly, so he didn't have the same references as the rest of us. His natural ability for parody was mainly film-based, or if there was a reference to TV, it would be to old soaps like *Compact*, or rare, strange TV. He liked to mix up ideas, like when we did a film called *Strike!*. It was about a writer, played by Lexei, being asked to write a movie for Hollywood about the miners' strike. So, there were lots of levels — as much a comment on LA gloss as it was a chance to do impressions (Jen as Meryl Streep as Mrs Scargill, me as Cher playing Joan Ruddock, Pete as Al Pacino as Arthur Scargill, etc.), as it was a satirical, topical romp.

Pete was always prepared to push us as far as he could to get 'the shot'. Both the crews and ourselves worked ridiculously long hours, some-times sleeping on the set, sometimes for only six hours before we were back on again. I can't imagine doing that now, or even asking a crew to do that, but we all loved it and loved him, so no one really minded. We were young, no one had kids or hatchback cars yet, and anyway, why would we want to go home or have days off when all our best mates were on the set?

A lean and handsome fellow, Pete was wound up as taut as a coiled spring and would lose his temper as quickly as he would become helpless with childish laughter. I was on the receiving end of his irritability once when I took against a last line he'd written to a film I was in, called *Susie*. My character, the eponymous teacher, was, not unusually, a bit of a nymphomaniac and had bonked virtually every guy in the story. In the last scene, after shooting with Ade in a wheat field, I was in an ambulance. The scene required Susie to flirt with the paramedic to prove how irrepressible she was, even in the face of death. It was very funny but the last line was awful and lame, and at the read-through weeks earlier we had all agreed (including Pete) that it needed a rewrite. The moment came to shoot it, the light was fading and it was the last shot of the day. I asked Pete for the rewrite. I had already asked that morning and again at lunchtime. Nothing. He didn't have the rewrite because he had absolutely no intention of rewriting it. I realised this, so was a bit hesitant to insist. He ignored my further request for the new line by looking at me when I asked for it but pretending not to hear me, just looking straight through me. It was a very weird, defiantly stubborn thing to do. The atmosphere in the tiny ambulance with all of us crushed inside was electric. Everyone knew this was a stand-off. We were all in such close proximity, the tension was hard to ignore. On Pete's command, the ambulance started to move, and he called for 'Action!' I did the scene exactly as written, until the very last line, whereupon I paused, looked at camera and smiled. All in character. But I did *not* say the awful line, whatever it was. Pete shouted, 'Cut!' and then said, 'You seem to have left off the last line, Dawn', in a strict geography-teacher sort of manner. I repeated that I was not going to say the line, that it was bad, and would let the whole film down, as we had *all* agreed. He studiously ignored me and called for the shot to commence again. 'Action!' Again, I stuck to the script till that last moment, then I said, 'La la la la la la la.' Pete shouted, 'Cut!' The ambulance stopped again and Pete asked me to step outside to 'discuss' it. The crew were silent. I climbed out of the ambulance onto the country road where Pete was waiting, red with rage about this mutiny. The veins on his neck were visibly pulsating his fury, and his eyes were blazing. The 'discussion' very quickly escalated from some pretty muscular accusations to full-on squaddie-style loud streams of obscenities (from both of us) until suddenly, Pete started to poke me hard in the shoulder screaming the repeated chant: 'You will say it! You will say it!' I replied, just as loudly: 'No I won't! No I won't!' The poking became pushing, pushing became shoving, shoving became tussling which took us off the side of the road into a field of corn where we had a proper wrestle (hilariously echoing the scene we had just shot in the wheat field), just like I used to do with Gary except without the laughing and the drool. A genuine fight, an actual ruck! Eventually we both stood up, brushed ourselves off and he hissed one final seething 'You will say it!' I so much wanted to stand firm and respond with an equally decisive 'No I won't', but the spat had unnerved me, and woken up the latent girly girl inside me who decided it was a good time to cry. Bugger and bollocks! Just when I wanted to be tough. So the tears streamed down my face, while Pete had a quick drag on a roll-up and then went back to the ambulance. I composed myself as best I could, readjusted my wig and climbed back in. I sat in my place. There was no air, just tension, and I said, 'I will say the appalling line, Pete, but then I will go back to the hotel and leave immediately.' We still had four more days of shooting so I knew that would scupper the film. He looked me straight in the eye and said, 'Action!' I started the scene, but the lovely cameraman, my friend Peter Middleton, stopped the filming and told us that the light had gone, and on top of that, my face was too blotchy from the crying, that it wasn't continuity and it wouldn't cut together. Pete gave up with a groan, and we drove back to the unit base in a silent huffy huff. Once out of costume, I headed back to the hotel, hell-bent on packing and leaving. Of course, Pete came into my room to placate me and eventually we sat on the bed apologising to each other profusely for such revoltingly childish behaviour. We went to the bar for a drink and, naturally, continued the filming the next day. Incidentally, the last moment in *Susie* is the first take, the look to camera, the smile . . .

The episode served to confirm to me Pete's complete passion for our films. He is one of those people who is nine parts genius to one part knob, and he is one of my closest friends. I almost love the knobby part of him the most. Not his actual knob, you understand, just the part that is a bit of a knob.

Nigel Planer was always a really good actor. He is now also a poet and a writer, but back then I only knew him as an actor, and as a colleague of course. He was the most fastidious of us all, employing proper techniques to find his characters — like getting the shoes right and caring a lot about the costume, and learning the bloody lines! He is attentive to his health and well-being and he didn't get drunk as often as many of us. Nige is kind and sensitive and willing to take a risk. He can play small and subtle and real as easily as he can choose bigger broader strokes, as he did in *The Young Ones*, which meant that he could play literally *any* part. And he did.

Alexei is a force of nature. I smile immediately when I think of him. Back then, he enjoyed his reputation as a larger-than-life, prickly firebrand. An angry political comedian. A spitting, shouting, foul-mouthed commie ranting on about evil social workers and the loathsome middle class. Oo-er, he was a bit scary. True, his

310

stage persona, which was a heightened representation of his real self, *was* aggressive, but hey, this
was the era of punk and retro-ska and two-tone
and skinheads. Lexei was all of that and more.
His physicality is the first thing you notice. Sort
of angry panda. He is Russian in physique.
Muscular and hairy and yet strangely light on his
feet. He's a good dancer, agile and very musical.
He is highly intelligent, widely read, good at art,
good at writing, good at jokes, good at driving.
He is an intriguing mass of lovely contradictions;
he seems to be a big sulky bear but actually he
has great patience. He looks like a fighter but is
in fact a peacekeeper. He appears to be angry
when in fact he is often perfectly content. He is
thought to be motivated mainly by politics, but
actually he is just as comfortable with the silly
and the surreal stuff of life. He looks like he
wouldn't give a toss when in truth he is a
thoughtful and attentive friend. He is a tart for a
laugh, and when he does laugh, it's big and
round and full. Consequently he's the sort of
person you *want* to make laugh. You want his
approval, his generous warmth wrapped around
you. He is quite shy at times and so it can take
some trial and error to creep into his affections,
but when you're there, it's grand. Lexei was to
be the conduit through which I was to meet Len,
although of course I couldn't know that back
then.

Ben Elton was unbelievably supportive to us,
always encouraging us to try new material and to
be brave. He was prolific, coming up with acres
of his own new gear every night and absolutely

no one matched his writerly ability. Passionate, determined and hardworking, he forged his own unique path with breathtaking force and commitment. He didn't consider himself an actor, I don't think, but he is certainly one of the most powerful stand ups I've ever witnessed. As for his writing, his huge successes both in print and on stage speak volumes about how popular his particular brand of incisive comedy is.

Robbie Coltrane joined us for the films and very quickly became a regular because we couldn't face filming without him. He made us laugh like no one else on set. His big, chippy, Scottish style was so different to everyone else. He played around a lot on set and yet, on camera he is clearly in utter control. He was the one who had big feature film-sized presence. Shame he's got such a small cock . . . in comparison to his magnificently impressive body I mean, of course.

Keith Allen was a reluctant member of our team. He was torn between enjoying the work and the company, and his ever-demanding need to appear cool. Being part of our group was so *not* cool. He was a solitary, renegade, lone wolf of a figure and the thought of an association with us was so obviously abhorrent. However, he was, I think, very fond of Pete and when he deigned to take a part, he was always very good because he is such a talented actor. Keith's desire for a reputation as a bad boy was a key factor in his demeanour. He decided, somewhere along the line, to be a threat so that's how he presented himself. He relished the disruptive power of turning up unannounced at the Comic Strip and

312

setting up his band without so much as a by-your-leave while somebody was mid-act. It must have been exhausting to be so Keith Allen.

Arnold Brown was one of my favourite people of that time in the eighties. He's a Scottish comedian in a tidy brown suit and tie. He had been an accountant for most of his adult life and was giving comedy a go at a much later age than the rest of us. He stood out. In a good way. His comedy was gentle and self-deprecating. He spoke quietly. He was then — and still is — a fabulous oddity and a truly funny man. He didn't join us on the films because he didn't really do the acting thing — his strength is live stand-up. I recall, though, his enthusiasm for our double act and his encouraging me to listen to tapes of Gert and Daisy which he found for me, alongside Mike Nichols and Elaine May improvising on albums. Listening to both of these double acts was a revelation to me. I realised that a relaxed, truthful representation of a friendship, however odd it may be, is the key factor in any long-standing, successful double act relationship.

So, Dad, that was the line-up of people I spent the best part of 20 years working with. People who are, for the most part, still my good friends today. People who helped shape who I am, and who directed me towards a greater understanding of just how bloomin' lucky I was to have such a great living. All that stuff you and Mum used to gently tell me off for, like being loud and showing off and being attention-seeking — guess what, Dad? That's my job!

Dear Dad,

When the live Comic Strip show was at its height, people I admired came to see it, people you knew of and appreciated, like Peter Cook and Michael Palin. I was stunned every time I was introduced to folk such as these, my comedy heroes. I remember sharing with Michael Palin the fact that we had received a bad review in the London listings mag *Time Out*, which I found very hurtful. He told me about the initial, appalling reception he'd had from the press for virtually every job he'd ever embarked upon, especially for *Monty Python*, and said to take heart, which I most certainly did. I have since endeavoured to avoid all reviews of any live work, until the very last night when I enjoy a little ritual of reading 'notices' with a glass of rum when I get home, after the party, when the whole shebang is put to bed. By this time the reviews can't hurt me or influence me or even puff me up, and if there is anything useful there for me to take forward to the next job, I can take it in. Reviews for TV work are different. The job is done, the show is made and usually my involvement is over by months. I will have watched it, maybe edited it, and so I have already formed my opinion of what I like or dislike about it. A review is handy for the audience perhaps, but even then you know very quickly if an audience enjoy something because they continue to watch, or not, and that's reflected in the viewing figures. The response is that tangible, that quantifiable. I learned a big lesson when the first series of *The Vicar of Dibley* received one memorably vile review which was especially personal about me. When the same series was repeated later in the year, the exact same fool wrote a glowing review claiming that Richard Curtis and I must have taken heed of his previous comments because this second (so he thought) series was much better, blah blah . . . I also have a clear memory of inviting reviewers to see a preview episode of an anthology series of comedy films I made in the eighties called *Murder Most Horrid*. I had worked so hard on it for a year or so, and here was the big Judgement Day. We hired a posh room and set up a screening. There were refreshments for everyone, a buffet and drinks. It was about 11am. As more reviewers tipped up, I started to notice what was happening. They fell upon the buffet like starving gannets and sloshed back the drink like camels fuelling up for a Saharan crossing. By the time we started the film, a good third were already asleep and those that graced us with their attention had egg on their ties and dried dribble on their many chins. Was this who I had been so scared of? I decided then and there not to mind any more what they wrote.

Anyway, sorry, meandered off-piste and up my own bum there. I was telling you about the various remarkable folk who came to watch us at the Comic Strip. One night, I heard very loud, distinctive, deep, rolling laughter in the audience. It was constant, throughout the show. This was the kind of big infectious laughter you crave when you're a comedian. You hunger for it. If chuckles are canapés, this was a bacchanalian feast. Someone generous-spirited was *really* enjoying the performance. We all felt it, and it was lovely. That person turned out to be Lenny Henry. He and Chris Tarrant were in to see the show, and especially to see Fatty and me because they were doing a new, late-night, adult version of *Tiswas* called *O.T.T.*, and were looking to cast some women. Don't get me wrong, I loved *Tiswas* but I found Len a bit loud, too broad, for my taste. They came backstage. I don't really remember much about it except thinking what a huge, impressive-looking man he was. To this day, he remembers every word of that first meeting and can repeat them back to me, as a kind of torture, doing a far-too-accurate impression of the much younger, misguided me who was at pains to explain that 'we take ages to write our stuff, yeah? And I'm not sure we could be involved with a show where we aren't, like, totally in control of it, we're just not going to do that, OK? And we don't want to be token women, right, that's not what we are, we're not just token, we actually *are* women and that's not really the point anyway, cos we're performers, not women, and anyway, if there's gonna be women in bikinis we wouldn't honestly be involved anyway. Cos it's demeaning. Sorry.' Yes, that is how much of a pretentious arse I was back then.

I didn't come across Len again till maybe a year or so later when Alexei was in a TV show called *Whoops Apocalypse* which was filmed in front of a live audience at London Weekend Television. I went along with my friend Angie to support Lex and while we were waiting in the queue, I felt a tap on my shoulder and it was Len with his friend Davey who had also come to see Lex. Of course, by then they were good friends because Lexei had gone on to do *O.T.T.*, the show I had been so very sniffy about. So, we started chatting in the queue and ended up sitting next to each other in the studio. Throughout the show, I witnessed the close-up phenomenon of that big laughter I had heard before at the Comic Strip. Len loves comedy. He is the most effusive audience member I've ever known. He can't help it. If something tickles him, and plenty does, he just surrenders to fits of joyous laughter, longer and louder than anyone. It's a wonderful thing.

Something else, parallel, was going on that evening. My friend Angie was getting on *very well indeed* with Len's mate, Davey. They were flirting a-go-go. After the show, it was obvious the two of them wanted to go on somewhere else, to have a drink, so really, Len and I tagged along like lemons. Or is it gooseberries? Well, like some kind of tart fruit anyway.

We went to a bar and had a few drinks then Angie suggested we all went back to the flat I shared with my friend Gaynor in Paddington.

She was the leaseholder and I was the tenant. I had taken over the back bedroom from my Welsh friend Lyn when he'd moved out and I couldn't believe my luck because it was so swanky. It was small but smart, with a balcony that looked out over leafy Cleveland Square. Gaynor was a precise, neat person, which is why the flat was so lovely and clean. Along with clean came rules, of course, which were pretty stringent, but it was her place so I tried to abide by them. No noise late at night, clean kitchen, clean bathroom, clean living room, clean cat-litter tray, etc. Gaynor was a teacher, but she was much more diligent than I'd ever been, and went to bed early each evening with earplugs in to get a good night's sleep. I was always tiptoeing around in a concerted effort not to disturb her. I enjoyed living in that flat, but I never entirely relaxed in it. Sometimes Gaynor went home to her family at weekends and I knew she wasn't there on this particular night, so it would be OK for the four of us to go back.

By the time we tumbled into the flat, it was pretty obvious Angie and Davey were hot to trot, and before long they had commandeered my bedroom. Len and I were left to chat on the sofa with the giggles and shrieks of their fun time as the sound-track to our evening. We were both a bit awkward at first, but then, slowly, we chatted and relaxed. It was so revealing, Dad. I was witnessing a whole other side to him, the quiet, bright, interested person he really is. Quite serious and, even more unbelievably, shy. We talked and talked and talked. It must have been four in the morning or so when we realised the bedroom had been silent for some time. They must have fallen asleep in there. We were also pretty weary, so I pulled out the sofa bed in the living room, and we camped down on that. It was all so innocent. Two gooseberries taking comfort in each other's company, that's all.

By morning, I was in giant love with him. In proper, big, marvellous, astonishing love. It completely shocked me, Dad, how in tune we suddenly seemed to be. I hadn't experienced anything like it before. Most wonderful of all, he seemed to feel the same and didn't want to leave. We both knew that something very big had happened. It was so sudden. So deliciously unexpected.

The other two had to be up and out but Len lingered on and I made a huge fry-up with the full works. He has never forgotten this breakfast, he remembers exactly what was on the plate and where!

He didn't leave the flat for the best part of a week. The morning of the breakfast, I was due to write with Fatty, but my head was in a spin and I totally forgot about the arrangement we'd made. She knocked on my front door and, seeing that it was her through the peek-hole, I opened the door half an inch and hissed, 'Go away!' She said, 'Don't be silly, let me in, what's going on?' I replied, 'Can't explain, can't work today, fallen in love, go away, sorry', and shut the door! Never before or since have I been so rude to her. But Len and I were genuinely in a love-fug, and I didn't want anyone to interrupt it, especially *not*

Jennifer who I always have regarded as an utter beauty and far preferable to me for any guy. Somewhere in the back of my insecure mind, I thought that if he met her, he would surely love her instantly, and I wanted to hang on to him even if it were only for a few more deluded days. This was a preposterous theory, they would have been an utter mismatch and I should have known better. I do now, but we all have little blips of self-doubt and that was one of mine. Luckily we are close enough, Fatty and me, for her to overlook this strange behaviour, and frankly, in the Book of Jennifer, a day where work is cancelled is a good day!

In that week, Gaynor got used to seeing Len around the flat. It wasn't easy because the flat was small and Len himself isn't exactly petite. In fact, let me describe him for you, Dad. He's about six foot two inches, very powerfully built, with a big chest and strong arms. His arms are amazing. They're long and wrap around me easily and that's no mean feat. He's got big hands (HURRAH! — thank you, God!) and the best legs I've ever seen on any man (with the possible exception of Gary Lineker . . . but . . . actually, no), long and sturdy, with much might in them. He is a sort of reinforced-looking person physically; he appears to be made with RSJs instead of bones. He is solid and strapping, which I love. When you're a big woman like me, you need a man who won't break. Len won't break. And his face, Dad, his lovely face. It's broad and open with appley cheeks and the most excellently expressive eyes, and a beautiful soft mouth. If he wants to, he can do things with his face that would persuade you to believe it's made entirely of rubber. He can move it about like a human shouldn't be able to, which led me to believe that perhaps he *wasn't* entirely human. Perhaps he hails from a long line of super-human rubbery-faced people, a notion he would love since his biggest heroes are indeed superheroes. Except Richard Prior. Usually, though, his face is in repose, and he maintains a lovely calm, quite serious demeanour. So much so that people often shout at him, 'Cheer up, Len!' The one thing he can't do with his face, though, is lie to me. If I need to know something, anything, and I ask him, his face speaks volumes he can't control. Of course, that doesn't mean he hasn't got or can't keep secrets, but if asked outright, he is an open book. It's like he's brimful of honesty and it overflows onto his face all the time.

Another important physical attribute, probably the most impressive, is his marvellous, incomparably fabulous bum, but it feels inappropriate to tell you about the many virtues of that, so I'll spare you . . .

That's Len physically, but Dad, what a tip-top chap he is. It sounds so trite to say I wish you could have known him, but I do so wish that. I don't waste my time dwelling on it but there is no doubt that, apart from Gary, you and Len have been the most important men in my life, and I would have had so much pleasure witnessing you discovering each other. I think both of you would have laughed a lot and I also

321

think you would have been quick to spot the softer, perhaps more troubled places in Len, and you would surely have been a good listener for him. But, hey-ho, that ain't how it turned out. The really wonderful thing, Dad, is that I often hear your advice in my subconscious, so maybe vicariously you are still influencing our lives in some significant way. Who knows? You certainly set the bar for me, as so many dads unknowingly do for their daughters. I knew I wanted a man who was as kind and supportive as you, and I certainly have that. Len is a gentle soul. He hates conflict and will do anything to avoid it. He is extremely romantic and continually surprises me with new ways to express his affection. He writes the most fantastic, moving poetry. He is a voracious reader and consequently has a really broad palette of knowledge and taste. The same applies to music, which is in every molecule, every atom of his body. He especially loves hip hop but he will listen to Radio 3 and get passionate about a symphony and listen to only that for a week. He loves blues, soul, jazz, rap, reggae, swing, grime, dance, jazz-funk, pop, rock, not country so much but Dolly Parton is allowed, not indie really, definitely not Dean Friedman (he 'lost' all my DF albums in one house move. I still haven't forgiven that). He can listen to acres of Brian Eno mood music and other strange soundscapes, or chanting or liturgical music, or world music, while he reads. He plays the piano really well. He has an amazing voice. He has a band. He has great taste in suits. He always carries a bag on his shoulder that is heavier than his own body weight. He loses stuff all the time. He's clumsy and he breaks things. He doesn't like pets but he has loved all of our dogs more than he cares to admit. He has enormous feet and has to have his shoes made. He smells great. He gets very dry skin and rubs coconut or almond oil all over. He can do a very funny dance featuring his privates. He loves movies. All kinds. He hates *Big Brother*. He is open to learning new stuff. He actively pursued the education he'd been deprived, starting when he was in his twenties, taking O levels while doing a summer season in Blackpool. He followed that with an Open University degree and now he's doing an MA. He writes all the time. He is a great dad. He strives to be a better person, always. He investigates his inner, spiritual life. He loved and still loves his beloved mum. He values his family. He loves wine. He loves food. He cooks. He loves Sundays. He loves kissing . . . and stuff. He loves his daughter till he's in pain. He doubts himself. He is not afraid to fail, and learn from it. He drives too fast. He gets lost a lot. He leaves the cooker on. He leaves the back door open (burglars, ignore please). He gets lonely easily. He lives and breathes stand-up comedy. On occasion, he's quite grumpy. He will help anyone. He's a Commander of the British Empire. Sometimes we refer to him as 'Commander'. He can ride a horse. He can play tennis. He will NOT swim until he's ready. He's curious. He loves Bootsy Collins. He loves Cerebus. He loves all things Neil Gaiman. He loves *The Sopranos*. And *The Wire* and *Entourage*. He fancies Judi Dench and Sinéad Cusack and Jessica Lange. He does the school run with no complaint, ever. He reads Harry Potter books aloud, doing all the voices. He knows lots of good jokes. He is a great, great man. A big, great, dignified, bright, beautiful man.

The first time I saw him perform, in about '82, I'd gone with him to a gig at an army base and we were held up in traffic en route so he was late. The crowd of squaddies were baying for his blood and were chanting racist stuff. It was a horrible, aggressive atmosphere. He came on to the tiny stage and within five minutes he was utterly, masterfully in control of a potentially explosive situation. Anyone who continued to pipe up was very quickly dispatched with a clever put-down. It was totally his room and he made them laugh solidly for an hour, until they were calling for encores. Of course, I'd seen plenty of comedians work, but all the lads I knew worked in comedy clubs where the audience were usually receptive. Len's apprenticeship was in working men's clubs and nightclubs where he was eighth on the bill so he had to learn to win people over, and be heard above the din.

Eventually, after a few messy moments, when we both had to extricate ourselves from relationships we were in, we 'came out' as a couple to our friends and family and did lots of introducing. By then, I was living in a house in Goldsmith Avenue in Acton, with Fatty. Len was much better known than me, and that's when I got my first taste of unwanted press attention when a couple of photographers loitered around in front of the house for a week or so, taking pictures of us coming and going. I found it excruciatingly embarrassing. I still do. He's always handled it better than me. He is obliging and courteous but brief. The only time I've seen him lose it was when press people were shoving our daughter and he couldn't abide that. What good dad would?

A key moment in those early days was when Len took me home to meet his mum, the remarkable Winnie, or 'Momma'. What a woman! As tall as Len, she towered over me — the whole family did. It was like walking into some kind of Jamaican episode of *Land of the Giants*. Len is one of seven siblings. The eldest is Hylton, who is an impressive six foot six, a benevolent, soulful fellow. Then comes Seymour, a true Jamaican with a passion for his homeland, always with a new plan hatching, cooking up some ism or schism. Then there's Bev, the spiritual, bountiful mother figure, the respected, wise older sister, the focal point in the family. Then Kay, the generous, ambitious, determined, tenacious, career-minded, spunky sister. She was the one who made Len pretend to be Paul McCartney, her hero, so's she could get hitched to him in a play wedding when they were eleven or something. Then comes Lenworth George, the first to be born in England. Then Paul, the younger brother, who lives in a small town outside Dublin, who is funny and observant, a brilliant chef and a writer. Then the baby,

Sharon, or the 'Queen of the Mad Bitches' as she likes to be known. She is a supremely bright young woman with a sharp tongue, coruscating wit and a degree in minxiness. And that's the Henry Posse, who were headed up by Momma, an extremely powerful force of a matriarch.

She told me that in the fifties she had travelled alone on a boat to England, following the lure of the promises made to so many Jamaican people, of amazing jobs and fortunes to be made in the UK. She lived in grey old Shepherd's Bush, and shared a room where she slept in the bed at night and someone else who did night shifts slept in it during the day. Imagine, coming from the bright warmth of Jamaica where fruit grows on trees by your back door, to rainy Shepherd's Bush where it doesn't, and where she had various menial jobs. She put in long hours of back-breaking work and suffered a great deal of abuse on the streets. In the end, she headed up to Dudley to settle near family members who had already secured jobs in factories there. She went without, saved her wages and gradually, one by one, she brought all of her Jamaican-born kids over to join her. She gathered her brood and her husband to her and went on to have three more children on British soil. She had always worked hard and I loved the evidence of that in her huge hands. She was very proper with me, right from the off, and made me feel welcome. Momma ordinarily spoke with a strong Jamaican accent but she sometimes used to temper it with careful, posh pronunciation to help me understand her. When I first knew her, she used to get the best china out for me. That nonsense stopped pretty quickly when I, thankfully, passed the Momma test, which I think was set for any potential incomers. She was an amazing cook and she sat me down at her table where I was presented with 'mi dinna', which was a plate piled about a foot high with rice and peas, curried goat, salad, plantain, okra, fried chicken and cucumber, with slices of buttered sourdough bread on the side and a 'nicecoppatee'. I did not hesitate. My task was clear. Eat it all or leave now and never return. I was undaunted. The grub was delicious, and I set about it. It took some time and a few rest breaks, but I did it. A clean plate — save a few bones. I passed. I was in. Momma and I always got along. So long as Len and I were happy, she was happy. She visited us many times and I have the most touching films of her wandering around our garden on Len's arm. This film is precious because she was diabetic and when complications with ulcers later set in, both of her legs were eventually amputated and she was confined to a wheelchair. She was an enthusiastic born-again Christian, and when I think of her, I remember her in her smart dresses, her Sunday best, wearing her special hats proudly like crowns, beatific in the bliss of her beliefs. Her faith was awesome, solid and unflinching, and sustained her through a prolonged and painful illness. We would visit her in hospital where Len and Billie, who was then about seven years old, would read aloud from the Bible while I moisturised those strong unforgettable hands. The same hands that held

Billie when she was a newborn and were bigger than the baby's whole body. Strong, safe capable hands. We held her hands often while she spoke, without fear, about her inevitable, imminent, sacred and holy delivery into Christ's hands.

I sometimes wonder how it works after death — does this notion of a welcoming committee exist? If so, were you on Momma's welcoming committee? Was there a heavenly reception for her with a soaring celestial gospel choir, where she was offered her favourite drink, Guinness punch, made with Guinness and condensed milk and nutmeg, where she could sip on Saturday Soup and eat hot peppers from the jar and where she would have her beloved Jesus? And legs! And she could look down and say, 'Oh good, I've got legs again — I haven't had legs since Whoppie killed Philip. It's very nice.' I do hope so.

The day I missed you more than any other day, Dad, was our wedding day. It was bloody fantastic! By then we were living in Sinclair Road, Shepherd's Bush, in our first ever joint home, a little basement flat that backed onto the nuclear train track. We had a brass bed and a cat called Aretha who was the Greta Garbo of cats. Gorgeous but unavailable. Len bought her for my birthday, which was a selfless thing to do since he openly loathes pets, especially cats. I very much enjoyed teasing him about 'the correct way' to introduce a cat to its home. I told him that a tried and tested way to stop her running off was to smear butter on her bum and lick it off. His face crinkled into a rugose mask of horror, as he digested this information. I explained that it was just replicating what the mother cats did, that it would be over quickly, that everyone who had a cat did it and to hurry up. He considered it for a good minute and was about to do it, but I couldn't keep a straight face long enough to see it through. I also knew I wouldn't want to kiss him if he did that.

Anyway, the day of the wedding drew close and the excitement mounted. I had, stupidly, decided to embark on a ridiculous diet. For some reason, I didn't think it was OK to be a fat bride. What was I doing?! Another momentary lapse of judgement, due to insecurity I guess, but anyway, I had started a rigorous regime which involved paying a fortune to a Harley Street charlatan, getting injections of what I later realised was probably speed, taking orange and green pills (probably more speed — I didn't ask) twice a day and only eating meat and citrus fruit. By the day of the wedding, 20 October 1984, my body had really eaten itself. I was down from a bonny size 20 to a starving size 12, and my breath stank like a decomposing cadaver from all the rotting meat inside me. Yeuch. Len had asked me to stop and questioned who I was doing it for. He reassured me that he loved me the way I was and was concerned for my health. Still, I continued till the actual day, and my friend Sue who made my dress (an inspired combination of shepherdess and whore, realised in champagne satin, net and ribbon — well, it was the eighties) had to take it in twice. The whole time I dieted, I was obsessed with thoughts of food, and I couldn't wait to get to the reception to EAT.

On the day, I got ready at our flat. The mums, so different, tall and short, chalk and cheese, went off in a big car, the BF and the bridesmaids — Len's nieces Babette and Donna — went off in another, and I was left for the last few single-girl minutes with my lovely brother, who was being you, Dad. He poured us both a gin and tonic and urged me to have a few calm moments to gather my thoughts. He wisely reminded me to clear my head of all extraneous fuss and clutter (of which there is plenty for any bride on her wedding day), and to focus on what it was really all about. It was about me and Len, and he told me to concentrate only on that, to look at Len and to be in the moment and remember what I was saying and why and how very important it all was. It was such good advice, which I always try to pass on, because otherwise my memories of that day would have been full of unimportant nonsense about arrangements and shoes and buttonholes, and veils and napkins and cake deliveries. Instead, I remember Len. And his face. And how happy I felt, how in love.

Before we left the flat, Gary made one last, vital check — 'Do you want to go through with it, Moo?' 'Yes. One hundred per cent,' I said. We raised a toast to you, Dad, and off we went, with him at my side walking me up the aisle in St Paul's Church, Covent Garden, towards my old school chaplain, Reverend Gordon Cryer, with the soaring, joyful strains of the London Community Gospel Choir ringing around the beautiful Christopher Wren building. I was aware of all that was happening, but all I saw was Len.

Yes of course a pigeon flew in and shat on people. Yes of course the price was still on the bottom of Len's shoes for all to see when he knelt down, yes of course we were interrupted by the din of the street performers and fire-eaters in the piazza outside, and yes of course Len stood on the train and ripped the dress. That's us, we always get it a bit wrong. We don't do perfect, but I tell you, Dad, that day was as near perfect as I ever want a day to be.

I stored my bouquet, with its traditional sprig of myrtle from the Bishops Garden at St Dunstan's, in the freezer at home while Len and I went off on honeymoon to Kenya. On our return I brought it down to the Blue Monkey church in St Budeaux in Plymouth, and I quietly laid it on the tiny little plot where your ashes are, for you.

Dear Alla,

Thirty minutes ago I was on my feet clapping
like a greedy seal at Sea World, celebrating your
encore at the Hammersmith Apollo. Who would
have thought that 25 years on 4,000 people
would roar for the triumphant return of Yazoo! It
was so touching to see you hand in hand with
Vince, lappin' up the love, and what a bloody
lovely night it was. I was expecting a comforting
retro meander down electro-pop lane among a
bunch of my-agers, only occasionally straining
our middle-aged knees and rising to our feet to
bop along to favourites. Not a bit of it. I'd
forgotten how sharp the art is when you two are
together. Of course, being a techno freak, Vince
is on it with state-of-the-art music technology. It
was cutting edge and performance art-y.
Something about his cool mastery brings out the
supreme soul mistress in you, to cut across his
electric soundscape with your vocal supernature. There were extraordinary moments when
the booming bass was so loud that the vibrations
were commanding my own heart to throb to
their more urgent and syncopated beat. The
walls were thumping and my ears were full of
swirling noise. Everybody was dancing and
sweating and remembering. It was fabulous. We
all tried to sing back at you the songs you gave

us, singing so loudly you would be in no doubt how much we know and love them. Some particular songs we wanted you to sing only as the backing track for our tribal rendition, like 'Only You'.

I watched you in the environment where you are most at home. So easy in front of a mike, being a sexy mofo and exploring the extraordinary shining excellence you are blessed with — your phenomenal, phenomenal voice. Are you ever as amazed with the sound it makes as I am? Does it surprise you when you reach so far inside and find those notes that no one else can make? You are a vocal archaeologist, finding treasures in hidden places and digging them up for our pleasure, then parading them in a bravura display. Is it right that notes are made up of three other notes? Someone told me that once, and tonight it struck me that what I hear with you is all three parts of each note. The top, the middle and the bottom are all there in one glorious whole, a consummate resonance.

Quite besides the utter pleasure of the gig, I watched you with awe. I feel massive pride when it comes to you, and I am properly honoured to be your pal — maybe because I admired you before I knew you.

We met, I think, at a party at the Wag club in Soho in the eighties. I don't know why I was there, though I have a vague memory of the party being something to do with Elvis Costello, who we both knew a bit. Anyway, I remember spying you across the room and getting very overexcited at the nearness of you. After much

333

unsubtle staring, you eventually returned my glance and then we sort of flirted with each other by having a kind of competitive funny-dance-off from a distance. (If I remember it rightly, you started it with your rendition of a silly dance I'd done in *Dirty Movie*, the porn parody we did as one of the Comic Strip films.) How divine it was to enjoy those surreptitious moments with a kindred spirit. No one else was aware of what was going on, just us, in our own little bubble, displaying our comedy feathers to each other like peacocks while carrying on conversations with our individual groups, behaving for all the world like we hadn't just had the synchronised epiphany of finding a fantastic new friend. It wasn't long before we spoke and we haven't stopped speaking since really, have we? Two forceful birds with plenty to say, that's us. A clash and a jangle and a whoop of insistent, persistent friendship. Our time together is so limited that sometimes we speak simultaneously so's we can cover more ground. I speak, you speak; I also listen, you also listen — just all at once! We don't always agree, and we aren't afraid to flesh out a difference of opinion at considerable volume. I love that. The thrust and parry. You find beauty in the small, the detail, the nuance, the insinuation. You are often fascinated by people's carelessnesses and oversights and equally by their generosities and abundances. You are moved by much that happens around you. Maybe that's why your lyrics are so insightful — you notice everything. I am less precise, more of a bletherer, keen to experience everything quickly, soon, now — usually without thinking enough about it first. I am a doer, you are a thinker.

We have been good counsel for each other through many phases, I think. There have been so many times where you have been the one who says the key, opinion-changing, intelligent thing which provides the pivotal moment. The start of the new thinking process. The change of the mindset. When Len and I went through a rough patch, I talked endlessly with my mum, my BF, Fatty, my brother, all of whom were supportive and helpful, in so many ways. But you were the one who spoke to me about what forgiveness really means. How it isn't something you withhold for power purposes if you truly love someone, about what a weight it is, how much lighter you feel the more of it you give away. Give it freely, you said. Not recklessly, make sure to learn from what's happened, but don't amass a backlog of fury because it will kill you. Be generous and understanding and kind. That's what you told me. Don't judge, just heal. Help each other to heal. It was the only thing that made sense to me. It was right, and good advice. You also reminded me of what a remarkable man he is, just at the moment I could have tipped myself, for an inviting wallow, into a vat of Len faults. You nipped that in the bud, which was a tad frustrating at the time. We all enjoy a good self-pitying moan, don't we? But you knew it wouldn't help and would only serve to extend the unforgiving time. The dangerous time in any conflict where one person takes a higher ground from which to do their superior judging. A waste of crucial time when both of us needed to be together, equally, making decisions about how to move on. You reminded me how much Len loves me and you cited literally hundreds of instances when you had witnessed that love. Again, of course, you had noticed the small things, the detail, the numerous subtle gestures, as much as the showy overtures of which there had also been many down through the years. You drew a picture for me of a man I adore, a family I belong in, a world I've invested my life in. Then it was obvious that I should fight to keep it and make it stronger. To concentrate on the important stuff and to ignore the crap. And that's what I did.

We continually share a lot about our kids, you and I, and help each other by reminding ourselves that we are benevolent, well-meaning women just trying to do some good parenting in the face of the frightening tsunami that is teenagehood. On many occasions, we have come to agree that teenagers are selfish little buggers who are, for all their faults, the fundamental point of our lives, the basic underpinning of our reason for being here. *They* are what has made us different and better. *They* are the leaven that has raised us up from being the selfish big buggers we were before they came along! Shit — we realise they are vital and amazing, and we *have* to be annoyed by them because any minute now they will be gone. If we still over-loved them like it was easy to do when they were teeny, the inevitable separation would be so traumatic we

336

would surely collapse and die from utter grief. This way, their behaviour forces us to create a distance, to slacken the ties and allow the disconnection. Let it happen now, so that the eventual uncoupling is gentler, not so much of a heartbreaking tear. They will still be moored to us, just by a long, long, long, long rope.

We often spoke of how much we would love to work together. Work together properly, that is. We had already had a few little jaunts, like the time Fatty and I appeared in your video for 'Love Letters' and when I shook my tailfeather on your 'Whispering Your Name' video. One of my greatest thrills was coming onstage with you at the Albert Hall and shoogling around you like a demented eejit. (I am your comedy dancing puppet, use me as you will, any time.) But as well as all these daft times, we wanted to find a proper opportunity to work together, didn't we? On reflection I've got a feeling that we were simply taking a rather circuitous route towards the basic fact that we wanted more time together. We could have booked a holiday for God's sake, but instead we embarked upon an extraordinary adventure which resulted in us both appearing in a West End play called *Smaller*.

Do you remember the brief? We wanted to commission a piece from a tip-top writer, something that gave us both a chance to flex our muscles (if only we had muscles . . . I haven't had sight of a muscle on this Mr Bumble-ly spherical body I live in for years!), and operate slightly outside the ol' comfort zones. You had done a bit of acting when you did *Chicago* and I had never done any proper singing, and was unlikely to start tormenting an audience with that this late in the day. We knew that the play had to mean something and, without being pretentious, it had to speak to people our age about the complex nature of the relationships women have inside a family. This was a recurring theme in our history and an area we had foraged about in before, fully aware that it was hazardous, stony ground.

To begin with, we imagined it would be a two-hander. Simple and stark. Very early on I called Kathy Burke, my great friend and the most knowledgeable person I know about new writers. She always has her ear to the ground for formidable new talent. Her first instinct was the person we eventually approached, Carmel Morgan, who was part of the award-winning writing team propelling *Coronation Street* towards top plaudits at the time. Kath is a *Corrie* addict, and said that every time Carmel's name was on the credits, the episode was extra muscular, that she seemed bold and unafraid, and properly funny. So, I met up with Carmel, who, by the way, wins the prize for best swearer I've ever met. What a potty mouth. Top. She told me straight away that she had an idea for a play that had been brewing for years, involving two women, a mother and a daughter. The mother, whose life was becoming slowly 'smaller', was in the grip of a powerful degenerative disease, and the play explored the claustrophobic relationship between the mother and her daughter, the carer.

Carmel suggested that she could well add a sister into the mix, your part, and that would bring another dimension she hadn't considered before. Plus you would be providing the music for this play. Not a musical but, rather, a play with music. This meant that you had to write songs specifically for the piece. Songs that would inform the play, and would combine with Carmel's words to give it a raw emotional thrust. Songs that your character would, naturally, sing. I know it takes you time to write and I know it was a tall order, but Alla, the songs you brought to that first rehearsal were unbefeckinlievable. The best I had heard you sing or write for ages.

To begin with, I was reticent about asking Kathy to direct. She has a powerful, clear idea of the work she likes to do, and I know she often likes to be involved in the initial development of an idea, so I feared that this project might be too advanced already for her to want to be a part of it. I called her and reminded her that Carmel had been her suggestion. Both of us were delighted when Kath agreed to oversee the writing process and direct the play.

And so we all started on an equal footing of shared risk and overwhelming excitement. Kathy is a careful and thorough director, who encouraged us to sit and talk about the play for a whole week or more before we got to our feet. By that time we had June Watson on board to play the mother, we had classes on lifting a disabled person, we learned about the wasting disease our mother character had, and we talked endlessly about the confines and the freedoms of this explosive triangular relationship. I watched Kathy slowly and surely convince you that you could act by making you aware of the natural skills you have, and your powerful presence onstage. She winkled you out of your shell of self-doubt with such maternal care. And sometimes, like all good mothers, she was strict with you, with us, insistent that we face our worst fears and deal with them in what was a truly emotional roller coaster of a play.

I remember the day we realised that there was need of an extra song. A really important song that you would sing in the funeral scene when finally the two warring sisters are united in grief for their dead mother. Initially we had thought the music in that part of the play would be something that already existed, some Bach or perhaps a liturgical chant. Kathy knew instinctively it would be better if it was original. Your face on realising that you had to write another song was a study in frustration and fear. It was the very thing you had asked us not to do. To put you under pressure to write a song quickly. You left on the Friday with an air of grump to propel you into the weekend. On the Monday you played us the Catholic funeral hymn you had written in two days, with your buddy Pete Glenister. Alla, that was one of the most splendid moments of my life. What talent. The hymn, a quiet then soaring paean of exquisite love and beauty, a gift from a daughter to a mother, and most importantly a holy and sacred song, reduced me to tears every night I stood next to you and heard it.

I had one other blissful moment like that with you. Do you remember when we went to Jamaica on holiday? You and Malcom and me and Len. What a laugh. Splashing about in the pool noticing our tits were the same size as our husbands' bums, scoring some wacky baccy in the local market and putting it in our tea only to realise it was sage or some such herb; being flirted with on the beach by Rastas calling us their 'heavy babes' and trying to mate with us. Then, most clearly of all, I remember when we went on a lazy raft trip. Len and me in front. You and Malcom on the raft behind. We floated aimlessly down the river in the gorgeous sizzling heat. All was calm and silence till you were taken with an irresistible urge to sing. You sang out, clear and strong, filling the air with magic. I couldn't see you but I could hear you, your beautiful voice, direct from God, providing the soundtrack to a heavenly, perfect moment.

I knew then that, as you often tell me, I would always 'love the bones of you'.

Calling all members of the Lazy Susans,

Greetings. As some of you may already know, I am writing a book, a kind of memoir, in the form of letters. It will be much like an album, I think, offering glimpses, snapshots if you like, that define and describe my life. I cannot conceive of such a book without reference to you, to us, to our highly clandestine society. However, I am, of course, mindful of our strict code of honour, and the need for discretion at all times. I intend to include a photo of us in our very first club outfits, taken at one of our gatherings in about 2002, I think. We do, of course, have new uniforms now, which will *not* appear. I will, without question, adhere to our confidentiality agreement and I will block out the faces of each member so that no identities will be disclosed. It is my utmost intention to preserve the integrity, secrecy and infrastructure of our organisation. I will not, repeat NOT, be revealing details of our passwords, handshakes, colour-coded livery or group rituals — especially not the one involving an axe and a carton of fake blood. I will not be disclosing the ingredients of our secret beverage and I will not be recounting *anything* of our exploits together on this continent or any other where we may, or may not, have met. Like any true Susan, I promise that our assignations and our purpose will follow me to the grave. This I swear on the life of my fluffy kitten heels. If you object to my suggestion, please let me know in the usual way, being careful at all times that you are not followed, or bugged.

Specialis infinitas, pinas coladas,
Dawn Susan

Dear Len,

Really, this book should be called *Dear Len* and simply be one big long love letter to you. It's hard to know how to sum up everything I want to say to you in one letter. We have been married for 24 years now, and we were together a couple of years before that, so half of my whole life is you. You. You. Obviously there are things I can't and won't write about in these pages because we both, but especially you, are quite rightly very private about our life together, but when I think hard about who you are to me, and what I really want to say to you, it is, essentially, thank you.

THANK YOU for filling out the all-purpose, multiple-choice questionnaire I devised for you when we first met. This helped me to ascertain whether you really wanted to eschew all opportunities of bendy dancer girlfriends and go out with a Weeble such as me. It also told me whether you could take a joke or not. You could.

THANK YOU for getting down on your hands and knees and helping me to trim the carpet at Gaynor's very clean flat with nail scissors (all I had) when you had stepped in the cat-litter tray and walked the poo round the whole flat, and she was due home in 20 minutes.

THANK YOU for doing 86 astonishingly accurate impressions of different famous people saying Happy New Year to me on New Year's Eve, and for knowing that, for some reason, New Year makes me gloomy, and I needed cheering up.

THANK YOU for being the kind of person who fell for the lady in the shop's patter and therefore bought the most expensive ring with which to propose. Thank you for wrapping it in six increasingly bigger boxes for added surprise. Thank you for not having a suitable face to go with the moment, so twitching like a demented Disney rabbit in anticipation. Thank you for not minding in the least that the ring has spent 24 years in a safe because it is beyond hideous.

THANK YOU for not chucking me when I took you to a romantic place I told you was 'magical' which turned out to be an old railway carriage set into the dunes on a beach in Cornwall where we were both very cold because it was winter. You kept a huge sheepskin coat on, inside and out. Thank you for making good jokes about not using the loo when stationary. Thank you for patting my back when we spent most of the week vomiting because we ate the stew my mum had cooked, which we had left in the sun on the back shelf of the car, and then refroze. Which was the wrong thing to do. We both threw up from both ends for days and it wasn't pretty or romantic or even slightly 'magical'. Thank you for still kissing me after seeing sick in my hair.

THANK YOU for taking me to Jamaica to meet your wider family. For not minding when I laughed a lot after you were trying out your best Jamaican accent and the man you were asking directions from just looked and said, 'You is an Englishman.'

THANK YOU for doing a five-month summer season, two shows a day, seven days a week, at the end of the North Pier in Blackpool, to pay for the wedding.

THANK YOU for insisting that all birthdays are celebrated, even when I can't be arsed. I remember when you insisted I go to Le Gavroche posh restaurant on my birthday despite my many protestations that I was too knackered to go out because I was filming. I begged you to let me stay at home and celebrate with a candle in a Big Mac. You persuaded me to go because when my supper arrived under its silver dome it was revealed to indeed be a hamburger with a candle in it, Gavroche-style. It was delicious and the kitchen staff were buzzing with excitement — they'd never ever served a hamburger before.

THANK YOU for buying me a white Pagoda soft-top 1964 Mercedes.

THANK YOU for putting up with the many pets, all of which you hated to begin with, and only three of which you came to love. Aretha the Cat, Delilah the Dog and Dolly the Smaller Dog are winners, but Hale and Pace (goldfish), Rodent (hamster), Oscar (guinea piglet who was eaten by Delilah the Dog on Christmas Day, the day he arrived), Holly (replacement guinea pig bought on Boxing Day), Hoppy (rabbit), Dracula (vampire rabbit) and Stickys 1–23 (stick insects) were *not* beloved by you.

THANK YOU for introducing me to your

friends, especially the Lokshen gang, whose mums cooked you soup when you first came to London on your own at 16 years old. The Haftels and the Greens have always been the most loyal buddies, with whom we have shared much light and any bit of shadow.

THANK YOU for opening up a world of music to me. Music I would never have listened to if I didn't know you. Thanks for all the tapes and CDs you've made, especially those which were for special reasons, like when I did *Smaller* with Alla and every song had something to do with small or little, or songs to celebrate anniversaries or songs with stories or songs with gags or songs that start with talking or songs that start with the letter D.

THANK YOU for not minding too much when, embarrassed and horrified by the price, which we could ill afford, I returned the very early model of a computer you'd bought me as a birthday gift, in 1983, to the shop. Sorry I've never learned to use one yet and thanks for printing things out for me or even occasionally typing things for me. I will catch up eventually. Probably. Will I? No.

THANK YOU for being such a loving son-in-law to my mum, and starting jokes 'My mother in-law is *so* nice', ' . . . *so* genial', ' . . . *so* supportive', and so on. I guess I felt the same way about your mum. The only time it was dangerous to be around them was the regular Christmas Turkey Tussle. We used to cook it very slowly overnight, remember? My mum likes the turkey to be moist but fairly plain with perhaps an onion up its bum for flavour. Your mum would sneak down, yank out the onion, slam in some peppers and a pineapple and cover it in rum; two hours later my mum would creep down and remove all that and replace with an Oxo cube; your mum would later discard that and add chillies and sweet potatoes, and on and on all night. The wars of the mums. Whoever raped the turkey last was the victor, leaving the other one to pout and sulk, lemon-lipped, over the Christmas dinner table. Yuletide joy!

THANK YOU for, unprompted, saying my mum can live with us when she's too old and infirm to change her pants. I've got news for you, she tells me that day ain't never comin'. She would rather live in a pond of her own wee at waist height and shoot at strangers through her letter box than be a burden. Let's see, shall we?

THANK YOU for offering, without hesitation, to let me put our house up as collateral to get the loan to start my big girls clothes business, 1647 Ltd, with my African partner, Helen Teague, in 1991. Still chugging along 17 years later, we haven't made a penny, but we have provided lots of big girls with some decent clobber that fits their bootylicious bums!

THANK YOU for never complaining when endless streams of friends and family come to stay, often bringing further, even more unwanted pets into your life.

THANK YOU for understanding the nature of my very close relationship with my cousins Keiren and Ellie and knowing that I never want to be without them, and so allowing our door to

348

be open to them at all times of night and day. Sometimes people are placed in our lives for a purpose and these two have 100 per cent been given to me so that I may learn about the profundity of family love. (Are you and Keiren going for some kind of world record when it comes to memory tests about old movies and music, by the way? Is that what boys do when they're alone together?) Thing is, you see, I looked out for them a bit when they were younger and now they return the favour and look out for our kid. There is a natural symmetry in it all.

THANK YOU for your patience and understanding and total commitment to the endless rounds of heartbreaking IVF failures we endured together, while quite often simultaneously celebrating yet more arrivals of new babies in the lives of our chums. The sneaking in and out of clinics, often at night, to avoid press interest. The discoveries of various problems, on both sides. The support we gave each other. The awful, painful injections you had to administer to me at home and your sweet crinkled face, so reluctant to hurt me with them, but so determined to try and make it work. The isolation of not being able to speak about it to others, for fear of alerting the media. The endless prescribed todger-tugging for samples and specimens. The jokes about it. The miscarriages and the grieving. Two of us quietly forging ahead together in our great yearning for a baby. The giving up. The reawakening. And then, the uphill adoption process. The hours of interviews, the reports, the questions, the counselling and the minute scrutiny of our marriage by strangers. The intrusion. The enforced dieting, the breath-holding and, eventually, the utter joy. Thank you so much for being such a mensch through it all. We sailed together in one small boat on this most private and personal sea of troubles, safeguarding each other throughout. We brought a baby back to a united and happy home.

THANK YOU for being such a genuinely great dad. For breaking a mould and being the kind of dad you had no example of, for making it up as you went along. For holding fast through terrible twosomeness tantrums which lasted ten years and immediately turned into tricky teenage tantrums, most of which appeared to involve the exact same dialogue.

THANK YOU for reminding me that, 'every day, clean slate'.

THANK YOU for riding the bucking bronco that is a household of hormonal women when you are the lone chap.

THANK YOU for doing so much devoted parent stuff during all those nights I couldn't be there when I was onstage. I've counted up the evenings of my absence from bedtimes since Billie turned up. It's over two years' worth. You had all those evenings on your own with her and you never once complained. Thanks for giving her that unquestionable security, the surety of her dad's love. I, for one, know just how important that is as a foundation for every other relationship she will have. She doesn't know it yet, but she will.

THANK YOU for telling me the truth when, like most marriages, ours was buffeted by a tornado. There's a reason we vow to love each other for better and for worse. It's because there will always be a *worse*. Otherwise how do you know what the better is? Or the even better? Ironically, I think you and I have always shared a kind of unspoken misbehaviour gauge, below certain levels of which much naughtiness is excusable and fairly harmless. We work apart a lot, we meet interesting attractive people and they are interested in and attracted to us. Some stuff's gonna happen and mostly, so long as no one is hurt or embarrassed, it's unimportant and ignorable. I genuinely believe that. We are, none of us, robots or perfectly perfect people. We are flawed and weak and tempted. Often. What compounded the situation in this particular instance was that certain facets of the press decided to whip up an infidelity maelstrom. You had made some grave errors of judgement, yes. It was frightening and humiliating to be door-stepped in the night by two journos in macs who I was convinced were police. You were driving home from a gig that night, so when I saw them I thought that they were here to tell me you had died in some awful crash. Instead, they were at my door to gleefully dump their buckets of sleaze and schadenfreude on me. Oddly, I was relieved! I thought you were dead. You weren't dead; you were just careless and a bit daft. No one wants to hear bad news like this, and no one wants the entire country to hear it, and worse, no one wants the entire country to hear a bizarre, and in

351

so many instances, fabricated version of it. BUT we are in the public eye, and when you trip up, unfortunately everyone's going to know about it. What the public never, *ever* get to hear is the *entire* truth with all its twists and turns, so there is rarely a balanced account of anything so hotly gossiped about. In an effort to lure us out of the silence we chose to keep, several newspapers ran supposed 'Exclusive Interviews' where we were both apparently quoted verbatim. Since neither of us has ever spoken to anyone about it, those brazen lies really shocked me. That they were willing to go that far down lies lane. I guess we all know it happens but, like the old cliché, until it happens to you, you ain't got a clue. Meanwhile, we were forced into a strange utter-cards-on-the-table kind of congress at home, both of us. We needed to know every single incident, harmless or otherwise, from 16-odd years of marriage, so's we could be armed against the bomb attack. It actually became quite tedious recalling any tiny or big moment that could be construed or exaggerated or reported in any form that would harm or threaten our life together. We started to invent wild scenarios to keep our interest up, remember?! The most remarkable thing was that, once again, our natural instinct was to pull tighter, towards each other, unite, hold hands and walk through the storm together. There was no single moment when separation was a possibility. Quite the opposite was the case. We needed to remind each other what was worth fighting for, and my darling Bobba, you really are worth fighting for. The most terrible thing about the whole palaver was that it had all come at a time when you were already feeling a bit midlife-sad, your mum had died and you were in the grip of that slippery old snake, grief. You had thrown yourself into too much work, both TV and touring, and you were knackered. All of this humiliating shit publicity on top of already feeling shit made life shit to the max. That's when you had a total wobble and I knew you needed to talk to someone, to work out what was really wrong. To see if you could work your way through some pretty challenging self-doubt and consequent destructive choices. That's when you went into the Priory, which was the last place on earth I would have wished for you to be, believing like so many others that it was a guilt hideout and spa for frazzled pop stars. Of course, the reason so many people go there, mostly unfamous, is because it's frickin' good, simple as that. The main doctor who was recommended to work with you couldn't treat you unless you went there, and we particularly needed his help. The Priory is not a spa, it's a hospital, with many people on the edge of their lives, for one reason or another. You didn't have an addiction, I don't know if you really had a depression in the truest sense of the word, but you certainly had a life-toppling, debilitating crisis of utter, all-consuming sadness and it was awful to see. You firstly needed sleep, proper big long sleep, and you needed to be safe in the hands of someone who could help you unpick the mental mess you were in. You are emotionally bright, you could put yourself back together so long as you could understand why you fell apart. Which you did. Quite quickly. You were hungry to understand, to dissect and analyse huge chunks of your life. It was amazing to witness you logically fitting your personal jigsaw back together. You love reason, you get it. It was a fabulous example of proper help for emotional and psychological trauma. I so wish this was the avenue my own father had been able to take. He struggled on alone with his private torments till it was all too much and he sought his own, tragic way out. You didn't. You took quantum leaps of courage and examined your flawed self, you drew conclusions and made decisions about how to live your life to avoid that sadness as much as possible. That, for me, has been the most remarkable, courageous and bloody brilliant achievement you have had, in what is a life chock-full o' achievements, frankly! I bloody loved your fortitude and your humility and your openness at this frightening time. I saw your phenomenal backbone righting itself and I saw you walk upright again, in the face of much scorn and derision. And certainly the comedy fraternity know how to heap scorn upon a fellow comic. Ouch. So, I thank you for your determination, for not scurrying off, for facing your fears and your mistakes with supreme dignity. I also thank you for, at that time, going to the homes of everyone on both sides of our immediate family and sitting them down to tell them what happened by starting with 'Look, I've been an arse . . . I wonder if you can forgive me?' By dint of that humility, you is SO not an arse.

You is a proper man.

THANK YOU for all the poetry, the letters and the cards. You haven't let a month of our marriage go by without reminding me of something meaningful. You *always* point me towards the bigger picture when, oftentimes, I'm busy doing frantic colouring-in with felt tips in the corner.

THANK YOU for not giving me surprise parties. I would *hate* them.

THANK YOU for always working so hard to keep our family (including the many and various dependants who you also never complain about) ticking over. You have always reckoned you are blessed and that if someone else in your family had been the recipient of the good fortune, they would be looking after you, so it's only right to share. You are so selflessly generous, it sometimes takes my breath away.

THANK YOU for showing such strength in the face of the inordinate amount of racism you experience. Knowing you has shown me a whole raft of mainly insidious, quiet racism that I had no knowledge of before. Those tiny, constant snidey jokes at industry gatherings, like 'I know the invite said black tie, Lenny, but that's taking it too far, sonny' from a much respected older comedian. Strange how the reference to you as 'sonny' is the more painful dart in that jibe. I remember you being interviewed on radio by a presenter who consistently referred to you as 'this little black boy from Dudley' throughout. Stealth racism. Fast and low and quiet. And *always* present. The references to me in the papers as 'his blonde girlfriend'. I've only ever been blonde once, for three weeks. It meant 'his *white* girlfriend'. Of course, we have had the big showy stuff too, the excrement smeared on the front door, the scratching of racist names on every panel of the car, the lit petrol-soaked rag through the letter box, starting a fire on our doormat at 3am. Luckily, I smelt it in time. The many letters with lurid racist obscenities sent to both of us. The most memorable of which came to you at a gig, threatening to kill you after the show because 'you are a filthy cone'. Racists can't spell so well, it seems. Remember when a Jiffy bag dropped through our door and it contained a broken tile with the image of a knight on one side and on the reverse it said, 'You have been visited by the Ku Klux Klan'? No we hadn't. We hadn't been visited. Visitors make themselves known. And stop for tea and cake. People who drop something hateful through your letter box and scurry off into the night aren't called visitors. They're called cowards.

THANK YOU for knowing that, although I am usually resolute, sometimes my strength fails me. Thanks for sensing when.

THANK YOU for coming to Cornwall with me. It's not your home, it is mine. You will inevitably be the only 'black in the village' and you are a long way from the beloved bustle of the city. We will, of course, have dollops of that, when we need or have to, but mostly we will be together quietly, in what I genuinely believe is the most beautiful place on earth, and where I truly belong. It didn't help, did it, when we were first thinking of settling down there and I took you to Padstow to seduce you with delicatessens and Rick Steinyness and great pubs and great music and art and stuff. My heart sank when locals regaled us with stories of their famed annual celebration of 'Darkie Day' . . . where they black up and dance in the streets . . . I knew it would be difficult to reverse out of this arcane cul-de-sac with any iota of reasonable explanation. I tried a pathetic attempt at: 'It's ancient, it's to do with fertility, it's not racist, it's tradition.' 'Yes,' you replied, 'traditionally racist'. But, but, but . . . There is no decent defence. We had some silence. Then I ventured: 'It's a bit like the Black and White Minstrels — you know, sort of odious and outdated but with nil malicious intent.' I had you at that. The Black and White Minstrels? Hadn't you been the first genuine black man to perform with them? I know you hate being reminded of it. I know it's a hideous blip in your past, I know we don't have it on telly any more for VERY GOOD REASON, and Cornwall might be some way behind when it comes to catching up with PC ancient rituals. But . . . you said, 'OK, so what do I do on annual Darkie Day? Do I have to stay indoors? Or will I be burnt for the amusement and general warmth of the gathered townsfolk?' We have yet to see, but anyway thanks for risking life and limb.

THANK YOU for loving me so very well, and for being an all-round tip-topmost chap.

Dear Fatty,

I don't know because I wasn't there, but apparently, there was a man who had an orange for a head. Can you begin to imagine how awkward that would be? Could he see? Could he hear? Was it from Seville or South Africa or Florida? Could he drink the refreshing tangy juice of his own head or is that just too revolting and cannibalistic? Anyway, anyway, anyway, he must have been thirsty because he popped into a pub for a drink. Presumably NOT orange juice, but I don't actually know for sure. Seemingly, as he was ordering this drink, the barman was transfixed by the whole orange-instead-of-a-head thing, and ventured to ask him how it had come to be thus. I think that's a *bit* rude, and I wouldn't have been so nosy, but I'm glad he did, because there was quite a comprehensive answer to his somewhat intrusive question. The orange-head man explained that once upon a time, when he had what's referred to by a narrow-minded society as a 'normal' head, he had been walking down a street, probably on his way home or maybe to work, but I don't know that sort of detail for sure, so don't take it as gospel, and he came across a magic lantern. It was at this point that I began to suspect this story was some kind of elaborate ruse, because

358

honestly, have *you* ever seen a magic lantern? Come on! It just sounds silly and bogus, doesn't it? And how many times do we hear about bloody magic lanterns being the answer to everything? They're not, they are utterly implausible. Anyway, anyway, anyway, shelve the doubt for a second because what happened next was very interesting. The man rubbed the lamp — how predictable. (Would you? I wouldn't, I would try to sell it to a junk shop or on TV to David 'Chips' Dickinson.) And lo and behold, a genie appeared! Right before him. Now, OK. I accept the genie, they have as much right to appear from a magic lamp as anyone, but why oh why is it ALWAYS them? Would it be so very wrong if just occasionally a civil servant, or a refugee, or someone who works for Hewlett-Packard, or an orthodontist, appeared from a lamp? Or an Eskimo? They might even be more use. But no, yet again, this was a genie, as usual, ho-hum, and of course, yep, you're there before me, he only goes and grants the man three wishes, doesn't he? Did you know, by the way, that the unwritten rule about being granted three wishes is that you are forbidden to use any of your wishes to ask for more wishes? I see exactly why they've done that. Very clever. Otherwise you would, wouldn't you — just endlessly top up on your wishes, sort of wish-as-you-go, save one wish back always to use for future wishes. Yep, that would really clog up the remaining, unused wish-availability numbers, and would likely also encroach upon other people's wish quota, never mind the amount of genies who would be out of work. No, it would be chaos. it would never do.

Anyway, anyway, anyway, the man very quickly decided what his three wishes would be. Maybe he was so ready with his choices because he'd always fantasised about it. The way people fantasise about being asked on *Desert Island Discs*. They plan it ahead so's not to be caught out. I haven't personally done that because I have a genuine allergic reaction to Sue Lawley, she actually brings me out in a raised, itchy, angry rash, and I'm not the only one. Of course it's not her any more, is it? Mmm, might be more interesting to consider doing it now it's Kirsty Young who's much cleverer, and frankly, not a twot, but I still don't walk around with a ready list of discs in my head . . . Except . . . Who would I choose? Well, of course there would have to be Alla, probably singing 'Ne Me Quitte Pas' — love that. Louis Prima would be in there with 'Embraceable You', maybe Ella Fitzgerald, Gavin Bryars' album with Tom Waits where the old tramp sings 'Jesus' Love Never Failed Me Yet' over and over again. Mirelle Mathieu, Stevie Wonder, Jessie Norman, Prince, Paolo Conte, Elton John with that amazing 'I Want Love' song where the video was all in one shot with Charlie Chaplin mouthing all the words. Not the real Charlie Chaplin, don't be silly, Robert Downey Jr, the fine actor and former drug addict, of course. Would *have* to have Toots and the Maytals and the Weather Girls with the original 'Raining Men', Eric and Ernie singing 'Bring Me Sunshine' and Joan Armatradings' 'Willow'. And Sinatra, and Elvis of course, ooh but what about Joni Mitchell and Fanny and Dean Friedman and the Beatles and the Fleet Foxes and a bit of Bach and Maria Callas and Jasper Carrott's 'Funky Moped'? It's too difficult. I'm not going to bother with finalising it now. I just can't.

So, anyway, anyway, anyway, the man told the genie his three wishes. First, he wished for his family to be rich as Croesus and they suddenly were. Amazing! Second, he wished for peace in Ireland and there was. Fabulous! He hesitated a little bit before his third and final wish, so the genie asked him why he was deliberating so hard. I wonder if the genie spoke in Arabic. What is the native tongue of genies? I expect they are magically able to make themselves understood in the language of the lamp rubber. There must be some system because it's been working for thousands of years and to my knowledge no one has ever complained of incomprehensible genie babble. So anyway, anyway, anyway, the man answered the genie, explaining that he knew full well what he wanted for his third wish, but that he felt reluctant to say because it was such a selfish wish, something he had always dreamt of, something he had always wanted but never been able to have, till possibly now. The genie encouraged him to say it, to wish for it, after all, he had been a hard-working, good man his whole life, and he had also just donated his first two precious wishes for the benefit of others. He was a truly altruistic human being, the genie told him, so go on, have something for yourself, crack on. The man was eventually persuaded to speak

361

the wish that would make all his dreams come true, that would give his life meaning. In a faltering, trembling voice, he said, 'What I would really truly like, just for myself . . . I would love to have . . . an orange for a head.' Can you believe that?

Dear Sarah,

I've never had a sister, but I always wanted one. Badly. Then my brother married you and suddenly I had one!

Here's what I want to say to you. You are quite simply the best person he could possibly have chosen. He is such a spontaneously emotional man, and when he was younger, I sometimes feared he would let his impetuosity get the better of him and he would choose someone wildly wrong. But he didn't. He chose you. And you are so perfectly right. Your tolerance, your patience and your optimism are the gifts I'm so grateful to you for, because inside your love, my brother has come to know and trust how loved he truly is. He carried a heavy load at too young an age from the moment our dad died, and with you he can share that and be lighter. You have been there, side by side with him, through lots of potentially scary decisions. I know your support gives him courage. Please don't ever for a second think I don't notice that. Can I thank you, too, for making my favourite niece and nephew and letting them come out to play with me so often? How sublime it is to know that we will all be there for each other whatever happens . . . (Unless of course you murder someone, in which case I won't be there for you at all. I will show no mercy or forgiveness and I will reject you and all your family in a heartbeat. Otherwise, I'll be there for sure.)

I thank God for you, and I love you.

Your sister-in-law

Dear Richard,

Been watching the news? Big hoo-ha about the possibility of female bishops for the Anglicans. Obviously there are those for whom the notion is abhorrent, a monstrous offence against God. They're probably the same protestors as last time, who then couldn't deal with the idea of female vicars. Remember them? They were the ones who were furious about our series, quite often sending me tracts promulgating the sin of women being allowed to speak in church *at all*, citing verse 35 and the like. I could never have anticipated receiving hate mail from Christians.

Of course, they were a tiny minority and I guess their fear was that you might write something funny enough or popular enough to normalise this new situation in the way that television so easily can. In that respect, their fears were well founded, because I think that's exactly what you did. You and Paul Mayhew-Archer together posited the idea of female priests as a natural and sensible state of affairs. That as the given, you were then free to write a sitcom about a vicar who landed in a village of mutants, which was by far the funnier and more traditional premise. Only occasionally did anyone object to the fact, or even notice, that she was a woman, in the series. Mainly, Geraldine just got on with the job of ministering, didn't she? Along with plenty of snogging and chocolate scoffing of course, which ought surely to form a large part of any decent vicar's life. Thanks, by the way, for all the choc. I know it didn't often figure in the original plot but was crowbarred in as an added component for my delectation. Some actresses might have objected to the large quantities that were required to be eaten on camera, but in that respect, I am extremely fortunate because I have such an active metabolism that I can scoff tons of chocolate and it doesn't seem to show on me at all . . .

I can't remember exactly, but I think it was sometime around 1992 that you first mooted the idea to me of *The Vicar of Dibley*. I think you'd been to a wedding where a female lay preacher had officiated in some capacity and I knew you thought it made total sense, seeing as it's nearly always our mums we run to for support and guidance in times of emotional or personal need. Anyway, I remember you giving me an outline of an idea which I think I read on a plane — maybe on the way up to the Edinburgh Festival? — I can't quite recall. I do remember, however, thinking that this was a very Richard Curtis kind of a project. The idea of a parish council full of odd bods, most of whom were no doubt based on people you knew or knew of when you were living, as you were then, in a tiny little cottage with wild roses round the door in a village in Oxfordshire. I couldn't understand why quite so many men of your age working in telly lived in

Oxfordshire until it eventually dawned on me, like the dolt I am, that, of course, you'd all been to Oxford and sort of stayed there. A bit like modern day lost boys.

At the time, I didn't really have much to do with you Oxbridge lot. We at the Comic Strip regarded you as the privileged, old-school-tie brigade who would, naturally, be propelled into top jobs at the BBC because all your mates and forefathers and everyone you ever knew were already there, ready and willing to usher you in through the back door while oiks like us from less prestigious unis or, God forbid, polytechnics or stinky art schools were prevented entry. Although founded in a certain amount of truth, this theory was laced with bitterness and chippiness, which didn't make for great relations between you, the toffs, and us, the proles. You, of course, ignored the general wrath, in true Curtis-style, and crossed the divide when various of our tribe like Rik and Robbie Coltrane appeared in *Blackadder* and when almost all of us did various bits 'n' bobs on the very first Comic Relief stage show and subsequent video, and every Comic Relief event ever since.

I've always admired you, Dick, for being such a persuasive and soothing negotiator. It is virtually impossible to deny you anything, when you make the case for why we should make the right choices. I'm sure anyone who's ever worked with you and for Comic Relief will agree with me. It must be exhausting for you to be so constantly pleading, scrounging favours and explaining, on behalf of others, but only you can do it with such panache. You launched Comic Relief (with Len alongside you) and it certainly would have crumbled without you continually driving it forward like a posigrade rocket.

I first encountered your irresistible, devilishly clever powers of persuasion after I had read that first brief document about how you envisaged the series. I could see it would be rural and green and British and pretty. I could see why all the characters were extremely funny. Except mine, who appeared to be a sweet, kind, wise, nurturing sort, around whom everyone's stories and troubles would swirl. She was to be the fulcrum, the heart of the village. All good — 'cept where's the cockin' jokes? I wondered. I couldn't conceive how the lead in a sitcom could be so bloody nice and still be funny. My personal favourite sitcom characters were big ol' monsters, full of pomposity like Captain Mainwaring or misguided snobby twots like Basil Fawlty, or louche fashion victims like Edina and Patsy, not nice, kind vicars like Geraldine. I made a brief and pointless plea to play Alice, to no avail. Do you remember meeting a few times in your rosy cottage to talk it through? To flesh out the problems as I saw them? That was the first of many times I saw a glimpse of that stubborn chap who lives inside you and is, I suspect, constantly screaming 'For fuck's sake, hurry up, catch up and get it, then just say yes, then you'll see, you cretin!' inside your head. Am I right? You ran out of patience with me and my procrastination quite quickly and sent me a list of other, more talented and available actresses including Miriam Margolyes, Alison Steadman and Julie Walters. That certainly jolted me into affirmative action. Thank God I said yes, because honestly, making that series for the next 13 years with you was some of the most fun I've ever had.

For me, coming to work with you every day was the ultimate lure. I suspected it would be fascinating to watch you sculpt the scripts with Paul, at close hand. I suspected I would learn a lot about teamwork and tolerance and keeping an open mind. I suspected I would laugh all day. I suspected we would forge lasting friendships and feel part of a loving, generous family. For all of that, and much more, my suspicions were confirmed. What I *hadn't* anticipated was how much I would come to love you as a true, loyal, decent, understanding, lifelong bosom pal. Having your friendship is honestly one of the most fulfilling things that's happened to me.

Let me remind you of some of the lasting memories from what were, for me, golden days:

- Meeting the legend that is the wondrous Reverend Joy Carroll, one of the first young women to be ordained and your inspiration for the character, and bombarding her with intimate questions. Watching her officiate with great tenderness at a funeral. Going to her wedding and having her on set to advise us and be our ally. Having her blessing. Realising that knowing her is a blessing.
- The day Paul Mayhew-Archer brought his

369

teenage son to work on 'go to work with your dad' day. How much Paul wanted to impress his son, so he leaned back on his chair with his arms behind his head at the read-through table, in an effort to appear cool and thoughtful and writerly. Of course, he leaned too far and toppled right over backwards. His son was consumed with embarrassment (as was Paul) and informed his father on the journey home that he was a total 'fuckwit'. Henceforward Paul carried that nickname. He is, needless to say, nothing of the sort.

- Jon Plowman's famous warm-ups and introductions of the cast before every show in front of the live audience. His dedication to and support of good comedy programmes being so impressive but his decision to refer to our lovely audience as 'silly cunts' on one particularly memorable occasion with my mother in the audience, not so very good.
- You, Dick, running in after every take, sometimes with a cushion strapped to your aching injured back, always nervously twanging an elastic band between your fingers and grinding your teeth, with some inspired new thought or suggestion to try.
- Giggling helplessly with James Fleet.
- Seeing Trevor Peacock's willy, when he did his Full Monty routine.
- Listening to Roger Lloyd-Pack trying valiantly, but failing, to master the tuning of 'Oh Happy Day'.
- Delicious gossiping with Emma Chambers.

- Listening to John Bluthal's old stories about Spike Milligan.
- Sly conspiratorial glances with Gary Waldhorn.
- Liz Smith's utter inability to pronounce the word 'taramasalata' in front of the audience.
- Getting plastered in thick gooey chocolate custard from the chocolate fountain episode, which had to be the last shot of the day. Getting in the shower to clean up and realising when I got out that everyone had gone home and I was locked in at Pinewood.
- Being stuck in a strange Dibley amber, age-wise. You not allowing my character to grow older while my genuine increasing decrepitude was patently obvious to all and sundry. E.g. I celebrated my 40th birthday as Geraldine when I was in fact 47, and you even suggested, for a brief deluded moment, that I should have a baby with my new 'husband' when in grown-up real world I was 49. Ta for the compliment but I'm a broad who welcomes age and all its creaky, dry and hairy wonders.
- Having the following shouted at me more often than I can cope with:

'More tea, Vicar?!'
'Hey, Vicar, where's Alice?!'
'Let's see your knickers, Vicar!'
'Hey, Vicar of Dimbleby!'
'Hey, Vicar of Doubleday!'
'Hey, Vicar of Dribbley!'
'Hey, Vicar of Drimbly!'
'Hey, Vicar of Dumbledore!'
'Hey, Vicar of Dublin!'

- Having a secret wee in the water of the huge puddle I had to jump into. Twice. Two jumps. Two wees. It's not secret now.
- Upsetting Hughie Green by having a reference to how some bus line hadn't run since he'd died when he hadn't died yet. Ooops.
- Filming in beautiful Turville, under the shadow of the windmill high up on the hill. Finding out the windmill was the one in *Chitty Chitty Bang Bang*. Doing a little jumping dance of excitement about that.
- Finding out a *Sun* photographer lived in a cottage on the green and constantly took photos of punchline moments and gave them away.
- Noticing all our kids growing up as they regularly visited the set over the years.
- Hearing my then 4-year-old daughter explain to one of the extras that her 'mummy is a vicar' and her 'daddy is a chef'.
- Witnessing the nightmare of Emma, who is allergic to animals, having to be in the tiny church with 27 different varieties of them during the pet service.
- Me getting an actual crush on Peter Capaldi. Then me getting an actual crush on Clive Mantle. Then me getting an actual crush on Richard Armitage. Then me getting an actual crush on Johnny Depp. Me realising I am an actual dirty harlot.
- Having fab directors like Ed Bye and Gareth Carrivick and Dewi Humphreys who returned again and again.
- The beauty of seeing your own breath in the

hushed churchyard in Turville at 3am on a dewy night shoot.

- The undeniable holiness we all felt when we shot the Christmas episode where the Christmas story was told in a farmyard, ending up with Alice giving birth in a stable. There had been lots of jokes all day, all evening, then suddenly, at midnight, when the little newborn was handed to Emma for that final shot, we were silenced by how sacred it all was.
- You, Dick, being unable to speak in the presence of the divine Miss Kylie Minogue when she came to do a guest appearance. You reverted back to being a stuttering 11-year-old with a tent pole in your trousers.
- Receiving written requests to perform actual christenings, weddings and exorcisms for actual people in their actual lives!
- Sitting quietly in Turville church and giving thanks for such a splendid job.
- Witnessing the regular 4pm doughnut and cake tray turn up on the set, and by 4.02pm every crumb would be inside a Turville resident rather than the intended crew or cast member.
- Not being able to continue filming for some time when Trevor Peacock as Jim Trott spoke his astonishing lines about wanting to have sex with a poodle. Neither the cast nor the audience could continue until we had a little break to compose ourselves.
- Great parties. So much dancing. So much vodka. So much errant misbehaviour. I

remember doing some extremely overenthusiastic dancing to Shakira's 'Hips Don't Lie' during which I actually dislocated my hip and had to walk with a stick for four weeks. So thanks, Shakira — the bald fact is your hips *do* lie, madam.

- I very much remember at the wrap party, after the final episodes, saying a tearful thank-you and last goodbye to everyone. Then, as I was leaving, the producer came up to me and said, 'Just so you know, Richard's asked us to store the set . . . ' So, Dick . . . what was I saying about those female bishops . . . ?

Bless you.

Dear Madonna,

The news is just comin' into my ears and eyes from reliable sauces like the mag what is *In Heat* that you might be doin' the divorcin' of the posh gangsta-style Ritchie boy. What a cryin' shame if that be true. I know doin' marriage is tough and hard to pull off for a long time, but from what I has been led to believe, you two was doin' it quite goodly. As goodly as a huntin' shootin' fishin' filmin' drinkin' Englishy *can* do with a gyratin' pumpin' singin' lookin' wearin' Yankee-doodle icon. It was seemin' to be good together. I thought he might be doin' the tellin' of the truth to you, who may only have some very few people not paid to do, so they might have to be lickin' of the icon bum to keep a job. But I could be wrong there, it could of been something entirely else, like he might have had bad habits which drove you round the crazy. Is he a comin'-in-too-late-after-the-pub sort of chump, not tellin' you of his whereabeens therefore leadin' you to suspects? Or maybe he just forgot to keep doin' the romance? Like no more special heart love notes or flowers for the lovely lady, or puttin' down of the cloak for you to not step in a puddle right up to your middle and frighten Miss Madge away? Or, of course, you could have been fancied by another while Guy of Gisborne was lookin' the other way. You is much highly regarded as top totty by many, so it wouldn't be the biggest surprise all year. I is amazed you would find the time for naughty secret hotstuff, with all the busy keepin' up with the younger musics, the home kiddie crèche from all rainbow colours, the strict maintainin' of the pecs, the constant lookin' at new dresses for image-reinventin' purposes, the endless meetins about important stuff, let alone the attendin' at the Kasbahlahlah. Phew! How do you do it all?! You is a mighty wind, that's for sure!

Look, the point is none of us on the outsides knows what is goin' on on the insides of you. So, if you is needin' to have a big hissy fit chuckin' down the weddin' band ring and shoutin', 'I'm goin', Guy Fawkes, and I ain't never comin' back!' then you do so. Better out than in. One word in advice though, *don't* let him take all your old Dionne Warwick or Earth, Wind and Fire LPs pretendin' they're his. They are not. They are yours, you bought them yourself with your first *Desperately Seeking Something* wage cheque. Along with all your Kylies and your J-Los. Hands off, Ritchie Rich!

I hope it's just a big silly ding-dong over who's got the biggest willy or something, so you can get over it quick and do the lovely make friends, make friends, never never break friends, and then have a quick cuddle and say sorry, no *I'm* sorry, no *I'm* sorry, before you have to rush off to do another rude dance with Justin Timberland Boots. If you *do* manage to do the rescuin', might I put forward one other tiny good advice?

376

This might be lies all scurrilous lies, all is false, but if it *is* true — *please* don't be takin' the raspberry and blackcurrant machine to bed with you both any more. It is a phone cum day-to-day personal organiser and interweb surfer and has no right place in the bedroom where the incomin' beeps would be disturbin' all the good good lovin'.

Just thinking ahead, that's all.

Dear Alfred

I think I would have missed out on my foray into the world of opera if it hadn't been for you. When the call came through in the autumn of 2006, from the Royal Opera House, I thought it was some kind of elaborate joke. Please would I consider being in the Donizetti opera *La Fille du Régiment*? Me? Just for one tiny deluded, pathetic second, I found myself feeling flattered that perhaps, just maybe, someone had over-heard me singing and realised that my voice was an undiscovered jewel, a hidden treasure, raw, naive and beautiful. So soaringly, supremely magnificent that I needed to be centre stage at the Royal Opera House immediately, with no training whatsoever, so that as many people as possible could witness the wonder. The world deserved to know. Who could have guessed that I possessed such a latent, undeveloped well of brilliant virtuoso talent? Nobody could have guessed. Nobody did guess. Because, of course, in reality my voice is remarkably average. Below average really. Average to poor. Pants, in fact. My voice is pants.

Did I ever tell you about the day this was proven to me in the most humiliating and painful way? The producer and the director of *Mamma Mia!* asked if I would consider being the funny fat one in the film version. I hadn't even seen the stage show at this point so I hurried along to take a look. Never before have I felt like such a pooper at a party. The audience were *lovin'* it and, apart from the great Abba music, that's a given, I couldn't connect with it at all. I didn't get why the broad humour was so appealing, and I didn't feel remotely emotional about the story. Yet the entire rest of the audience most certainly did. There's no doubt it has a magic, the show. Maybe only some people can feel it? Fortunately for all those involved, it's MOST people in the world since it is such a massive hit EVERYWHERE! Anyway, they told me that Meryl Streep was on board to play the main role. Wow — Meryl Streep! Big heroine of mine. She's got great taste, maybe I was wrong about the show, maybe it's utterly brilliant and I'm the only person in the world who doesn't get it? God knows, that's a familiar enough situation. I had to admit I *was* a bit excited by the thought of meeting Meryl and forcing her to become a new close friend. Oh, the stories we'd trade about our Hollywood careers. Well, the stories I'd hear, anyway . . . So, drunk with the idea of working with her, and also just a little bit actually drunk, I agreed to take the next step, which was a voice test. I was quick to explain that I am NOT a singer, that all the singing Fatty and I do in our shows is written by us and arranged by our trusted musical-director chum Simon Brint (ex Raw Sex band leader and all-round genius) and that he goes to great pains to fix everything so's it's in the right key for us and so on. In other

379

words, he makes the music fit our very limited ability. *It* comes to us, so to speak. With the Abba music, I would have to go to *it*. Everyone knows and loves this music. It would be awful to sing it badly. I voiced all of these concerns and they reassured me that with Björn in charge of the music, everything would be fixable, taken slowly and carefully honed. They explained that even if I bellowed like a cow in labour, they would be able to cope, but they encouraged me to have a safe little plinky-plonky no-strings friendly singalong with their musical director just to check I had the merest whiff of ability to hold down the most rudimentary of tunes. I agreed to this, with the proviso that we do it somewhere ultra private. Singing is so embarrassing if you don't do it much, and I knew I would clam up if there were spectators. 'Of course,' they reassured me. So, I pootled along to HMV and bought an *Abba's Greatest Hits* and punished the air in my car with some pretty confident renditions for a week or so. I hate it when you're caught singing your head off by other drivers on the motorway, as I often am on the M4, and you have to pretend your gaping jaw action is all down to dreadful toothache and start looking at your mouth in the vanity mirror, don't you? Oh, don't you? It's just me then.

Anyway, the day came to meet the music guy. The audition was arranged in a 'quiet' room at the very top of the Palace Theatre in Cambridge Circus. The lift was broken so we walked up the 8,462 floors to the top. A small, pert man, he bounced up the stairs ahead of me. A big, fat, lumbering woman, I hauled myself up behind him, puffing all the way. By the time I reached the top I knew I would need to sit down and recover with a KitKat and a cuppa for about three weeks, without moving, never mind singing. He introduced me to a bevy of bright-eyed chaps working in the office next door to the room we were to be 'private' in. A couple of the dandies made comments like 'Ooh, we're so excited', 'Can't wait to hear you warble' and 'This'll be our lunchtime concert, we're not going out today, we've brought packed specially' and suchlike. Oh God. I asked Mr Music if we really would be 'private' as requested. Yes, of course, he assured me. We went into the small room, which had a sofa and a keyboard. Oh double God, the keyboard. There it was, taunting me. I sat on the sofa and started wall-to-wall nervous fast gossiping so as to delay the awful moment. I noticed that I could hear the guys next door quite clearly and deduced that the reverse must also be true. Oh triple God. I thought we might start with some gentle scales, a little warm-up perhaps, but no, he sat at the keyboard, invited me to share the piano stool, and off he went pounding away at the keys with the fervour of Bobby Crush on acid, and before I had time to draw breath, we were away, singing like mad, one song after another, 'Dancing Queen', 'Take a Chance on Me', 'Chiccyteeta' or 'Chicken Tikka' or whatever that one's called. It was fast and loud and furious. Each one was worse than the last, and the first was appalling. For some reason I don't understand, not only did I sing dreadfully, but I sang worse than I ever have before. I kept saying, 'Hang on there, fella, something's wrong, let me get my breath and have another crack at that,' and off we'd go again, ten to the dozen, and it would be dire. Worse than dire. An entirely tuneless, croaky, wailing, drony caterwaul of a noise. Inhuman really. The noise the dead might yawl as they roast and screech in hell's inferno. A caw unburdened by tone or key. Horrible, horrible, horrible. All credit to Mr Music, he was tenacious, he was trying to remain optimistic, but very quickly I sensed he was beaten. After half an hour or so of this excruciating slaughter, the punishment was over and Mr Music bade me farewell with tears of pain in his eyes reflecting the damage to his ears. I rushed out, offering a hasty 'Bye!' to the poor witnesses next door, most of whose hair was standing on end and all of whom couldn't look me in the eye for shame. My shame.

As I beat a speedy retreat, I turned my phone back on to see if there had been any calls, and it was ringing with my agent's name, 'MAUREEN-OFFICE', flashing on the tiny screen. 'Love, it's not going to work out.' 'But, Maureen, I've only just left — ' 'It's just not going to work out, love — ' 'But they said you'd have to sing worse than the noise a cow makes in labour ... ' Silence the other end. 'Maureen ... ?' 'It's not going to work out, love ... ' So that was that. I can't sing. At all. Fatty was very supportive when I told her about the horror of it all, and in defiance, and an effort to reclaim some self-esteem, we decided to sing 'Thank You for the Music' at the end of our show on tour every night. We sang it loud and proud and I was gradually, nightly, clawing my way back out of the pit of zero confidence voice-wise and was really enjoying performing it with gusto until someone told me there was a reference to the song in a review which said we were 'hilariously out of tune'. I surrender to the gods of music, to Pan, to Apollo, to Björn, Benny, Agnetha and Frieda. I am not your servant or your handmaiden or your daughter. I am your jester. That much is clear.

Anyway, sorry, Alfred, back to the opera. Of course they didn't want me to sing. They had wisely decided to go with the odd professional for that. No, they wanted me to take a speaking part, a comic cameo normally played by an older soprano like Montserrat Caballé. Well, I had no reference for such a proposal so I called you toot sweet. You are, after all, not only my beloved buddy but also my oracle, my encyclopedia of all things opera. Anything, and it is a teeny amount, but nevertheless, *anything* I know about opera, I know because of you. I love our ritual. You call up, you have tickets, it's *vital* to see this particular production because of this singer, that director, this conductor, that composer, etc., etc. I come to your flat in Fulham, we eat scrambled eggs and smoked salmon, we listen to a recording of said opera, you educate me about the story, the background, former productions and, my most favourite part, the gossip. Which diva is shagging which divo. Who is so fat they take up three plane seats. Who was booed off at La Scala and had a hissy fit, all that stuff. You are not only the font of all high information, you are the deliciously dirty dealer of the low. You are the *Heat* magazine of opera. Hurrah. That's what makes it all the more intriguing for me. I can then watch the opera appreciating not only the soprano's excellent coloratura, but also her bravura bosoms, knowing which dirty divo has had his mitts on 'em!

So, do you remember when I called you and told you about the production? 'Who is in it?' you asked. I told you. Juan Diego Flórez is the tenor, Natalie Dessay is the soprano, Laurent Pelly is the director, and so on. 'There is only one word to use regarding this decision, Dawn,' you said, 'and that word is 'must'. You MUST do this. If you do not do this I will kill you. No, seriously. Kill you. A slow, lingering, merciless death. Understand?' Message received. You went on to explain that these people are the *corps d'élite*, prodigious talents at the top of their game, and the time was right, this particular opera hadn't been performed at 'The Garden' since Pavarotti and Joan Sutherland did it in the sixties. It's rarely staged because the tenor has to hit nine extremely difficult high 'C's in one demanding aria and there are very few singers alive who can do it well. Juan Diego is one such singer. And what's more, you explained, he's Peruvian and drop-dead gorgeous. Sold.

What a bloomin' roller coaster! Opera is such a different world to the kind of theatre I am used to. My part was in French so I had to attempt to conquer that, which I never fully did, so we decided Franglais was a good, funny, alternative route. To be directed in French was quite an experience. I found out that operating in a language which is not your first language is potentially limiting, especially for comedy, because the nuances, the playing around, is curtailed. I couldn't have as much verbal fun as I usually would in a rehearsal room, with shared jokes and running gags. I had to make myself understood with gesture and posture, which is suitable for big opera in a big opera house. I was also aware that my part was tiny and that a great big muscly machine of a production can't wait about for one fat ol' comedienne to arse about. It needed to be grand and slick, and funny. This, after all, is not my audience. They might loathe my intrusion, my style. Gulp. In the rehearsal space the singers mark their parts by blocking out their actions, but not singing out too loudly, in order to save their voices. The day comes eventually, when, after endless costume, shoe, wig, jewellery, make-up tests and fittings, you actually get on the stage for a dress rehearsal. Finally, the many different elements who've been rehearsing in many different rooms come together at last. That's when the chorus are there to join in and when the singers sing out for the first time. That's when my head was nearly whipped off with the full force of the sheer blast of power of their huge impressive voices. It was fantastic!

Luckily, the show was well received, and no one seemed to mind me, the impostor, too much. When opera audiences love a show, they *really* love it. We would bow our way through ten curtain calls with the entire opera house on their feet. It was utterly thrilling and I'm so glad I took your advice, Alf, to do it. I made some good friends, and I had a front-row, in fact onstage, seat every night to hear and see such phenomenal talents at their peak.

During the run, I kept complaining that I would finish my time at the opera house having never sung a note. Surely, I ought to be entitled to *one* note?! Then I'd be able to claim for ever that I had sung onstage at the Royal Opera House Covent Garden. My final exit each night from the stage was a big huffy flounce off, accompanied by a loud angry roar because my character had been thwarted. It comes about three minutes from the end. So, on the very last night, instead of roaring I decided to sing that last moment of fury. I waited, I waited. The moment came, and I sang out loudly, one note, one word, 'Merde!' — and exited. Yes, ladies and gentlemen and my beloved Alfred, I have indeed sung onstage at the Royal Opera House Covent Garden. I thank you.

BRAVO! And Toi Toi Toi!

Dear Dad,

We've never been a family where any one person's achievements matter more than anyone else's, so I really want to make sure you know about all the amazing stuff Mum and Gary have done.

Gary, it probably comes as no surprise, has been adventurous. He's travelled a lot, especially in his twenties and thirties. He would work hard for a couple of years to fund each next journey, where he would have phenomenal experiences — for instance, actually building the main part of a hospital in a leper colony in India, or living with and helping Tibetan refugees. Then, when he'd exhausted his funds, he'd return and put his nose to the grindstone again. But even the grindstone has been an area of huge personal achievement about which he has been very quiet, very self-effacing. He's worked mostly in housing, both in London and in Devon and Cornwall. At one time, he was finding housing for people on probation for whom life was pretty tricky, and he was later the instigator of an amazing 'Foyer' scheme in Plymouth. He'd seen a version of this scheme working on the Continent, where young homeless people are given a place to stay while they have access to an IT centre and careers advice which they can use to springboard them into jobs and consequently further housing. They are given counselling and lifestyle advice to help them bridge the gap between home (for many, this is a major problem area) and work. A crucial stepping stone for the young, vulnerable and disaffected. It sounds like the sort of thing you would have been involved with, Dad. Perhaps he is more of a chip off the old block than we know. He has married a fantastic woman, Sarah, with whom he has had two gorgeous kids, Hannah (the Heavenly) and Jack (the Lad). He is a great dad, for whom family comes before everything. They live happily in Cornwall, where Gary and Sarah both worked hard in housing — until recently, when Gary made a huge decision of which you would be so proud. He decided to change his life completely. No longer does he work nine to five for the city council, where he was snowed under with bureaucracy. He runs the cafe that overlooks Burgh Island at Bigbury-on-Sea in Devon. He is his own boss, he cooks the grub and makes the decisions. I've rarely seen him so happy. He is knackered a lot of the time, but he starts and ends his day with a cup of coffee, looking out to sea knowing that life is more than memos and meetings. Who knows what he'll do next. He is willing and open and creative. He knows, as we all do so well in our family, that nothing is worth getting depressed about, that you have to expand your horizons and 'follow your bliss', as Joseph Campbell said. Gary knows himself and has listened to his heart. He's still fiery-tempered, always fighting for the rights of the underdog or the unheard. He is remarkably unmaterialistic and generous of spirit, and he is a great listener. Certainly for me and for Mum. He loves his dog, his family and his friends, he loves to sail, he loves to read, he loves music, and chickens and pigs and food and Cornwall. Simple stuff really. Properly achievable, tangible happiness is his motivation and I really think he's done that rare thing, and found it.

Mum rose from the ashes like a phoenix. She turned her grief and her loneliness and her fear into a snowball of energy that gained and gained momentum. One Christmas, maybe 1982 or so, I noticed she had an unusual amount of cards on her fireplace. As I read them each one was more effusive than the last, *Dear Roma, you are the light in my darkness, To Roma, thank you for saving my life*, and on they went. When I asked who these people were, it turned out she was opening her home to all comers, glue-sniffers and heroin addicts and alcoholics alike, to have a place to come and talk. Although it was a generous gesture, I was a bit concerned for her safety, and I felt that she would be more use to people if she had the proper training. Well, Dad, she was amazing. Mum, who had left school at 16, took herself off for, firstly, a foundation counselling course, then further qualifications to enable her to help the people she most wanted to. She was gripped with a desire to change what she saw was useless practice and bad law when it came to young mothers with drug problems. The typical process was that, once the mothers were discovered to be addicts, the social services would immediately take the children into foster care until the women had been through rehab and proven they were clean. It all had to go through the courts, so very often this process could take years, during which the mother and children were separated. Mum's theory was: keep them all together in a safe place. They must recover and heal together because the kids are the 'affected others' and need to witness their mum's recovery in order to trust her again. It's no good separating them, it only causes heartache and alienation; but if the mums and kids are to remain together, it has to be controlled and supervised for the kids' sakes. Meanwhile, alongside the rehab, the mum also gets cooking and parenting classes, the kids go to local schools and they all work together to slowly, carefully feed the family back into society when they're ready.

In order to achieve this, Mum had to find the funding to buy properties that could be transformed into safe flats for the families, with a rehab centre attached. She somehow (I suspect by fair means AND foul, you know what a Boadicea Mum is when she sets her sights!) raised the cash, through a mixture of charity, fund-raising and the local council, to set up with her colleague, Bob Underwood (the ex-police chief), first one house, then two, then more, which became the Trevi House Project in Plymouth. The ongoing success rate was so good that the government, specifically Mo Mowlam, consulted with them to use their method as a blueprint for other projects around the country.

As if that wasn't astounding enough, she went on to acquire the magnificent ex-admiralty Hamoaze House at Mount Wise from the MoD, and with a dedicated team she created a drop-in centre there for drug and alcohol abusers and their families in Devonport, Plymouth, which has been a huge success. She has worked tirelessly for other people's benefit for 30-odd years now, and when she retired a couple of years ago, the city gave her a posh lunch to thank her for all she'd done. And, like Gary, she's done it all quietly. No hoo-ha. I took your lovely mum, Grandma French, along to the official opening of Hamoaze. I looked around the room and saw that there were four generations of our family there. If ever a family have been committed to the improvement of a city, the Frenchies have been to Plymouth. Your city, Dad.

Mum lives happily alone, by the sea in Cornwall, on a cliff overlooking a fishing village, where she's lived for nine years now. She says the view and the air are healing. She's very high up. I think she feels closer to you there.

Dear whomsoever it may concern,

I write to wholeheartedly recommend Miss Kathy Burke for the position of Queen of England. I am aware that the post is not technically open to applicants presently, but I expect you must be tossing around a few names, just in case, surely? I'm also aware that there are other, more seemingly suitable contenders. Members of the royal family for instance, who may appear to be the obvious, if not the legal and constitutional, choice. Prince Charles springs to mind as the first thought of course, and actually I like him very much. So much so that I've always fancied the idea of ruffling his hair up during a tumble in a royal bush on a lazy Sunday afternoon in September. Yes, I would have to concede that he would do well as Queen. BUT, don't be too hasty. Hear me out.

Miss Kathy Burke is the quintessential Englishwoman, and loved by all. She is firm but fair, she is maternal but disciplined, she is creative but focused and above all she doesn't suffer fools, she tells it like it is. She is instinctive and clever and funny and she would really, really suit a crown. So few can pull that off and I genuinely believe that she is one of the lucky ones in that respect. Kath wouldn't hold with long boring formal dinners for foreign dignitaries unless there was a bit of entertainment, so I reckon life at the Palace could liven up a bit. She also doesn't like to stay up too late if she's working, so the staff would be certain of reasonable hours, unless she was in her cups in which case I'm sure they would be free to join in.

I've heard tell that a large contingent of Palace staff are as gay as a really gay thing, and again, Kath would be perfect because she is nothing if not a splendidly well-qualified and experienced friend of a friend of the odd Dorothy.

Please consider my reference. This country needs her, so do your duty and anoint her with the Holy Gism. Soon as.

Yours in anticipation,

Dawn French

(possible future lady-in-waiting to Her Majesty)

Dear Scottie,

I want to own up at last to what happened with your ashes. Much as you predicted, your death was quite a drama, and I'm glad that you decided to put me in charge of it because then, at least, I had something to do to distract me from the misery of it all. I love a bit of organising, you knew that.

I clearly remember when we met, as we so often did, for supper at Julie's restaurant, it must've been about 1989 or so, and you told me you had HIV. I felt the ground beneath my seat shudder. I tried to remain calm, but one of my best friends was going to die quite soon, and I didn't feel calm at all. I felt scared and panicked. Typically, you had everything in hand and you told me your plans. You'd always been in control like that. I remember loving that about you when I first knew you at Central. That and the fact that you were virtually the only actor who spoke to me for the whole three years at college. We had that in common, we were both people who like to have the organisational stuff, the arrangements of life, done and dusted quickly so there's time for fun. I hate not knowing what's happening. It unnerves me. You explained that you were going to the States where they were more familiar with HIV and where there were more advanced medicines available. You knew where you would stay, where you would go for treatment, everything. My job was to support from a distance, visit you occasionally for the craic in New York and be ready for your return, which you told me would indicate that you were in the final phase. And who knows, you explained, they might find a cure in the short time you thought you had left, but probably not. So, hey, that's enough of that, you said, let's talk about important stuff like which one of us is the more likely to get a shag with George Michael. If he was blindfolded. On a desert island. With only us two to choose from. Yet again, I was the loser, just like in the same game previously, featuring K. D. Lang.

So, you went to America. When you weren't ill, you had a great time. You fell in love. He had HIV too. Then you came back in 1992 and the serious business of dying began.

The Middlesex Hospital was the venue, and the Broderip Ward, an Aids ward which was the campest place in London, was your deathbed of choice. There were nurses in drag, and a cocktail trolley at 6pm. I remember your key nurse, Mark, very well. He knew and loved you and was determined the finale would go as well as it could. With boas and glitter wherever possible.

You were pretty bad by the time they moved you into a private room. We all took it in turns to sit with you, and while you were still conscious, we managed a lot of laughs. I remember one evening when you and I were alone and you indicated (you couldn't speak too well by then)

395

you wanted a joint. This had become a regular comforter and pain reliever for you each evening. I knew where your stash was. I also knew it meant I would have to roll it for you and help you to smoke it. Being a stranger to dope, and indeed to smoking, what ensued was an utter fiasco. I could see the frustration in your eyes as I dropped everything and cocked it up so badly. The spliff looked like a fat sausage, there was far too much of everything in it, and it was splitting at the side like some kind of illegal pitta pocket. I knew that because of your various problems, you couldn't actually hold it or properly draw on it, so I had to smoke it and puff the smoke into your mouth for you. This is when I realised what a very poor hippy I would have made. I was rubbish at smoking, with bits of roll-up paper stuck to my lip, and burning tobacco and weed all over the bed and all over us. It was a dangerous, chaotic half an hour that left us both in hysterics. Sorry I didn't do drugs better. I never have, and it's unlikely I ever will.

Although I arranged the funeral, you had, of course, stage-managed and designed it to perfection way ahead of time. The music, the coffin, the flowers, all chosen for perfect dramatic effect. You chose the quiet room at the Lighthouse, the Terrence Higgins Trust hospice, for the ceremony and decided exactly how the room should be set out. As we sat there, crying to Louis Armstrong singing 'What a Wonderful World', I looked at the coffin and I couldn't erase the thought of your tired and ravaged body inside it. Then my eye wandered to the artwork on the wall beyond, which was a huge photographic triptych of a mass candlelight vigil in Trafalgar Square with thousands of young gay men singing. Then, I saw you. Right in the middle, young, healthy, with your hopeful happy face bathed in candlelight and your lover's arm around your shoulder. The old Scottie. It was a fabulous final masterstroke, you absolute drama queen.

So, to the ashes. I know you asked for them to be flung off the top of the Empire State Building while simultaneously incanting favourite lines from various show tunes, BUT it wasn't that easy, Scottie. Len and me and the BF and her fella Barrie went to New York for New Year specifically for that purpose. We had booked a table for supper at the Windows on the World at the top of the World Trade Center for 10pm to see the New Year in and to raise a glass to you. So, earlier on in the evening, your old friend Michael Way joined us as we traipsed up to the viewing platform at the top of the Empire State Building with the urn containing your ashes (which, by the way, had involved hefty amounts of paperwork to 'export' from the UK to the US). On arrival we discovered that there are fine mesh nets all around to prevent people jumping off, or falling debris killing innocents on the street way below. We didn't want you to be caught up in that mesh, so we changed to plan B, climbed in a yellow cab and drove to the river on the West Side to scatter you there. But, of course, there are huge fences and barricades, so we climbed back in the taxi and asked the now impatient and confused driver to take us back to our hotel via Times Square. That way, at least you'd be scattered on Broadway. We thought that was fitting. By now it was raining and the cabbie really couldn't understand why we needed to divert through the busiest square on the busiest night of the year. It would be chaos. We eventually persuaded him and Len distracted him while we attempted to get the ashes ready in the back of the cab as we approached Times Square. Who knew they'd be so industrially well wrapped? We prised the lid off the urn using a key edge as a mini crowbar, then we hacked through at least three thick polythene liners with mini scissors from a Swiss army knife. Then, to our horror, we realised that the cab window only opened two inches, so we had to sort of flick you gradually out of the cab in the fervent hope that most of you would end up on Broadway. Sorry if you got stepped on, but it was the best we could do in the circumstances. Job done, and recovering from the fit of hysterical giggles the whole process had reduced us to, we headed back to the hotel to get ready for the evening. We paid the driver and gave him a fat tip for the favour he didn't know he'd done. As I stepped out of the cab, and watched it speed away into the night, I saw that the majority of your ashes were smeared all the way down one side of it, stuck to the rainy door and bumper. We consoled ourselves with the thought that at least you'd see more of New York that night than ever before . . .

Later we stood against the windows at the top of the world at midnight, looking down on all the firework displays. We improvised a quick show-tune medley, and raised a glass to you. To Scottie. The gayest and fairest of them all.

Dear Fatty,

So, here I am, nearly at the end of my book, and here we are nearly at the end of *French and Saunders*. I'm glad we decided to do one last tour, aren't you? It feels right to finish it as we started, with a live show. Don't you think it's amazing how we have jointly and happily come to this decision to stop now? It feels completely timely and undeniably the correct choice to say goodbye to that part of our work lives while we still love it, and while we still have the audience for it. I know you felt like I did, privileged and grateful, to be taking the show around the country and personally bidding farewell to our audience from the stage each night. It has been so rewarding to experience the appreciation, and to notice that there were often three generations of the same family who came to see us. Blimey, how old are we? I'm only 50 as far as I know, and aren't you the same? Yet we have the support of three generations. How bloody gorgeous is that?!

Doesn't it get your goat when interviewers *always* ask how often we fall out? To my knowledge, I don't think we *ever* have, have we? Sure, we have a few grumpy moments and an occasional bit of skilled sulking goes on and some extremely enjoyable ranting about whoever or whatever has annoyed us, but as for outright fury *at* each other, I can't remember any. I think we have a well-tuned mutual gauge of each other's mood, attitude and taste. We know what could be potentially awkward so we don't travel there. Why bother? I'd rather spend time seeking out and enjoying what we both love about each other than rooting about in what we might dislike. There are those who would call this avoidance. These are the people, in general, to avoid. Avoidance is good. It's what compromise and maturity are made of. In order to avoid, you have to identify that which you are avoiding, and know that to avoid it is a choice. More often than not, a wise one, made after consideration and with an unspoken instinctive understanding of the complex nature of the other person. Avoidance is a loud and clear inner language, which we all speak and hear with various levels of clarity. You and I know each other. *Really* know each other. And so I think we make these intricate and sophisticated decisions *all the time*. We try to work out what matters to the other one, what would make us happy or sad, and we make constant, attentive fine adjustments so that nothing needs to come to such a head that it unbalances us, knocks us off-kilter. We rarely need to 'have that conversation' because so much mindful benevolence has already taken place. I think that's why our partnership has endured. We relish our similarities and respect our differences, of which there are many of course.

Can you remember the people we were when we first met? We've shed a few skins since then, I think, but essentially we are the same two bods who have grown through so much, learning all the time. There's no massive alteration of character, or personality, or habit, there's just the natural metamorphosis that age brings.

I have such vivid memories of our friendship. Mostly, it feels like we came out to play as often as possible, both with work and home life. Long before we ever imagined such a career as we've had (did we ever imagine it? — I think not), I remember drinking in a pub on England's Lane and noting two fat old men who used to sit in the corner, near the door to the Ladies, and leer at every woman who passed by. They'd wink and click at the girls, then at each other *about* the girls. It was as if they thought the girls should be flattered by and grateful for the attention of two old farts, so fat they couldn't possibly have seen their genitals for years. This amused us greatly and of course we stored that image, along with many other shared experiences, which popped up later in our show.

I remember you going off on Sundays to cook for the local firemen to earn a few extra quid when we were students. One day you were running the customary 30 minutes late and so you borrowed my foldaway bike to make up time. I watched from the top-floor window of our flat, as you sped away on the bike, then I watched the bike folding away underneath you as you frantically pedalled, gradually bringing the handlebar closer and closer to your hilariously bewildered face. You must have forgotten to put the necessary pin in or something. This image tickled me so much, I laughed about it for weeks.

I remember, later, writing *Girls On Top* in Ruby Wax's flat in Holland Park. You fell asleep a lot, so your character ended up as a sort of dormouse who didn't speak much. Thank God for Ruby, whose energy was the generator for both of us. No wonder she was often exhausted, she was constantly pushing the two of us lazy lardbuckets up the comedy hill to work. Do you remember Ruby pretending to be blind so's she could utilise the disabled taxi pass she'd mistakenly been sent in the post? The chutzpah of the broad. I think in Ruby we found another Jobo. A clever, funny, self-deprecating and daring woman who motivated us, and who made us laugh all day long.

How lucky we were that the BBC took a long-term view of our career there. And how lucky we were to have the remarkable Jon Plowman as our faithful producer, who always defended and fought for our jokes. Our first series was well meant and showed glimpses of promise but was pretty shabby, wasn't it? In the present climate at the Beeb, we wouldn't be permitted to go any further for sure. Back then, the head of 'light entertainment', Jimmy Moir, decided to take a gamble on us, (or, in his words: 'I've got my dick on the table for you ladies'), to give us time to develop and learn, to nurture us, and to take the long view. Thirty years later, we still wonder occasionally if they want us ... I think it's quite good to doubt. It puts us on our mettle. Forces us to keep inventing and experimenting with new ideas. (And persevering with some old ones. It's funny, isn't it, how Madonna rejecting our endless requests for her to come on the series has turned into a superstition of ours, the show just doesn't seem right without her familiar 'NO! Go away!') This desire for fresh challenges is why it's so important to bid farewell to our sketch show. We need time and room to work on new, different ideas. Stuff we've been cooking up together and individually for years, but which there's been no time to concentrate on. Besides which, I think we both agree that sketches are a youngster's game, they're so demanding. Personally, I look forward to cheering on the next batch of female funnies — I wish there were more, to be honest, but nevertheless, big respect and good luck from the old mamas to the young missies like the divine Catherine Tate, and Miranda Hart, and Katy Brand and Karen Taylor and Josie Long and Gina Yashere and Laura Solon and Ruth Jones and Beatrice Edmondson . . .

Talking of change, how did you manage to change so skilfully from being the mistress of effortless understatement in the early days of *Girls On Top* and *Comic Strip* and *French and Saunders*, to the queen of pratfalls and big, broad, loud monsters, like Edina and Viv Vyle? I guess the switches were imperceptible over time, but on reflection you have run the gamut and back when it comes to versatility.

404

How very annoying to discover that everyone has noticed your huge talent. I selfishly imagined it was for the benefit of my own private pleasure.

Do you remember once, when we went to see our friend Gareth Snook playing Prince Charming in panto in about 1986 or something? Buttons came on to play games with the audience. I love panto and was already a bit overexcited when he held up a giant troll (like those ones with brightly coloured hair that sit atop a pencil going up their wazoo, except a hundred times the size) and explained it was the prize for the winner who had the lucky number on the back of their programme. I glanced at the back of mine — number 13 — huh, not much chance. I wasn't surprised to see such an unlucky number, I'd never won anything in my life, never. My concentration was wandering slightly when Buttons shouted, 'Number 13, come on down!' I simply could not befeckinlieve it. I'd won! I'd won the giant troll! Thank you, God, I'd always wanted one of those ... I remember screaming at you, 'I've won! It's me!' as I stood up to rush and collect it. I felt you clawing at my clothes and urging me to sit down. But no. I wanted that troll, I deserved to claim my rightful prize. I pushed past everyone in our row and ran down to the front, with such euphoric glee, waving my programme with my prizewinning lucky number aloft as proof of my great good fortune. It was only as I reached the stage, and I started to tune in to the resounding laughter, that it dawned on me that this was a joke — EVERYONE in the theatre had number 13 on their programme. It was only me that didn't click until it was too late. The elderly had got it, the children had got it, the three rows of mentally challenged people at the front had got it, the whole audience had got it. It was just me, twatty thick ol' me, that hadn't. The walk back to my seat took five years. Thanks for trying to comfort me in my utter humiliation, by the way, and for not disowning me at that awful, cringing moment.

Another memory that stays with me is the time, many years later, when we performed with Darcey Bussell onstage at the Opera House in a benefit for the Benesh Institute. We achieved a major ambition of mine that night, by simply having, on the door of our dressing room, a gold star and a list of its occupants as follows: Miss Darcey Bussell, Miss Sylvie Guillem, Miss Viviana Durante, Miss Jennifer Saunders, Miss Dawn French. Oh my good, good God. We were prima ballerinas for the night! What a laugh it was. We did our silly sketch where I pranced about, echoing Darcey's steps in a giant mirror (a routine we later repeated on *Vicar*), and you played a bossy dance teacher (good toes, naughty toes). We had been asked to bring alternative costumes to wear for the finale, so I had a friend make me a preposterous outfit where I looked like an old-fashioned ballerina in a tutu over a huge swan with tiny dangling knitted ballerina legs hanging over the swan's back. The swan's neck was held by a handle and its legs were, of course, my legs in black tights with huge ungainly flippers for feet. It was inspired by Bernie Clifton and his ostrich. The effect was just plain silly and hopefully very funny. Well, *we* laughed anyway. I know I looked ridiculous, that was the point. Ordinarily when you do a big jokey sketch with a big jokey costume, you endeavour to get out of it pretty quickly. When the gag's over, it's over. Unfortunately, as you may remember, that night we all had to remain onstage to receive the Royal Blessing of the institute's patron, Princess Margaret. She obviously knew a lot about ballet and seemed familiar with many of the dancers onstage, who were the crème de la crème from around the world. She moved along the line, chatting and congratulating everyone till she got to me. She leaned around the swan head to shake my hand, and looked me full in the face with full-on pity in her eyes, quietly said, 'How brave,' and moved on. I think she thought I was special needs or something, being given a chance to jump about with the real dancers. On second thoughts . . . she was right really, wasn't she? Tee hee!

I love it that we still have so much fun together when we come out to play in our civvie life. Like when we started a book club to encourage us to read more, and to have a chance to meet with our favourite mutual female chums for literary criticism and alcohol in equal measure. Or going to see Dolly Parton over the years, witnessing both her waistline shrinking and her genius ever expanding. And I love that we have been part of each other's family. I'm so glad you had three girls, all older than my daughter, all very different, who I could watch and learn from. I have gained so much from seeing you and Ade bring them up so beautifully. The kid tips you gave me — some I took, some I ignored — all helpful.

I will never forget the cloak of protection you flung around me when the press were on my tail trying to exacerbate an already sensitive and tricky situation with Len and me. We'd just started a new sitcom, *Let Them Eat Cake*, at the BBC, and I was trying to be light-hearted and funny, when I was actually feeling hounded, and anxious for Len. You were like a Gladiator, fiercely guarding me, and calling for coffee breaks whenever you sensed I was a bit wobbly. You deserve a proper Gladiator name for that. How about 'Defender'?! Yeah, sounds good. 'On my first whistle, you will fight off predators with a giant cotton bud. Defender, are you ready?!'

I watched you the other week, at your 50th birthday party, looking more radiant and confident than ever, basking in the love of those who care so much for you, and I was reminded in one blinding instant how lucky I am to have you.

So, as I say, here we are, at the end of an era. Saying goodbye to *French and Saunders* with a last shout in London at the Theatre Royal Drury Lane. I've said some important work goodbyes recently — *Vicar, F+S*, and so on. You'd think I would feel sad. I don't. I feel more alive and more creative than I have for years, and I can't wait to say hello to LOTS of new projects. I think both of us are now busier than we've ever been, in every way. But we mustn't forget to stop for a breath occasionally and enjoy the moment. Because it's a glorious moment. We're 50. And it's bloody fantastic! There are only two things to look out for as we get older. One is loss of memory and . . . I can't remember the other one. I bow to you, and bring on the next 50!

As we move our gear into yet another dressing room for the last time, I remember all the other dressing rooms. How they are all so different and yet the same. The sharing of hairdryers and make-up and rollers. The chocolates and the nuts and the Berocca! The speeded-up running of lines in a bid to reassure ourselves that we know the show. The no-nonsense notes to each other, no punches pulled, no time for politeness: speak up. Wait till I've finished before you move. Don't do that thing to the audience at that moment. Energy. Pace. Clarity. Don't blether. God, I hate this. Are your flies done up? God, I love this. This is going to be a good one. Remember they've paid. I need the loo. I need a Quirk. Make it a Robson instead. A quick handshake for luck. You arsehole. You twat. The *F+S* theme tune. The lights. We're on!

There's just no buzz like it.

I think we might miss it, you know.

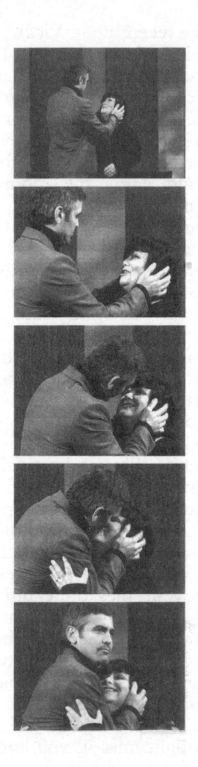

410

Dear George Clooney,

Look, mate, it was one kiss, on Michael Parkinson's chat show, in front of millions of people. It would have been better if you'd decided to display your undying love for me in a slightly more discreet way, maybe backstage or something, y'know, pull me gently into your dressing room and kiss me hard up against the wall, something like that, but no, you chose to go public. I know you were elated, and swept up in the moment, so you couldn't resist declaring your uncontrollable lust, and hallooing my name to the reverberate hills, and making the babbling gossip of the air cry out, 'Dawn, oh Dawn. For she is my love!' I *know* that, and I went along with it because I felt sorry for you. I didn't want to spurn you or shun your advances and embarrass you in front of a whole nation. But George, babe, it's over. Really. You must come to accept this and leave me alone. Please. I am happily married, sorry. I've tried to think of ways we could perhaps meet, fleetingly, in various Premier Inns around the country for a series of secret, hurried and passionate liaisons, but it just isn't going to work out. My satnav is on the blink, I'd never find you. It would be hopeless and, frankly, tawdry. So just turn and go, George.

411

Don't look back. Remember the good times and try to find someone to love if you can, someone who's nearly as great as me.

Good luck, darling. Farewell.

Moo French (age 50)

Dear Dad,

It's time to stop writing now, but I feel frustrated by all the stuff I *haven't* managed to tell you about. There's so much. Nearly a lifetime's worth. I've forgotten more than I can remember! It's clear to me that when I reflect on everything that's happened so far, it's not the work or the career I remember so much as the people. My life has always been, and continues to be, about an abundance of people. Somehow I've been on the receiving end of such plenty when it comes to the folk I know. It's an embarrassment of riches. I haven't even begun to tell you about my fellow Lark Risers and how they've come to be like a second family to me. Or about how much I love Catherine Tate, or about Bex Hale who decided to rethink everything she ever knew, or Helen Lederer, the third funniest woman in England, or Trevor Leighton, the easy, natural artistic savant, or Jon Fink, my writerly confidant, or Maureen Vincent, my trusted guide. Or Sue or Cyn or Linda or Davey or Ben . . . all of these people and more are the colour of my life. They are the ones who, along with my family and the BF and Fatty and so many others, shore me up and love me so well.

In the end, y'know, I'm wholly convinced that, as ol' Macca said, 'the love you take is equal to the love you make'. I'm further convinced that you can only know *how* to give love if you've been given it yourself. And I have, Dad, in bucketloads. Starting of course with you and Mum. My steady stream of unwavering love from you was stemmed far too soon, but Dad, for me to feel the lashings of self-worth I do, is a clue to how deep and wide that flow must have been. I only know how to love others because of your huge unquestionable love for me. And that's a gift that keeps on giving.

Don't misunderstand. I can certainly be ornery. I am extremely stubborn about probably far too much. I am unforgiving of those I don't trust or who have betrayed me, or who are needlessly unkind, or who threaten my beloveds. I can be cantankerous and cunty when it suits me. Come to think of it, it never actually 'suits' me. Does being contemptuous suit anyone? Whenever I catch sight or sound of myself in the full grumpy flow of despicable thoughts or words or deeds, I repulse me sufficiently to try and stop, thank goodness. It's far preferable to seek out the good than dwell on the bad which is so bloody exhausting. A bit like Mum with the dogs in the parlour, I endeavour to give everyone at least a chance, y'know, before I condemn them to the eternal fires of hell!

It feels difficult to finish these letters. Even the simple act of writing 'Dear Dad' at the start of a letter has been comforting and has given me a closeness to you I have missed so much. Dad. It's such a short, dapper word. Just like you. The palindromic perfectness of it is beautiful. Dad. A

414

little word that contains a whole world of meaning. Like 'Mum'. I use that word often, I use it on the phone to her, I call it out when I'm with her, I use it to check if she wants a coffee, or to see how her day is. I use it to write in my diary about her, or to include her in a list of things to do, or an invite, or on a note that goes with flowers, or a card at Christmas or on her birthday. Or for a thousand reasons. I've written that word 'Mum' so often. But I haven't written 'Dad', I don't think, for about 30 years when it's directly to you. I write it now — 'Dad'. There, with such tenderness. It's a treat to write it, an excellence. I want to keep on writing it, 'Dad Dad Dad'. It's like a jewel, a precious thing. I don't want it to stop . . .

But it must. It must stop because it's time to properly say goodbye, isn't it? After your funeral, when I was 19, I stood on the shoreline at Rock, feeling entirely bereft without you, feeling that you were gone with the waves sinking back into the ocean. Writing these letters to you has helped me to wade out a little way, and dive in. That's all I needed, to swim about and play for a while. To connect with you and feel your nearness again. I'm surprised how easy it is to do. I didn't know how near you are. You are close by, aren't you?

About five years ago I went to Skibo Castle and one evening a medium from the Black Isle came to tell us our fortunes and read our tarot cards. It was all for fun, a light hearted distraction. I went in, a little worse (or maybe better) for whisky and sat down. She was quiet, and then she looked at me and said, 'Oh, I see your dad is with you!' This shocked me. Just for her to say such a thing shocked me. 'Yes, there he is, standing right behind you with his hand on your shoulder. I hope you're not offended by this but he's calling you 'Dumpling' and 'Moo'.' I had to leave. I wasn't offended, I was heart-thuddingly touched. How did she know? Was this trickery? I went for a walk outside and sat on a bench in the clear moonlight. I don't know if you, or some form of you, was there, I don't really hold with 'all that' ordinarily. Actually, it doesn't really matter what she said or saw, her words to me transcended the rational. What mattered that night, as it has mattered to me through this whole book, is that we are always connected, you and I. Always. It's the memory of you and the love you gave me that remain. Death is merely the horizon, the love is eternal. Undoubtedly.

There's an astronomical term, 'syzygy'. It means the alignment of celestial bodies in the same gravitational system along a straight line. The celestial bodies are actually stars and planets and stuff, I think, and apparently it's rare when it happens. That's how I think of what has happened between you and me in this book. For a brief, excellent moment, we have aligned in the same gravitational pull, and we've been together. But now it's time to go about the rest of my life. I don't know what you'll do. I like to imagine you in a sort of five star dead men's dorm with Eric Morecambe and Elvis and Kenneth Williams and Tommy Cooper for company. For

God's sake, don't let Bernard Manning in if he comes a-knockin'!

As for me, I pootle on, with you in my heart for warmth and fortitude, and I do all I can to have a good life. And it is a good life . . . with knobs on. And then some . . . Some more knobs!

Chio then, Dad.

Dear Fatty,

Quickly now, I need to tell you about a phone call I just had with an actor friend of mine who works in LA. I wouldn't work in LA, would you? I don't think I could be bothered any more to pack everything up to move there, to be honest. And what about my geraniums? They're just starting to take, so I wouldn't want to abandon them for a life of glitter and gloss and enormous wealth beyond my wildest dreams. Would you? Besides which, frankly, no one's asked.

Anyway, anyway, anyway, my friend — it doesn't matter what his name is, you don't know him — was hanging around with a load of old *Star Trek* actors and found out something he couldn't wait to tell me, something really shocking, something I need to impart to you immediately. Get this. Why do you think Lieutenant Uhura smelt so strange? Because William Shatner . . . The dirty dog. Can you believe that?

ACKNOWLEDGEMENTS

So many huge thanks to the following, they know why.

Len and Billie, big love
Sue Hunter for everything
Hannah Black for everything else
Abi Wilson for all the other stuff
Maureen Vincent, Chris, Ruth, Robert and all
   at United Agents
Mr Finkle
All the Frenchies
All the O'Briens (especially Keej and Ellie)
Brian Nicholson
Ray Faulkner
Rachael Martin
Jennifer Parker
Sabrina Lillicrap
Yasmin Lillicrap
Charlie Duffy
Cheryl Phelps-Gardiner
Trevor Leighton
Helen Teague
The Green Family
The Robinson Family
The Amihyia Family
The Barrett Family
Cynthia, Linda and Jeff, Ben, Davey
Mr D'Arcy, Gordon, Rory and Anna
My amazing Godchildren:

Sophie
Hannah L
Hannah F
Ella
Aba
Oscar
Florence
Jack
Rocco
Spike
Cameron
Jake
James
Joe
Naomi
Max
Mum, Gary and, of course, the Mighty BF.